OVERCOMING THE HURDLES TO ACADEMIC SUCCESS

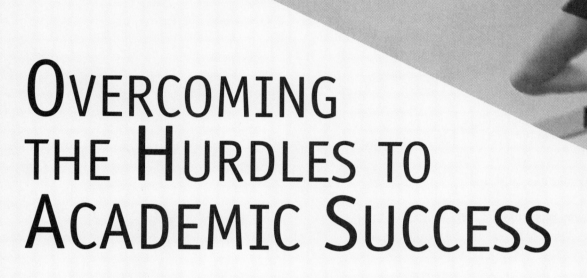

OVERCOMING THE HURDLES TO ACADEMIC SUCCESS

STRATEGIES THAT MAKE A DIFFERENCE

Darrell Anthony Luzzo
Arapahoe Community College

Marilyn K. Spencer
Texas A&M University—Corpus Christi

Houghton Mifflin Company
Boston   New York

Editor in Chief: Patricia A. Coryell
Associate Editor: Shani B. Fisher
Editorial Assistant: Andrew Sylvester
Senior Production/Design Coordinator: Sarah Ambrose
Senior Manufacturing Coordinator: Jane Spelman
Marketing Manager: Barbara LeBuhn

Cover image © Alan Thornton/Tony Stone

College Survival
A Program of Houghton Mifflin Company
2075 Foxfield Drive, Suite 100
St. Charles, IL 60174

Hurdler photos © 2002 Photodisc, Inc.

All cartoons © Vivian Scott Hixson

Printed in the U.S.A.

Library of Congress Control Number: 2001133302

ISBN: 0-618-15039-0

123456789-QD-06 05 04 03 02

contents

Section Two | **MASTER STRATEGIES FOR SUCCESS 89**

11   prepare papers and presentations   182

12   PULL IT ALL Together   203

preface

To The Student

Congratulations! By enrolling in this course and purchasing this book you've made a personal commitment to overcome the hurdles to academic success. Whether you've just graduated from high school, have decided to "go back to college" after several years away from school, or have struggled recently to maintain a satisfactory level of academic performance, our primary purpose for writing this book is the same: To help you master a variety of strategies you can use to overcome the hurdles to academic success.

As you probably already know, many different challenges can prevent students from achieving academic success. For some students taking notes is particularly difficult. For other students, reading textbooks, writing papers, or studying effectively may be a problem. Still others consider taking tests or making class presentations to be the most significant obstacle to their academic success. Whatever specific challenges you face, the good news is that help is on the way! Our approach in this book is to offer you various options for learning as effectively as you possibly can.

In each chapter you'll find a variety of features and exercises that we've designed to help you learn about the academic success strategies that we present. These features include a variety of hands-on exercises to help you process the information in each chapter, as well as definitions of important terms in the margins, summaries of each chapter, and questions for critical thought. Critical thinking is a skill that will come in handy not only in this class but in all of your classes and even in extracurricular activities. Furthermore, engaging in critical thinking is an important part of succeeding not only in college but also throughout your personal and professional life. We hope that these **Questions for Critical Thought** will help you develop and fine-tune your own critical thinking.

Also included in each chapter are case studies. These examples demonstrate how college students we've actually worked with over the years have faced their own individual hurdles and have used a variety of strategies to enhance their academic success. As you read these cases, we hope you'll find appropriate ways to apply the experiences of others to your own personal life situations—both in and out of the college environment.

We want college to be an enjoyable and successful experience for you. It will surely be stressful at times, but it will be very rewarding at others. We sincerely hope that you'll enjoy reading this book and taking this course. We're confident that the skills and strategies you'll begin to master will provide you with the tools you need to overcome the hurdles to academic success.

Darrell Anthony Luzzo, Ph.D.
Marilyn K. Spencer, Ph.D.

To the Instructor

When we set out to write this book, one major principle guided our efforts: To introduce students to a variety of hands-on strategies they could use to overcome the hurdles to academic success. To sum it up in just a few words, we wanted to write a book that is engaging, that is written in a professional and informative—yet conversational—tone, and that is filled with dozens of strategies and examples to enhance students' ability to achieve their academic goals.

In the first section of the book we introduce readers to many different strategies they can use to prepare for academic success. Chapter 1 sets the stage by emphasizing the importance of adopting a positive attitude toward the learning process. Also presented in Chapter 1 is a set of four principles that should guide students' learning of academic strategies for success. We refer to these principles as the **Ground Rules** and invite students to apply the rules as they read through the textbook and learn strategies in class.

Throughout the first five chapters of the book we provide readers with over 50 practical strategies for thinking positively and critically, setting goals, honing critical thinking skills, creating effective study habits, and using academic support services. In the second section of the book we introduce students to over 150 additional practical strategies they can use as they engage in the everyday academic activities of college, such as taking notes, reading textbooks, taking tests, and writing papers.

Features and Exercises

Boxes and Definitions. As you preview the contents of the book you'll notice a variety of features and exercises (each denoted with an icon in the margin) that complement the book's discussion of academic success strategies. For example, at the beginning of each chapter is a box that summarizes the strategies presented in that chapter. This preview provides students with the opportunity to get a sense of what types of techniques they'll be learning about in the pages that follow. Other information throughout each chapter also appears in boxes as a means of emphasizing important concepts or helping students organize new information. Each chapter includes several definitions of terms or phrases that are common in the academic arena but may not be all that familiar to most readers. These definitions are featured as boxes in the margins of the text. Extra space in the bottom of the box allows students to make their own notes on these terms or to add other terms they need to look up in the dictionary.

Points to Ponder and Time to Reflect Exercises. Also found in the margins of each chapter are **Points to Ponder**. **Points to Ponder** are designed to highlight an important concept or principle discussed in the chapter. They are placed in the margin of the book as a means of drawing attention to them. Another feature found in each chapter is the **Time to Reflect** exercises that invite students to think back to principles they've learned earlier in the chapter or earlier in the book. Some of the **Time to Reflect** exercises ask readers to think back to earlier life experiences altogether. By engaging in this type of reflection, students will be able to connect some of the information they're learning in this book to meaningful experiences from their past. Furthermore, both the

Points to Ponder and **Time to Reflect** exercises can serve as excellent topics for journaling or brief writing assignments.

Exercise Breaks. Several hands-on exercises, referred to as **Exercise Breaks**, also appear in each chapter. These exercises vary in content and length. Some are a series of questions that ask students to react to the information they've read, whereas others involve gathering information outside of class and sharing that information with their classmates. In all instances, the exercises are designed to provide ample opportunity for students to apply the concepts presented in the book to real life situations. Several of the **Exercise Breaks** encourage group process work and are denoted by the group icon in the margin. Although such exercises are excellent opportunities to invite students to work in groups, instructors certainly have the option of changing those exercises so that students may complete them individually.

Case Studies. Each chapter also includes two case studies. These examples demonstrate how college students we've worked with over the years have faced particular hurdles in college and have used a variety of strategies to enhance their academic success. The **Time Out** feature that appears within each case study is designed to actively engage readers in the case. The **Apply This Now** feature that follows each case study encourages students to find ways to apply the experiences of others to their own situations as they build confidence in their ability to succeed academically.

Take it Away Summaries. Toward the end of each chapter is a section entitled, **Take It Away!** We want to make sure that as students finish reading each chapter they'll be able to "take away" strategies that they can immediately begin incorporating into both their academic and personal life. The **Take It Away!** section highlights the major strategies discussed in each chapter and encourages students to apply the strategies firsthand.

Questions for Critical Thought. Finally, each chapter concludes with a series of **Questions for Critical Thought**. These questions allow students to practice their critical thinking skills. They'll help students reflect on what's important to them, what their specific challenges are, and which academic success strategies are most likely to work for them.

Although this book is relatively short, we're confident that it includes the essential information about academic success that students need and presents that information in an applied, hands-on, and engaging manner. We believe the presentation and discussion of over 200 useful strategies, coupled with multiple opportunities in each chapter for students to practice those strategies, will help students achieve their goals and experience academic success.

Valuable Classroom Resources

College Survival Consulting Services: College Survival is the leading source of expertise, support services, and materials for student success courses. We are committed to promoting and supporting effective success courses within the higher education community.

For more than fifteen years, Houghton Mifflin's College Survival consultants have provided consultation and training for the design, implementation and presentation of student success and first-year courses. Our team of consultants has a wide variety of experience in teaching and administering the first-year course. They can provide help in establishing, or improving your student success program. We offer assistance in course design, instructor training, teaching strategies, and much more. Contact us today at 1-800-528-8323, or visit us on the web at collegesurvival.college.hmco.com/instructors.

College Survival Web Site: This web site offers new ways for students and teachers to learn. The *Overcoming the Hurdles to Academic Success* web site includes chapter quizzes, sample syllabi, additional case studies, and useful links to web sites that correspond with the topics in each chapter. Also available on our website are PowerPoint slides which may be downloaded for use on your computer or made into transparencies if PowerPoint is not available in your classroom.

Roundtable Discussions" Videotapes: These two videotapes, "Study Strategies" and "Life Skills," feature five college students who discuss and seek solutions to the problems they face in college and in life. Call Faculty Services at 1-800-733-1717, visit the College Survival web site, or contact your Houghton Mifflin representative for more information. A teaching unit for the videotapes is also available on the College Survival web site.

Myers-Briggs Type Indicator® (MBTI®) Instrument*: This is the most widely used personality inventory in history—shrink wrapped with *Overcoming the Hurdles to Academic Success* for a discounted price at qualified schools. The standard form M self-scorable instrument contains 93 items that determine preferences of four scales: Extraversion-Introversion, Sensing-Intuition, Thinking-Feeling, and Judging-Perceiving.

Retention Management System™ College Student Inventory: The Noel Levitz College Student Inventory instrument is available in a specially priced package with this text. This early-alert, early-intervention program identifies students with tendencies that contribute to dropping out of school. Students can participate in an integrated, campus-wide program. Advisors are sent three interpretive reports: The Student's Report, the Advisor/Counselor Report, and The College Summary and Planning Report. For more information, contact your College Survival consultant at 1-800-528-8323 or your local Houghton Mifflin Sales Representative.

The College Survival Student Planner: This week-at-a-glance academic planner is available in a specially priced package with this text. The College Survival Student Planner assists students in managing their time both on and off campus. The planner includes a "Survival Kit" of helpful success tips from Houghton Mifflin's College Survival textbooks.

---

*MBTI and Myers-Briggs Type Indicator are registered trademarks of Consulting Psychologists Press, Inc.

Acknowledgments

We thank Vivian Hixson, whose imaginative illustrations have provided inspiration and much needed humor over the years, for permitting us to use her previously published illustrations for this text, from her book, *He Looks Too Happy to Be an Assistant Professor*, the University of Missouri Press, 1996, as well as from numerous issues of the *Chronicle of Higher Education*. But we are even more delighted that Vivian Hixson created new illustrations for our text.

We wish to thank thousands of our students, who over the years have helped us learn so very much by sharing their hopes, dreams, struggles and courage.

We need to thank the following colleagues for their many valuable suggestions and other contributions: Monty Douglas, Pam Durrwachter, Rich Haswell, D. K. Ivy, Diane King, Denise Landry-Hyde and Richard Shepperd.

Special thanks goes to the following professors who took time out of their busy schedules to review the manuscript of this textbook. We are truly grateful for their questions, criticisms and suggestions:

Kathy Cid, Lincoln Tech Institute, NJ;
Beverley Davies, Niagra College, Ontario, Canada;
Carlotta W. Hill, Oklahoma City Community College, OK;
Linda Kleemann, Lewis and Clark Community College, IL;
Patsy Krech, University of Memphis, TN;
Signe Matson, University of Wisconsin, WI;
Kathryn E. Moore, St. Louis Community College, MO;
James Muniz, University of Scranton, PA;
Rebecca Owens, Texas Tech University, TX;
Elva Peña, Del Mar College, TX;
Celeste Thomas, James Madison University, VA;
Bev Walker, North Central State College, OH.

Barbara Heinssen, former Director of College Survival at the College Division, was the individual whose enthusiastic response to our project began our flourishing relationship with Houghton Mifflin. We are ever grateful to Barbara for her support.

We are so thankful for the opportunity to work with Melissa Plumb, our Developmental Editor. Without her help over many months, this text would not be what it is today.

We are MOST thankful for the continual guidance of Shani Fisher, the Associate Editor for College Survival at Houghton Mifflin's College Division. We're delighted to have worked with Editorial Assistant, Andrew Sylvester, for his important and timely help.

We also wish to acknowledge the members of our families, particularly David Spencer and Tanya Luzzo, our loving spouses, who supported us throughout this project. Their optimism and emotional support allowed our dreams of publishing this textbook to become a reality.

Darrell Anthony Luzzo, Ph.D.
Marilyn K. Spencer, Ph.D.

prepare for academic success

expect success

1 If you really want to succeed in college—even if you've had your share of academic struggles in the past—you need to keep your spirits high and remain confident.

2 Being responsible requires hard work. If you're willing to invest an adequate amount of time and energy, your chances of success are almost guaranteed!

3 Understanding why you're motivated to complete a program of study or earn a degree can help you stay on track when you experience challenges along the way.

4 When setting your academic goals, it's important to (a) be realistic, (b) be specific, (c) periodically evaluate your progress, and (d) maintain a healthy balance.

5 Once you've clarified your own personal academic hurdles, you can begin to work on them and improve your chances of achieving academic success.

6 It's important—at least every now and then—to rely on persons who willingly offer their support.

7 As you learn the many academic success strategies that will be presented throughout this book, you'll need to remember the four *ground rules*.

Maintain a Positive Perspective

Over the years we've worked with thousands of students who've struggled to achieve academic success. Some have had problems with specific academic tasks, such as remembering what they read or paying attention during class. Others have had particularly difficult times taking tests or writing papers. Regardless of the specific challenges, one factor seems to separate students who overcome their hurdles to academic success from those who fail to achieve their academic goals. That one factor is *perspective*.

If there's one message you could take away from this textbook to increase your chances of achieving your academic goals it is this: *expect success!* You may be thinking to yourself, "Easy for them to say. They're not the ones who are unsure about their ability to succeed while attending a **college** or **university**." That's true, but we also know that positive thinking is *absolutely essential* to succeeding in college. We may not be struggling academically at this point in *our* lives, but we've had numerous personal experiences that have helped us recognize just how important it is to expect the best.

 As we work with students who face a variety of academic challenges, one message becomes clearer and clearer. If you *really* want to succeed in college—even if you've had your share of academic struggles in the past—you need to keep your spirits high and remain confident. What would have happened to Michael Jordan if he'd quit playing basketball after being cut from the team in his sophomore year at high school? What would have become of Oprah Winfrey if she hadn't convinced herself that she could entertain people as a talk show host—even when others doubted her ability? And what would have happened if Abraham Lincoln had stopped when he lost two elections instead of continuing his quest to lead the country? All of these famous people experienced their fair share of challenges, obstacles, and disappointments. Yet all of them refused to allow their personal hurdles to prevent them from trying even harder to achieve their goals.

college: An institution of higher education that may be private or public and that bestows degrees and/or certificates.

◆ ◆ ◆

university: An institution of higher education that may be private or public. All universities offer bachelor's degrees. Some also offer associate's, master's, and/or doctoral degrees.

Time to Reflect

Think back to your elementary and high school days. What famous person do you remember having learned about who overcame significant obstacles on the way to accomplishing her or his goals?

_____

_____

In what ways did the person persist in the face of hurdles?

_____

_____

Success in college may not be as glamorous as winning an NBA title, hosting a TV talk show, or becoming president of the United States. But it's still important to remain positive and be willing to keep trying, even when the hurdles seem extremely difficult to overcome. As you continue to work hard to achieve academic success, don't underestimate the power of positive thinking.

Many times people undermine their ability to succeed in a task with negative thoughts about themselves. This is something psychologists call "negative self-talk." Your attitude about learning and your perspective about academic challenges directly influence your ability to overcome the hurdles you face. Keeping up your spirits—even if your situation seems hopeless at times—will help you stay focused and will motivate you to try success strategies. You'll begin to replace doubtful thoughts and negative beliefs with positive expectations. You'll begin to expect success!

Point *to* Ponder

■ As you continue to work hard to achieve academic success, don't underestimate the power of positive thinking.

Exercise Break 1.1

Several academic challenges you might face appear in the left column below. Statements that represent negative self-talk about each of the challenges are listed in the middle column. In the right column are blank spaces for you to list more positive ways of thinking about each situation. Before you continue reading this chapter, spend a few minutes thinking of more positive ways to approach each situation. Jot your ideas down in the spaces provided below.

After you complete the exercise, get together with a few other students in the class and talk about the more positive approaches each of you came up with.

The Situation	Example of Negative Self-Talk	A More Positive Approach
Poor performance on a test.	"I'll *never* figure out how to do well on tests."	"Perhaps if I study a little harder and work with a tutor for a few weeks, I can figure out what I can do to improve my test performance."
Poor grade on a written assignment.	"I am a terrible writer. I don't know why I even try."	_____ _____ _____
Taking notes in class that are incomplete.	"There's no way I can write down everything my professor has to say."	_____ _____ _____
Not comprehending the content of a lecture.	"I can't understand a thing my professor says in class. It's way over my head. I guess I'm just stupid!"	_____ _____ _____

| Difficulty finding time to study. | "How in the world am I ever going to find enough time to study for my classes when I have so much else going on in my life?" | _____ _____ _____ |
| Having a hard time figuring out priorities. | "I should never have watched TV for three hours last night! I'll never figure out how to prioritize my time." | _____ _____ _____ |

Accept Responsibility for Success

As you probably know already, college is very different from high school. In high school, homework is assigned and graded frequently. Quizzes and tests are given every week in just about every class. Students often have the opportunity to read their books and complete their assignments in class. In college, homework is rarely graded. Often, midterms and final exams are given instead of weekly quizzes. There's rarely any time during class for students to read textbooks or complete assignments. It's not that **instructors** or **professors** don't want college students to succeed. It's just that students bear the majority of the responsibility for keeping up and figuring out how well they're doing.

We've worked with thousands of students over the years who were successful in high school. Doing well in high school doesn't guarantee that academic success will come easily in college. In addition to some of the differences we've already discussed, one of the main differences between high school and college has to do with time spent in class. Although there are a few exceptions, most classes taken in college meet only twice or three times a week. That means that even if you're enrolled as a full-time student, you may be in class for only three or four hours a day. College students have the added challenge of managing their time to ensure that they're devoting adequate time to out-of-class learning and studying activities.

Are you prepared for the responsibilities of being a successful college student? This may sound like a condescending question, but it's not meant to be. What's important for you to realize is that one of the most challenging aspects of college is that you are personally responsible for your success. Being responsible requires hard work. If you're willing to invest an adequate amount of time and energy, your chances of success are almost guaranteed. College students who achieve academically are those who learn to be disciplined about using their time and who realize the importance of making the effort to master effective strategies along the way.

Despite the many benefits of a college degree, more than 40 percent of students who enroll in college fail to complete an academic program. Furthermore, about 25 percent of students who start college don't even return for their second year! Most quit college because they're struggling with completing academic requirements or juggling all of life's other responsibilities. We don't mention these facts to create additional anxiety for you. We

Point *to* ponder

Don't underestimate the power of discipline and effort as you continue your quest for success.

instructor: A title bestowed upon a faculty member who teaches courses at a college or university that does not use the professor system; a commonly used term at community colleges.

♦ ♦ ♦

professor: A title bestowed on a college or university faculty member by that college or university; a member of the faculty of a university who has reached a certain rank.

© Vivian Scott Hixson

"I'd like to go to college next year, but I don't want it to make too much of a change in my lifestyle."

simply want you to realize that it's *your* responsibility to do all that you possibly can to succeed in college.

The good news is that you've already taken at least one very important step in assuming personal responsibility for your success. By enrolling in this course and purchasing this book, you've made a personal commitment to overcome the hurdles that could otherwise prevent you from achieving academically.

case study 1.1

Consider Mario . . .

After several unsuccessful attempts to obtain a degree in computer-aided drafting, Mario began to think he simply didn't have "what it takes" to succeed in college. He couldn't understand why the computer-aided drafting program at his local community college was so difficult to complete. He attended all of his classes, regularly read the textbook, and turned in his assignments on time. Yet he struggled to maintain a C average. He was having particular difficulty with tests. After quitting and reenrolling in the program year after year, Mario was beginning to lose hope. Nevertheless, with the support and encouragement of his friends and family, Mario decided to give it another try.

When Mario went into the registration office to sign up for classes, an academic advisor in-

formed Mario that he was on **academic suspension**. This meant he would not be allowed to enroll in any content-area classes until he successfully passed a **prerequisite** course—in this case a study-skills course offered by the college. Mario was upset and embarrassed. He didn't understand why he had to take a basic study-skills course.

Time Out If you were in Mario's situation, how would you respond, and why?

_____

_____

_____

_____

1.1 (continued)

Despite his initial reluctance, Mario enrolled in the required study-skills course because he was motivated to obtain his degree. When the term ended three months later, Mario was amazed at how much he had learned in such a brief period of time. For the first time in his life, Mario was aware of various effective strategies for taking notes, reading textbooks more efficiently, and—most important for Mario—preparing for and taking tests. He remarked to several of his friends that he wished he had taken a course like this years before. He was sure it would have helped him avoid many of his earlier academic struggles.

By making the effort and devoting quality time to learning academic success strategies, Mario significantly increased his chances of achieving his academic and career goals. When he graduated from the program two years later, Mario expressed his heartfelt thanks to his academic advisor for requiring him to take the study-skills course in which he finally learned the tools he needed to experience academic success.

Apply This Now

Consider something you've recently accomplished about which you are particularly proud. What specific effort did you put forth to help you accomplish that goal?

_____

How might the absence of this effort have affected the outcome?

_____

_____

What courses do you need to take to help *you* prepare for academic success?

_____

Identify and Clarify Your Goals

■ *Determine Your Purpose for Attending College*

Why are you in college? Perhaps you're back in school after a few years away, having learned valuable lessons from your work experiences. Maybe you never really thought of college as an option until someone encouraged you to attend. Perhaps you know exactly what you want to do with your life, and college is necessary for achieving that goal. Maybe someone you admire finished college, and you want to follow in her or his footsteps. Or maybe you're aware that completing at least some college will help you earn substantially higher wages than you would otherwise.

Most students have several reasons for enrolling in college. And, believe it or not, many times their reasons for attending college in the first place aren't the same as their reasons for deciding to remain in college later on. Whatever your initial reasons for

academic suspension: A term used to indicate that a student's academic performance has fallen below a minimum standard, usually requiring time away from college; developmental work may be required before the student can re-enroll in classes.

◆ ◆ ◆

prerequisite: A course that must be successfully completed before a student is allowed to enroll in other courses within a particular discipline or subject area.

going to college, you are more likely to succeed academically once you're fully aware of reasons for returning to or remaining in college *at this time*. Understanding why you're motivated to complete a program of study or earn a degree can help you stay on track when you experience challenges along the way.

exercise break 1.2

In the space below, write down the two or three main reasons for your decision to remain in or return to college at this time in your life. Why are you here?

_____

_____

_____

_____

Point *to* **ponder**

You are more likely to succeed academically once you're fully aware of reasons for returning to or remaining in college at this time.

Set Academic Goals to Expect Success

Now that you've clarified why it's important to you to succeed in college, you can begin to specify the academic goals you want to achieve. This surely isn't the first time you've heard about the importance of setting goals. You've probably set many different goals throughout your life, and you've probably already achieved many of them. Spending some time thinking about occasions when you've set your own goals and followed through to accomplish them is a worthwhile endeavor. It can help you realize the importance of setting goals and doing what's necessary to achieve them. Setting goals for academic success in college is a particularly important process.

exercise break 1.3

Think about goals that you've set for yourself in the past that you eventually achieved. What was the *key* to achieving those goals? In other words, what are some of the essential things that you needed to do in order to accomplish those goals?

_____

_____

Keeping the four principles of effective goal-setting in mind, use the space below to identify four or five specific academic goals you hope to accomplish *this term* (see Box 1.1, opposite page).

_____

_____

_____

_____

_____

A goal represents something you hope to accomplish, something for which you're willing to work hard. Goals are very different from hopes or dreams. Goals represent realistic possibilities. Unlike merely hoping for or dreaming about something desirable, the process of setting goals requires you to (1) reflect on your personal strengths and limitations and (2) figure out what you need to do to make the goals become realities. As you begin to identify your own academic goals, consider the four important principles of goal-setting presented in Box 1.1.

BOX 1.1. **Factors to Consider When Setting Your Academic Goals**

1. Be realistic.	It makes no sense to create an overly ambitious set of goals. Doing so only sets you up for frustration and anxiety when you're unable to accomplish them. Be sure the goals you set are attainable, and don't set too many goals at one time. If you're in doubt, ask your friends or family members to provide input about whether your goals are realistic.
2. Be specific.	It's not a good idea to set goals that are too vague or general. State your goals clearly so that you'll be able to monitor your progress. A goal such as "succeed in all my classes" is much too vague. On the other hand, a goal such as "earn a B or higher in each class this semester" is much easier to evaluate.
3. Periodically evaluate your progress.	Many people set goals at different times in their lives. What often separates those who successfully achieve their goals and those who don't is the degree to which they evaluate their progress on a regular basis. If you want to increase the chances of achieving your academic goals, be sure to evaluate your progress every few weeks or months, and adjust your efforts accordingly.
4. Maintain a healthy balance.	As you create your goals and begin to work on methods for achieving them, don't forget that you have many other responsibilities and commitments in your life. Be sure to adequately maintain order in these other areas of your life while you pursue academic success in college.

■ *Overcome the Hurdles to Academic Success*

Stating your academic goals is the first step in the process of creating a firm foundation for academic success. You also have to prepare for the many challenges you're likely to face along the way. Sometimes students refer to those challenges as obstacles or barriers. Other times students choose to ignore the challenges, almost as if they're pretending the challenges don't exist.

We believe that words like *obstacles* and *barriers* imply that academic challenges are extremely difficult to conquer or overcome. We also believe that when you ignore academic challenges, you run the risk of not being adequately prepared to handle them. That's why we prefer the term *hurdle*. Just as track-and-field hurdlers practice important techniques and strategies to learn

Point to Ponder

Once you've clarified your own personal academic hurdles, you can begin to work on them and improve your chances of achieving academic success.

how to successfully jump over hurdles on a track, you can learn how to overcome the challenges you'll face as you attempt to achieve your academic goals.

The hurdles that may stand in the way of your academic success are personal. They depend on your own initial strengths and limitations as well as your external constraints. External constraints include financial circumstances, family responsibilities, and work obligations. The hurdles that *you* need to learn to jump over may be very different from the hurdles your friends or classmates are experiencing. Once you've clarified your own, personal academic hurdles you can begin to work on them and improve your chances of achieving academic success.

Exercise Break 1.4

In Exercise Break 1.3 you were asked to identify four or five academic goals you hope to accomplish this term. Write down each of those goals in the left column below. In the right column indicate the hurdles that could possibly prevent you from achieving each goal.

Academic Goals	Hurdles That Might Prevent Your Achievement of the Goals
example: Successfully passing Math 101.	I experience a very high level of anxiety every time I have to take a math test.

■ *Count on the Support of Others*

In addition to this book and this course, there are undoubtedly many other resources available to help you overcome the hurdles that might otherwise prevent your academic success. Perhaps you have friends or family members who are able to offer encouragement and support. Or perhaps your roommates or study-group partners are willing to lend a helping hand. Maybe there's a professor, teaching assistant, counselor, or academic advisor you're comfortable consulting when you're struggling with particular problems.

The important thing to recognize is that people in your life are available to support and encourage your efforts to succeed. It's important—at least every now and then—to rely on persons who willingly offer their support.

case study 1.2

Consider Rochelle . . .

Rochelle was a thirty-three-year-old single mother who was preparing to go back to college to pursue a degree in respiratory therapy. Because she had been away from school for almost fifteen years, Rochelle was concerned about her ability to successfully juggle her many life responsibilities while attending college. She had two young children to care for, a part-time job as a retail sales clerk, and an elderly grandmother who lived nearby. In addition, because of limited financial resources, Rochelle planned to complete the respiratory therapy program at her local community college in only twenty-four months, which meant that she was going to have to enroll full-time and take at least fifteen credit hours each term.

A couple of weeks before classes were scheduled to begin, Rochelle met with one of the allied health program advisors at the college. She wanted to find out whether the advisor had any suggestions about resources that she might find useful in coping with the multiple responsibilities she was juggling.

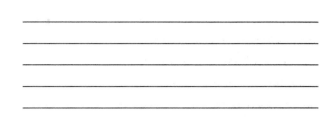 If you were Rochelle, what might you do to prepare for your return to college? Are there are any particular resources that you might want to access at the college? If so, what resources do you think would help you the most?

The advisor with whom Rochelle met began by providing a list of academic support services available on campus. This list included the campus location, phone number, and website address for such offices as the Learning Assistance Center, the Women's Center, the Returning Adult Student Support Office, and the Academic Advising and Transfer Center. After discussing on-campus resources that might be of particular interest to Rochelle, the advisor asked her to think about people she knew who might also serve as important resources over the next couple of years. In essence, the advisor challenged Rochelle to make a list of such persons, including their telephone numbers and e-mail addresses, and to post the list in a handy place so it wouldn't be forgotten.

Within a couple of days, Rochelle had put together a list of more than a dozen friends, family members, and church leaders whom she could count on for support. A couple of the friends could serve as emergency babysitters; a few family members were sources of temporary loans; and church leaders were a welcome source of emotional and spiritual support. Posting this list on her refrigerator provided Rochelle with a constant reminder that she wasn't completely on her own as she pursued her dream of becoming a respiratory therapist.

▪ *Plan to Overcome the Hurdles*

An important part of expecting success in college is to create a plan for overcoming the hurdles. In the first section of this book, we present more than a hundred strategies you can use to overcome many of the hurdles that may have prevented you from achieving academic success in the past. If you've had a difficult time figuring out the best way to learn new material in your classes, the strategies discussed in Chapter 2, "Know How You Learn," will help you

Apply This Now

In the spaces below, jot down names of people you can turn to for information, advice, encouragement, and support as you prepare to achieve your goals. Be sure to specify the particular way in which each can be of assistance to you.

Support Person (Phone Number)	Specific Way(s) They Can Help
example: My sister-in-law (555-1111)	She is willing to baby-sit my two young children if I need to visit my professors during the morning hours.
_____	_____
_____	_____
_____	_____
_____	_____

Make copies of this list and post one on your bulletin board or on the refrigerator and keep another in your wallet or purse. That way you'll know who you can call on for help if the need should arise.

Point *to* ponder

You'll be surprised how many services your campus provides to help you overcome challenges to academic success.

learn more about your preferred style of learning. If you've had problems concentrating on academic tasks and managing stress in your life, the techniques discussed in Chapter 3, "Focus Your Efforts for Success," will be of great value to you. If you've struggled to establish a successful study routine, the concepts presented in Chapter 4, "Create Effective Study Habits," will provide you with many answers to the question "How can I study to maximize my chances of success?" In Chapter 5, "Utilize Academic Support Services," we make sure you're aware of the many resources available on campus to help you achieve your academic goals.

In the second section of the book, we devote six chapters to a discussion of more than a hundred strategies for increasing your academic performance. These skill areas include taking notes (Chapter 6), reading textbooks (Chapter 7), enhancing your memory skills (Chapter 8), preparing for tests (Chapter 9), taking tests with confidence (Chapter 10), and writing papers and making presentations (Chapter 11). In the final chapter of the book, we summarize the most important strategies for you to consider as you work to overcome the hurdles to academic success.

Time to Reflect

Considering the basic content of the chapters of this book, which two or three chapters do you believe will be most useful to you?

_____

What specifically are you hoping you'll learn from these chapters that will enhance your ability to achieve academic success?

_____

_____

_____

_____

Point *to* PONDER

■ The best academic success strategies are the ones that produce the most effective results for you.

Bring the Strategies to Life: The Ground Rules

As mentioned earlier in the chapter, throughout this book you'll learn more than two hundred practical strategies to help you accomplish your educational goals and achieve academic success. As you learn about these strategies, it will be important for you to periodically review the ground rules we've outlined for your consideration in Box 1.2.

BOX 1.2.   **The Ground Rules**

1. Learn a variety of academic success strategies.	For us to claim that all students should use a specified set of academic success strategies, regardless of previous life experiences or individual learning styles, would be shortsighted. Perhaps the best way to figure out which strategies work best for you is to learn about them and then try out several different ones over time. For example, when it comes to learning about note-taking strategies (Chapter 6), you might try one note-taking approach one week and then try a different approach the following week. With this trial-and-error method, you'll quickly learn which academic success strategies work best for you.
2. Give each academic success strategy a try.	What might at first seem like a strategy that just won't work for you might end up being a very effective approach after all. If you don't like a particular technique after trying it once or twice, you can move on to another one. Eventually you'll discover the specific academic success strategies that work best for you.
3. Evaluate the success of each strategy.	Ultimately, the best academic success strategies are the ones that produce the most effective results for you. You'll want to regularly evaluate how well each strategy contributes to your academic success. An effective way to evaluate the usefulness of the strategies is to see how well you perform in your classes as a result of using them. For example, if you discover that

BOX 1.2.	**The Ground Rules (continued)**
	using a particular memory-enhancing strategy from Chapter 8 helps you remember information when taking a test, you'll probably want to keep using that strategy in the future.
4. Master the strategies.	Once you've selected the strategies you plan to use on a regular basis, you'll want to continue to practice them over time to master them. You'll be sure to benefit by learning some of the more intricate aspects of each technique and by finding out how to best use each strategy to maximize your academic performance.

Take it away!

Throughout this chapter we've asked you to consider a number of ways to increase your chances of overcoming the hurdles to academic success. Some of the important principles we've discussed include the following:

- *Maintain a positive perspective.* As you work hard to achieve academic success, remember to keep a positive attitude about college. Keeping your spirits up is a useful way to stay motivated and focused to expect success.

- *Accept responsibility for success.* It's important to realize that *you* bear the responsibility for ensuring your own academic success. If you're willing to invest your share of time and energy into the process, you'll greatly enhance your chances of achieving your academic goals.

- *Clarify your reasons for attending college.* Clarifying why you're attending college will help you stay on track along the way.

- *Set academic goals to expect success.* Setting goals related to your academic performance is the first step on the road to achieving academic success.

- *Identify the hurdles to academic success.* By identifying potential hurdles, you can begin to prepare to overcome them by acquiring appropriate skills and learning useful strategies.

- *As you learn about academic success strategies, remember the four ground rules:* (1) learn a variety of academic success strategies; (2) give each academic success strategy a try; (3) evaluate the success of each strategy; and (4) master the strategies.

   In Chapter 2, we discuss the importance of identifying your preferred style of learning and invite you to find ways to increase your participation in active learning activities.

Questions for Critical Thought

1. In Exercise Break 1.1 you wrote down positive ways of thinking about some hypothetical academic hurdles. What types of negative self-talk have you engaged in lately? How might you go about replacing those negative thoughts with more positive ones?

2. What are some of your out-of-class responsibilities? How might some of these nonacademic responsibilities affect your ability to succeed in college?

3. What did you report in Exercise Break 1.2 as the main reasons you're attending college? Do you think these reasons differ from your reasons a few months ago? How might your reasons for being in college change again in the future?

4. When you set academic goals, it's important to periodically evaluate your progress toward achieving them. In what ways can you evaluate your goals on a regular basis? Choose one of the goals from Exercise Break 1.3. How does periodically evaluating this goal help to ensure success?

5. What are some of the things you can begin doing now to stop the hurdles you listed in Exercise Break 1.4 from preventing you from achieving your academic goals?

6. Look back at the Points to Ponder that appear in this chapter.
   a. Which Point to Ponder surprised you the most?
   b. How does knowing this help you better prepare for academic success?

7. How does the information presented in this chapter help you in your life outside of the classroom and college environment? Which strategies discussed in the chapter are particularly relevant to success in your career and personal life?

Web Site

Visit the *Overcoming the Hurdles to Academic Success* web site for a chapter outline, review exercises, additional case studies, links to other online resources, and a practice test.

References

Peale, N. V. (1996). *The power of positive thinking*. New York: Ballantine Books.

Salili, F., Chiu, C., & Hong, Y. (2001). *Student motivation: The culture and context of learning*. New York: Kluwer Academic/Plenum Publishers.

know how you learn

Chapter 2 Strategies

1 If you're a visual learner, you remember well by reading and/or watching a demonstration; each presents the visual information in a very different way.

2 If you're a truly auditory learner, you're comfortable with learning through what you hear and say.

3 Speaking, a form of active learning, is a good way for you to reinforce your learning, especially if you're an auditory learner.

4 Writing to learn—using your own words to explain something you've learned — is an excellent way to reinforce your learning, in that it uses visual and kinesthetic senses.

5 If you're a truly kinesthetic learner, you learn best by doing; you enjoy the laboratory and field-experience portions of courses.

6 If an instructor allows time for a question-and-answer period, ask questions to let the instructor know which parts you don't understand.

7 If your assigned textbooks are written in a way that's difficult for you to understand, ask the instructor to suggest supplemental texts, or go to the college library to look for a text that you find more readable.

8 Take responsibility for learning the course content in class and outside of class.

9 One way to learn is to ask yourself questions about previously assigned material.

10 You and classmates can meet as a small group to see if together you understand and can apply new course material.

11 To see if you understand a concept, either alone or with your group, you can research the answer to a question before the next class.

12 Think critically about information by questioning whether it is accurate, com-

plete, and makes sense in a particular context, and if the source of the information is trustworthy.

13 To thoroughly analyze an interpersonal or professional situation or problem, try to state it from the other persons' perspective.

What Type of Student Are You?

In Chapter 1 you learned about the importance of maintaining a positive perspective as you set academic goals and prepare for hurdles on the track to academic success. You'll find out more about yourself as a learner in this chapter. The chapter will help you recognize your particular strengths and preferences as a learner, and it will show the importance of active learning and critical thinking. The chapter will also introduce you to problem-solving skills that can help you achieve academic success. By using your current strengths and greater self-knowledge and the new strategies you'll find in this chapter, you'll be farther along the track to success.

Most people, without even knowing it, often prefer to rely on one or two specific strategies to learn new information. For example, perhaps you prefer (1) reading or watching and seeing—such as attending a lecture or viewing a demonstration or film; (2) writing everything down; (3) hearing and speaking about what you've heard; (4) thinking about the subject logically for a while to see if it makes sense to you; and/or (5) having a hands-on or other type of physical experience. One of these may be your favorite way to learn. You may

Time to Reflect

Look back at the list of learning strategies in the previous paragraph.

1. Which one or more of these strategies do you enjoy using the most?

2. Which one or more of these strategies do you need to use the most for this course?

3. What was your *most* favorite class ever?

4. To be successful in that class, did you most often use the strategies you listed in (1) above?

5. What was your *least* favorite class ever?

6. To be successful in that class, did you most often use the strategies you listed in (1) above?

be most effective when you use a combination of these strategies, or perhaps a strategy that's not listed above. Or you may prefer one strategy to learn some things and other strategies to learn other things.

▨ *Increase Your Awareness of Learning Styles*

What are learning styles? The term *learning style* refers to the method an individual regularly uses to learn something new. Although every individual is unique, most people learn best by using one to three different methods, or learning styles.

All of the styles rely on one or more of our five senses. We take in information through our five senses, and sometimes we use more than one sense for information-gathering. We again use one or more of our five senses when we work to remember information that is important to us.

We explore a few of the widely used theories of learning styles in this chapter in order to help you see the variety of ways people learn. You'll surely recognize your most comfortable learning style or styles as described in at least one of these theories. Keep in mind how you use your five senses in the process of learning, and think about how different learning styles employ different senses and/or different combinations of senses.

Have you ever smelled a fragrance or aroma, or heard a sound or a song, that suddenly transported you back in time to an old, forgotten memory? Some information stored in our brains is connected to a particular sight, sound, fragrance, and/or other sensation. The more we involve multiple senses in the learning process, the more likely we are to be able to retrieve this information later.

In Box 2.1 and subsequent paragraphs, we describe some of the common classroom and studying activities you'll be engaging in. This will illustrate the first theory of learning styles that we present in this chapter. It concerns your use of three of your senses—auditory, visual, and **kinesthetic**—as well as thinking or reflection about what you've done. You'll see that some learning activities involve more than one of the styles. Most college courses don't have activities in which you utilize your sense of smell or taste, so we don't discuss these. But you could add them to the list for some fields of study, such as chemistry and culinary courses. As you study Box 2.1, you'll see that speaking and writing employ multiple learning styles. That helps make speaking and writing especially valuable learning strategies.

 Reading or viewing.   Reading and seeing a demonstration are both visual, but each presents the visual information in a very different way. Some people's memories are able to record and retrieve the written word very efficiently. Some can even "see" in their memories a particular page they previously read or a page of notes they wrote. Others have memories that are best at recording and retrieving "pictures" or "videos" of something they've seen. Some people are able to learn best by reviewing how visual situations felt. Some can remember an event as if they experienced it from several different perspectives.

Some people need to view something going on in front of them and then take time to reflect on what they've seen. These individuals prefer to observe what's going on, which also is a visual experience. But their learning really takes place when they think about the event in abstract ways—when they think about the reasons or theories that could explain what happened.

BOX 2.1. **Learning Styles and Learning Strategies**

	Auditory	Kinesthetic	Reflection	Visual
Learning Strategy				
Reading or viewing				√
Hearing	√			
Speaking	√	√	√	
Writing		√	√	√
Hands-on experience		√		√

Hearing and speaking. Both hearing and speaking are auditory. Truly auditory learners are comfortable with learning what they hear even without a visual image. They can learn if they close their eyes during a lecture, listen to an audio recording, or hear information over the telephone. They're able to record and retrieve the sound of the information. Auditory learners are most effective when they study by reading aloud, participate in discussions, and repeat statements and formulas aloud.

Speaking is a form of active learning. In other words, a speaker is doing something, not just watching and listening to someone else. So speaking is a good way to reinforce your learning, especially if you're an auditory learner. In some colleges, professors use "speaking to learn" or "speaking across the curriculum" techniques for the same reason that many use "writing to learn" or "writing across the curriculum." When students have the opportunity to speak and hear their own explanations and arguments, they know whether they really understand the material.

Writing. A number of colleges and universities require students to write about what they're learning in all sorts of courses. This type of writing is often referred to as "writing across the curriculum" or "writing to learn." It involves having students explain something they've learned in their own words. Sometimes students are asked to write about how they think they might be able to use new knowledge or even how they feel about it.

Writing is a physically complex activity; it is much more complex than reading or viewing. It involves both visual and kinesthetic senses, as well as reflection on what words to use. When you write, you use your eyes and hands to put pencil to paper or pound out words on a keyboard. When you read what you've written, you're not only learning in a much more active and involved way than by reading what someone else has written; you're also involving more of your senses in the process, and you'll be able to think about whether what you've written really makes sense to you. Later in this chapter and in other chapters, we talk about numerous ways to be an active learner.

Point *to* PONDER

Many colleges and universities require students to write about what they're learning—something referred to as "writing across the curriculum."

kinesthetic: Involving the sense of touch and/or bodily movement; actively engaging by using your hands and/or feet, or perhaps your entire body.

© Vivian Scott Hixson

"Actually, I'm not going to read them. See, I'm taking architecture, and
we've got this project where we're supposed to build a house out of
alternative building materials, and I had this great idea . . ."

 Hands-on experience.   Some people learn best by doing; they are the truly
kinesthetic learners. These people can take things apart and put them back together to understand them. They're much more likely to enjoy the laboratory
and field-experience portions of courses. They're the people who prefer actual
experiences and actively experimenting. They learn best by doing.

Hands-on activities involve visual and kinesthetic experiences and sometimes involve auditory (listening) experiences as well. Some people need to actively experiment to see if they can make concepts from class really work in
order to know for sure that they've learned. If you're this type of learner, you
probably like to find practical uses for what you're learning. The need to experiment means that these types of learners, by their very nature, prefer active
learning experiences.

exercise Break 2.1

In the spaces provided below, record your answers to the questions.

1. **What do you think is your favorite strategy for learning? To help you decide, think back to a favorite
course, teacher, or activity. Write a specific example.**

_____

_____

2. Do you remember the method you used when you learned to tie your shoelaces, or when you learned to ride a bike? Which learning style(s) discussed above do you tend to use most often?

_____

_____

3. In order for you to remember to do something important, what method or methods help jog your memory?

_____

_____

4. How do your answers to these questions help you understand how you prefer to learn?

_____

_____

■ *Use Your Learning Style for Academic Success*

This course may devote some time to helping you size up your strengths and limitations as a student and discover your preferred learning style. If not, your college's **career planning and placement center** and/or **counseling center** may have one or more learning styles tests (usually referred to as inventories) available to you at low or no cost. You can also find many learning styles inventories online.

Two of the more widely used instruments for better understanding your learning type and learning needs are the Learning and Study Skills Indicator (LASSI®) and the Learning Styles Inventory (LSI®). Even personality-type indicators, such as the Myers-Briggs Type Indicator (MBTI®), can help you discover which ways you prefer to learn.

In addition to these three, you may learn about other inventories that can help you find out more about yourself as a learner. The particular inventories recommended by your college could help you learn more about (1) the ways you prefer to learn, communicate, and make decisions; (2) what skills you might need to develop; and even (3) what careers you might be interested in pursuing.

Because these instruments help you determine your strengths as a learner, they can help you adjust the ways in which you study. As a result of your preferred learning style(s), some methods won't work as well for you as they do for your classmates and professors. But differences among types of learners aside, everyone needs to become actively involved in the learning process to truly succeed in college.

■ *Understand Multiple Intelligences*

According to the theory of multiple intelligences, at least eight different kinds of intelligence can be measured, not just the verbal–linguistic and mathematical–logical types of intelligence that are measured on standard intelligence tests. According to this theory, different people have varying amounts of each of these eight types of intelligence, and each type is associated with its own ways of learning. Box 2.2 briefly explains the eight major intelligences described by this theory:

Point *to* ponder

■ **Knowing that others learn in different ways can help you understand why some of your classmates and professors use learning and teaching methods that don't work as well for you.**

career planning and placement center (career center): A campus office that helps students learn about career choices based on individual interests, values, and strengths, as well as how to research job opportunities

♦ ♦ ♦

counseling center: A campus office that offers academic, personal, and group psychological counseling.

BOX 2.2. **Preferred Learning Strategies Based on Multiple Intelligences Theory**

Type of Intelligence	*Examples of Preferred Learning Strategies*
1. Verbal–linguistic: ability to work well with languages.	Listening, listening to lecture, writing, discussing, memorizing, interviewing, reading silently or aloud, group work.
2. Logical–mathematical: ability to form and use abstract models and to use logic to understand concepts.	Using the **scientific method**, using analogies, asking questions, measuring, finding patterns, sequencing, graphing, diagramming, coding and decoding, figuring out probabilities or geometric properties, calculating.
3. Visual–spatial: ability to form a mental model of a three-dimensional spatial world and to operate using that model.	Sitting up front, using flow charts, using other types of charts and visual outlines, **mindmapping**, using visual memory techniques, using visual aids with lectures, using art projects as a learning tool, integrating art and mathematics, highlighting and note-taking in color, making displays, board games.
4. Musical: ability to create and understand musically.	Using background music while studying, creating and/or using songs to memorize concepts, using music of the specific time or place to learn about its history and culture.
5. Bodily–kinesthetic: ability to use one's whole body to experience in order to understand.	Participating in theater and role-playing, creating simulations, going on scavenger hunts, taking field trips, conducting experiments, taking things apart and putting things together, building models, creating flow charts, telling stories through dance and other movement, keyboarding.
6. Interpersonal: ability to understand others and their motivations, as well as ways others work and how to work with them.	Reflecting on **service-learning** activities, role-playing from diverse perspectives, discussing, interviewing, practicing conflict management.
7. Intrapersonal: ability to form an accurate model, or understanding, of oneself.	Giving and receiving peer support, identifying and expressing emotions about topics, **journal** writing (also referred to as journaling), setting individual goals.
8. Naturalistic: ability to be in tune with natural phenomena, including cycles and seasons.	Classifying, categorizing, taking field trips, describing, grouping, conducting experiments.

■ *Take Charge of Your Learning*

You are ultimately responsible for what you learn. You're the one who needs to know the material in order to get the grades and the degree or certificate that will lead to a good job. You can't expect to change what your professors do in the classroom or what they expect from their students. However, if an instructor allows time for a question-and-answer period, you can ask questions to let the instructor know which parts you don't understand. This may be a little embarrassing at first, but your classmates will secretly thank you for asking the questions they were too timid to ask. In addition, your professors will probably think you're more interested than most other students.

Sometimes you might find that your assigned textbooks are written in a way that's difficult for you to understand. Your struggles to make sense of them may stem from any of a number of factors. Maybe the vocabulary or sentence structure that's used is very complex. Maybe the author of the text has a learning style that's different from yours. If so, ask the instructor to suggest supplemental texts, or go to the college library to look for a text that you find more

exercise break 2.2

In the spaces provided below, record your answers to the following questions:

1. Which of your textbooks this term is the most difficult for you to read? Why?

_____

_____

2. What strategy or strategies are you using to understand textbook material that is difficult?

_____

_____

_____

scientific method: A research method that starts with a statement of what you think is the right explanation, then tests it, and finally states a conclusion about whether the statement still seems correct.

♦ ♦ ♦

mindmapping: Note-taking technique in which you use branching lines to indicate connections among related concepts.

♦ ♦ ♦

service-learning: Learning through helping others, usually for service hours, that is built into the curriculum of a course; often a report about the service is required.

♦ ♦ ♦

journal: A written account of your thoughts and activities as you learn, sometimes including how you feel about the activities and about what you're learning.

■ *Time to Reflect*

Think for a moment about the intelligences described in Box 2.2. Reflect on your particular strengths.

1. Which two or three of the eight intelligences summarized in the table describe you best?

_____

_____

2. How does knowing this help you determine useful learning strategies?

_____

_____

_____

readable. Keep in mind that the texts the instructor recommends may be organized differently from the assigned text. Some books on the library's shelves may also be organized so differently or may be so old that they don't include information the instructor considers important.

The Importance of Active Learning

▓ *What Is Active Learning?*

Traditionally, students in most U.S. colleges sit in lectures more than in any other type of teaching and learning situation. In such classes, professors provide information on a subject, and students more or less passively take lecture notes. Even if students are confused, they seldom feel brave enough to ask questions. What strategies do you use if, like many students, listening to lectures isn't your preferred learning style? Conventional wisdom is that most students remember less than 20 percent of what they see and at most only 10 percent of what they hear during a class lecture. You might do better than that, but most students don't.

Active learning is the opposite of what we've just described. In this type of learning, students must take on the responsibility of doing something with the course content, in class and/or outside of class. In other words, students must take responsibility for their own learning. If you go back to the list of five different activities on the first page of this chapter, you'll see that attending a lecture involves only two of the learning strategies mentioned. And if you flip back to Box 2.2, the list of eight intelligences, you'll see numerous learning strategies for each intelligence. You can pick out active learning strategies from either of these lists to help you learn both during and after a lecture.

▓ *Become an Active Learner*

Your instructors may help you become an active learner in a variety of ways. They may ask questions about previously assigned material. Some of them may divide their classes into small groups to apply new course material to solve a problem. Some may ask you to research the answer to a question and to make a presentation to the class. All of these methods, and many others, require you to do more than sit, listen, take notes, and memorize.

To a certain extent, traditional laboratory courses in subjects like biology and chemistry have always required students to actively engage in their learning. Students run experiments or dissect organisms and then record what they did and what they learned. But often the procedure, the tools, and the end result are preprogrammed—almost like following a recipe in a cookbook. This leaves little room for the trial-and-error method that works best for many types of learners.

What if your instructors don't provide built-in active-learning strategies? What can you do to create such strategies for yourself? Here are a few ideas, and you probably have other ideas to add. On your own, you can ask yourself questions about the material previously assigned. With others you trust, you and classmates can form a small group to see if you understand and can apply new course material. Alone or with your group, you can research the answer to a question before the next class.

Time to Reflect

1. Refer back to the part of the chapter on multiple intelligences as you reread the paragraph above. What forms of intelligence make it easier to learn in a lecture? In a laboratory? In a class discussion?

_____

_____

_____

2. What types of classes are most appealing to you?

_____

_____

3. What active-learning strategies have you used effectively?

_____

_____

4. With two or three others, share the strategies you wrote in (3) above. Write down the ideas that you think are worth trying.

_____

_____

exercise Break 2.3

In the spaces provided below, record your answers to the following questions:

1. List a few of the types of active-learning strategies your instructors have used over the past two weeks. Which of these did you find the most useful? The least useful?

_____

_____

2. Do you think your answers are related to your preferred learning styles? What useful active-learning strategy could you have used on your own in the past week or two so as to increase your chances of learning and remembering new information presented in class or in the textbook?

_____

_____

How Active Learning Helps You

At first glance, active learning may seem like an inefficient way to learn. The students struggle to come up with answers their instructors already know, and students are sometimes even required to figure out the right methods to reach the right answers. Why go through all that? After all, colleges pay substantial salaries to experts to teach

active learning: Being involved in such learning activities as writing, discussing, categorizing, graphing, experimenting, drawing, setting to music, role-playing, and group work.

classes. Why should professors let students struggle when they can just give students the right answers?

The reason many professors promote active learning has to do with the ways people really learn. Because of the ways our brains store new information, active learning makes it easier to pull information out later, when we need to retrieve and apply it. Only if you can retrieve information and use it in a variety of ways is it a part of who you are and what you know. We retain very little of the information we take in passively.

How do you take responsibility for being a successful active learner outside of class? Many professors suggest studying two to three hours outside of class for every hour spent in class. If all you do is read the textbook and review your lecture notes during those two to three hours, your brain may have trouble retrieving the information later. Students who are successful at taking notes and reading textbooks tend to be those whose intelligences are best developed for listening, writing, and reading. But if your strengths are more musical, bodily–kinesthetic, interpersonal, intrapersonal, or naturalistic, these probably aren't the best strategies for you. You're better off if you come up with one or more different active ways to learn the material. This course and this text suggest numerous strategies to help.

case study 2.1

Consider Ahmed . . .

Ahmed's best learning style is bodily–kinesthetic; he learns best by manipulating objects, by experimenting, by using bodily movement, by drawing, and by using other active strategies. His mind is always wandering, and he has difficulty sitting still during fifty-minute class lectures.

After receiving his first graded test in his 8 A.M. class, Ahmed analyzed why he did so poorly. To his dismay, he realized that the test primarily covered course material the professor emphasized most during lectures. In order to earn a good grade, Ahmed knew he needed to devise a strategy to stay focused and pay close attention during class.

Ahmed tried taking notes the way his friends did, by focusing on and writing down all the key words and phrases. But he ended up doodling and wriggling in his seat. Then he met with someone from the tutoring center to try to bring up his grade.

 If you were Ahmed's tutor, what strategies would you suggest Ahmed try?

_____

_____

_____

The tutor showed Ahmed a variety of strategies he could use. As a result

- Ahmed began to do stretching exercises before the class started to relax his body.

- During class Ahmed periodically changed his posture and did some **isometric exercises** to increase his attention span and the blood flow to his brain.

- Ahmed began to use four or more different colored inks and pencils during lectures. He drew pictures to represent the professor's ideas and drew arrows and dashed lines to represent connections among the lecture topics.

- Ahmed began to rewrite his notes in various colored inks on numbered three-by-five index

2.1 (continued)

cards. He wrote concepts in one color, examples in another, and questions in a third color. Using cards allowed him to sort some of the ideas, examples, names, theories, definitions, and questions so that they made more sense to him. He could spread the cards out and re-arrange them on the table to look at different connections or to study facts separately from definitions and theories.

• Sometimes Ahmed would study by walking or marching around his room while reading the cards aloud.

Ahmed's bodily–kinesthetic style required him to make numerous changes in the way he prepared for class, took notes and stayed focused during class, and manipulated and studied his notes after class. After several weeks, these changes felt so comfortable and worked so well that he stuck with his new routines. He became so successful in his 8 A.M. class that he continued to use these strategies throughout college.

Apply This Now

In a group of two or three students, discuss whether any of you have tried the strategies Ahmed experimented with in order to stay focused and pay close attention in class. How well did they work?

_____

_____

Which strategies that were new to you do you think might be worth trying? Why?

_____

_____

_____

isometric exercises: Exercises that involve only one or a few muscle groups at a time and that do not involve gross movement, only tensing and relaxing muscles. For example, you could tense the muscles in your feet for five seconds, followed by relaxing them for five seconds, then tense and relax your legs and continue with progressive muscle groups up to your neck.

♦ ♦ ♦

critical thinking: Questioning information through a process of "healthy skepticism" to evaluate whether the information is accurate, complete, trustworthy, and applicable to a particular situation.

Critical Thinking: Why Is It So Critical?

▨ *What Is Critical Thinking?*

You may or may not have had teachers or professors talk about your need to make **critical thinking** part of the way you study and learn. Critical thinking means having a "healthy skepticism" about what you hear or read. This involves more than learning new concepts, understanding new information, understanding your emotional responses, or mastering a skill. Critical thinking is active learning because it requires you to challenge a new concept or new information. Thinking critically about information means questioning whether (1) the information is accurate; (2) the information is complete; (3) the information makes sense in a particular context; and (4) you can trust the source of the information.

When you've mastered a new skill, critical thinking allows you to question whether it's the correct skill to apply in a certain situation. A different skill might be a better choice and result in a better outcome. For example, you might find that some professors respond to your questions best if you ask them in person. Others might prefer a phone call. Still others might prefer that you use your e-mailing and writing skills to ask questions online. Applying the right skills when approaching a particular professor can be a very useful application of critical thinking.

Thinking critically about your emotions, or the emotions you see in others, means questioning why you (they) feel the way you (they) do and whether these reactions make sense given what you (they) are responding to. You might be feeling a strong emotional response to a stranger, only to discover upon reflection that she looks a lot like a former classmate you never liked. Or someone may be pretending to like you, when all they're really doing is trying to get your vote, borrow your car, or in some other way take advantage of you. How can you evaluate whether your feelings are accurate or whether others are being sincere? You need to ask yourself difficult questions about what might really be motivating you or the other person. You might need to talk about your situation with a trusted friend or family member to seek a more objective opinion. Or you might just need a bit of time to reflect, to "sleep on it," to come up with a conclusion.

■ *Thinking Is Critical to Your Success in College and Beyond*

We're bombarded with commercial messages on TV, radio, billboards, magazines, newspapers, and the Internet. Most of us question whether the advertisements are "too good to be true." Sometimes the message is direct: You'll look years younger after using the product for several weeks, or this mouthwash will make your fresh breath last longer. Sometimes the message is subliminal, not really stated. People in car commercials are almost always happy, handsome, and enjoying life in the car being advertised. People in soft-drink commercials are almost always popular and attractive. Your college's advertising brochure is likely to show only happy, physically attractive, and enthusiastic students. By an early age you probably learned not to trust most of these messages. By this point in your life you might not even realize that you regularly engage in this type of reality check. This skeptical evaluation is what we mean when we use the term *critical thinking*.

You may not be as practiced in questioning whether information in articles, books, news broadcasts, and other media is the truth, the whole truth, and nothing but the truth. How will you determine whether an author is an expert? If two experts disagree, how will you know which one to trust?

You'll be taking courses in which the amount of material that's covered on a single test can be daunting. You may encounter tests in which you have to remember which formula out of the ten you've studied is the correct one to use to solve the problem in front of you. In a course that's introduced several theories to explain human behavior, you might need to know which theory is appropriate to use in a specific situation. Throughout this book, you'll learn about several strategies that can help you succeed academically. How will you decide which ones to use?

Time to Reflect

Think back to the last time you had a problem deciding on a brand of toothpaste, shampoo, or cereal. How did you use your critical-thinking skills to decide on the right brand for you? Put a check mark next to the items you compared:

1. Prices _____

2. Claims of quality _____

3. Features of special importance to you _____

4. Recommendations of people you know _____

5. Recommendations of experts _____

6. Your own previous experiences with the products _____

7. Other:

_____

_____

How might your decision have been different if you hadn't used your critical-thinking skills?

_____

_____

_____

_____

_____

case study 2.2

Consider Deborah . . .

Deborah was required to write a research paper for her biology class. The assignment was to write about any issue related to environmental effects on organisms. Early in the semester, all students were required to turn in a single sheet of paper with a title, a one-sentence statement that explained the position the student was taking on the issue, and information about three articles to be used as references. The professor would check to make sure the student was on the right track and return the paper with suggestions.

Deborah realized that this topic was relatively new. So she did a subject search on the web. She discovered that thousands of articles had been written about the topic. Some of the easiest to understand argued very strongly that the global-warming scare was being advanced by liberals who wanted to force the development of alternative fuels. Deborah thought this was very interesting and handed in the following:

Title: Global Warming Grossly Exaggerated: Political Liberals Exposed!
Statement of position: This paper will show that we are being manipulated by the liberal press into believing that the use of fossil fuels has caused a warming of the planet called global warming, when there is no proof of this environmental concern.

2.2 (continued)

Deborah's one-page draft listed not just three, but five articles that supported her position statement.

Deborah was upset when the professor handed back her paper and she saw the following comment written across the top: "Please come to see me in my office as soon as you can to discuss your research, your choice of references, and your topic. Your references and your position are not scientifically sound."

When Deborah went to the professor's office, the professor explained that recent scientific studies all indicated the reality of global warming. Not all agreed on the cause, but all were concerned about the predicted effects on weather, rising oceans, and the numerous organisms that would be affected. The professor explained to Deborah that anyone can publish articles on the Web, and that she shouldn't accept all web articles as accurate.

 Have you ever looked up something on the Web?

If so, did you encounter any web pages that you didn't trust? Why didn't you trust them?

_____

_____

If you haven't looked up anything on the Web yet, how do you think you'd know if the information on a web site was accurate?

_____

_____

The professor then gave Deborah the names of some of the most respected researchers in this area and the titles of some of the most respected web journals on environmental research. The professor also suggested asking a reference librarian in the college's library to help her search for these references and others the librarian might know about. He asked her to resubmit the assignment during the following week.

Deborah followed the professor's advice and found articles by experts in the field of global warming. This time the professor accepted the new title, position statement, and three references.

Apply This Now

1. Suppose the instructor for this course assigned you the task of finding three expert references on the topic of multiple intelligences. How might you get started?

_____

_____

2. Suppose two of the articles you found gave conflicting information. What would you do to try to determine which one to trust?

_____

_____

3. If your professor or the reference librarian told you that both articles were written by respected scholars who disagree, how could you include both viewpoints in your paper?

_____

_____

College success requires you to practice critical-thinking skills. Learning to apply this healthy skepticism will pay off in your personal life and in your future career. Throughout this text, you'll encounter exercises and end-of-chapter questions that will allow you to use your critical-thinking skills.

exercise Break 2.4

1. Can you think of a recent situation in which you questioned something on the news or in a newspaper article? If so, what was it, and why were you skeptical?

_____

_____

2. Look back at the section in this chapter on multiple intelligence theory. Use your critical-thinking skills to answer the following questions:

  a. What emotional reaction do you have to this theory? Can you speculate why you're reacting this way?

_____

_____

  b. Which of the multiple intelligences seems to describe you best?

_____

_____

  c. When might the multiple intelligence that describes you best be appropriate to use?

_____

_____

  d. When would the one that describes you best be inappropriate to use?

_____

_____

problem solving: Devising a feasible solution to a problem, puzzle, dilemma, or difficult situation.

♦ ♦ ♦

core curriculum (general education): The courses selected by the faculty that are required of all degree-seeking undergraduates at a college or university.

♦ ♦ ♦

analyze: Try to understand the true nature of something, how or why something works, or its component parts.

♦ ♦ ♦

synthesize: Combine parts to make a whole; combine concepts, even diverse concepts, into a broader, coherent reality.

Critical Thinking for Problem Solving

In addition to increasing your ability to concentrate and manage the stress in your life, another important set of skills that is useful to develop during college involves your ability to think critically to effectively solve problems. Critical thinking and **problem solving** are both important in higher education. Your college's **core curriculum** (or **general-education** requirements) probably includes specific courses to help you learn critical-thinking and problem-solving skills. As you begin to think more critically about what you learn in college, you'll develop skills that will allow you to learn at a level higher than merely memorizing information. Critical-thinking and problem-solving skills require you to develop the ability to **analyze** a situation and to **synthesize** different skills and information to come up with an answer.

To thoroughly analyze an interpersonal or professional situation or a problem, it's sometimes necessary to find out who might be involved, why, what's at stake, how different individuals will be affected by different decisions, and what the various possible solutions or outcomes might be. It can be valuable to try to state the problem from other people's perspectives. You might ask them to state their understanding of the situation; then try to restate their words. If they agree with your restatement, you've accurately reported what they're saying. This strategy will help you understand their point of view. Once you understand another person's perspective, you may even begin to respect a point of view that you don't agree with.

When you synthesize, you're figuring out how different things fit together in order to come up with a new solution. You may need to bring together different aspects of a problem, different but related problems, and/or different individuals' needs. Synthesis is the most difficult and most creative type of critical thinking. You have to thoroughly understand the problem, who or what is affected by the problem, and, conversely, what affects the problem.

By analyzing and synthesizing information and others' perspectives, you might see ways to provide a solution or outcome that's better than other suggested outcomes. In an interpersonal or business situation, this may be an outcome that helps everyone—a "win-win" situation. Or it's possible that each outcome you propose might be beneficial to some but not all involved. In this latter case, it may still be necessary to find ways to compensate the "losers" that will be acceptable to the "winners," to turn the situation into a win-win outcome.

Time to Reflect

Turn back to the section on critical thinking. Write an example of how your critical-thinking skills have helped you solve a recent problem in your life.

_____

_____

_____

_____

_____

Point *to* PONDER

Critical-thinking and problem-solving skills require you to develop the ability to analyze a situation and to synthesize different skills and various sorts of information to come up with an answer.

Maybe you've taken tests that required you to demonstrate your ability to analyze and synthesize. Maybe you've completed complex assignments that have helped you develop these skills. Or maybe you've studied on your own or in groups, without an instructor's guidance, and done work that has improved your critical-thinking and problem-solving skills.

exercise break 2.5

When students decide to attend college, they often need to use problem-solving skills to decide which school to attend, what to study, where to live, whether to work full-time or part-time, and/or how to pay for their education, just to name a few. Name three problems you had to solve in making the decision to attend college.

_____

_____

_____

At some colleges and universities, the terms critical thinking and problem solving might mean that you have to make hypothetical decisions and justify them on an ethical basis. Usually such assignments appear in **upper-level** courses. They involve applying what you've learned to complex societal or professional problems. Some majors require one or more courses in logic, philosophy, and/or ethics to prepare students to think critically about such issues.

If your college has incorporated multiple opportunities for you to work on your critical-thinking and problem-solving skills, you'll be actively learning and working very hard. If you're successful at these levels of higher learning, you'll develop effective study habits and problem-solving skills that will come in handy well beyond college. This type of activity will have a big payoff later in your career and will make you a more knowledgeable family member, neighbor, and citizen.

exercise break 2.6

Suppose your professor told you that there would be problem-solving and critical-thinking questions on the next test. In the space provided below, explain why this requires more, and perhaps different, studying than questions that require you only to memorize or describe something.

_____

_____

_____

_____

upper level: Courses that require you to have previously completed foundation-level courses; a university course designed to be taken during the junior or senior year.

take it away!

Throughout this chapter we've asked you to consider a number of concepts and strategies that can help you become a more effective and efficient learner. Some of the important ideas we've discussed include the following:

- *Discover your favorite ways to learn.* Knowing the ways you like to learn allows you to use your preferred styles to study. If you don't already know your favorite ways to learn, find out if your college offers one or more of the learning-styles instruments that will help you determine your preferred style.

- *Experiment with new active-learning strategies that can work for you.* Try rewriting your notes, reading aloud, talking with others, singing, categorizing, or using one of the other strategies discussed in the section on active learning.

- *Apply critical thinking.* Critical thinking allows you to evaluate information, sources of information, emotions, and skills, and determine when it's appropriate to use particular information and skills. College success requires you to practice and improve your critical-thinking skills.

- *Learn how critical thinking is necessary for problem solving, and why problem solving requires you to more fully understand course material.* When you analyze and synthesize material or bring together various sources of information to solve a problem, you're bound to learn that material more thoroughly.

In Chapter 3, we turn our attention to several strategies you can use to increase your ability to focus your efforts for success. In particular, we discuss strategies for increasing your concentration and effectively managing stress in your life.

Questions for Critical Thought

1. Describe your strengths as a learner and your preferred learning strategies.

2. Choose any one of the courses you're currently taking, and describe its passive- and active-learning elements. What can you do on your own outside of class to add active-learning strategies? In what situations might active learning not be the best tool to use in this class?

3. You're more successful as a learner if you use which of the following: auditory, visual, or kinesthetic learning strategies? Why do you think so?
   a. Does the answer depend on what you're studying? If so, give examples of when you use one strategy instead of another.
   b. Can you think of a situation in which you combined two or maybe all three strategies? Did this work well for you?

4. Given what you've learned about multiple intelligences in this chapter, what three different learning strategies might best help you remember the main points of *this* chapter?

5. How did this chapter require you to use critical-thinking skills? Reflecting on your strengths and weaknesses as a learner, which kinds of critical-thinking skills do you need to work on most?

6. Look back at the Points to Ponder that appear in this chapter.
   a. Which Point to Ponder surprised you the most?
   b. How does knowing this help you better prepare for academic success?

7. How does the information presented in this chapter help you in your life outside of the classroom and college environment? Which strategies discussed in the chapter are particularly relevant to success in your career and personal life?

Web Site

Visit the *Overcoming the Hurdles to Academic Success* web site for a chapter outline, review exercises, additional case studies, links to other online resources, and a practice test.

References

Campbell, L., Campbell, B., & Dickinson, D. (1999). *Teaching and Learning Through Multiple Intelligences,* Second Edition. Boston: Allyn and Bacon.

Gardner, H. (1993). *Multiple Intelligences: The Theory in Practice.* New York: Basic Books.

3

FOCUS your efforts for success

S Chapter 3 Strategies

1 If you need to study and can't seem to concentrate, try sitting up very straight, standing, or walking around a bit.

2 If you're studying on your own, give yourself breaks. Try switching from subject to subject once you reach a good stopping point.

3 To jump-start a new concentration cycle, try to spend a minute or two sitting up straighter and doing a few isometric exercises that won't disturb nearby students.

4 In class act interested by keeping your eyes on the professor or on the visual aids, bending your body slightly forward, or nodding occasionally to indicate you're understanding and/or agreeing with your professor.

5 Schedule your meals so that you finish at least thirty minutes before your next class or exam.

6 Work with your body's natural rhythms. Your individual daily rhythmic pattern will include periods of major rises in the molecules that chemically regulate attention.

7 To maintain faith in yourself and your goals, think about a positive event in your life, meditate, or pray.

8 Exercise is a helpful strategy for dealing with bad stress.

9 One way to stop procrastinating is to promise yourself a reward *after* you've accomplished the necessary task.

10 Another way to keep yourself from procrastinating is to use the buddy system.

11 Thinking about how much you care for another person can motivate you to complete tasks that will please that person.

Methods to Enhance Concentration

In Chapter 2 you learned about the importance of determining your preferred learning style and the benefits associated with active learning and critical thinking. This chapter will help you increase your capacity to concentrate on your studies. We'll also teach you effective ways to manage the stress in your life.

Suppose your professor gives a standard fifty- or seventy-five-minute lecture, and your maximum concentration time is much less than that. Or suppose you aren't concentrating as well as usual, and your mind begins to wander. Numerous circumstances and skills can affect how much you learn—a gifted teacher, your ability to take good lecture notes, and much more. But if you don't concentrate on the material you need to learn, even the most ideal circumstances and most highly developed skills won't help. You simply *must* focus your attention in order to learn. This section offers numerous strategies for enhancing your ability to concentrate.

■ *Use Your Brain*

Scientists continue to learn more and more about how our brains work. Fortunately, with little or no extra effort, we can use much of what they're discovering to increase our capacity for learning. It just takes practice to follow some of the suggestions to make our brains work more effectively.

Blood flow to your brain.   During class and study time, you need to have as much oxygen-rich blood as possible flowing to your brain. When you sit up straight or when you stand up, your body is signaling your brain that you need to be alert. Your brain responds by sending more blood to various parts of your body. Doing the opposite, slouching or laying your head down, tells your brain that it's time for you to rest, conserve oxygen, and go into a relaxed, inattentive mode. If you need to study and can't seem to concentrate, try sitting up very straight, standing, or walking around a bit.

exercise Break 3.1

In your regular study space and at your next regular study time, try switching your study topics every fifteen to twenty minutes, taking a very short break between each topic. Then record below what you experience.

1. What did you do during your breaks?

_____

2. Was it easy or difficult for you to get back to studying after each break?

_____

3. How did taking short breaks periodically help you stay focused on the material you were studying?

_____

_____

Giving yourself some breaks.   Some researchers propose that you can't fully concentrate on anything for more than twenty minutes straight. Others say the cycle is up to ninety minutes long. Think about how well you're able to concentrate during class lectures or while reading your textbook, and try to figure out your maximum efficient concentration time.

If you're studying on your own, it's easy to give yourself a break. If you have two or more courses to study for, try switching from subject to subject once you reach a good stopping point. If you're studying only one subject, take a very short break to do something that requires a limited amount of time. What you do on this break should be something that requires little brainpower and that isn't at all exciting. Take out the trash. Brush your teeth. Start a grocery list. Sort the laundry. Do the dishes. The important thing is to take *quick breaks* to recharge your mental battery. If you switch topics at good stopping points and occasionally stop studying for a few minutes to accomplish something in your immediate environment, you'll discover that you really can study effectively for long periods of time.

Concentrate!

Assessing how well you're concentrating.   You've surely experienced being involved in a conversation or reading for a while, only to realize you can't remember a thing from the last minute or two. You totally stopped concentrating. To become good at studying, you have to become aware of your own level of concentration. To do this, you need to make a habit of monitoring your previous level of concentration whenever you take a break from your studies. In other words, you have to think about how well you were thinking.

What can you do to jump-start a new concentration cycle? One thing you might try is to spend a minute or two very deliberately sitting up straighter and doing a few isometric exercises that won't disturb the students sitting nearby. By taking just one minute every twenty or thirty minutes to keep yourself alert, you'll concentrate on the information being presented for a much longer period of time.

Sending the right cues to your brain.   This might sound weird, but it really works: Your brain learns more when your body sends it signals that indicate your interest in what's going on. You don't even have to be truly interested; you can fool your brain on this one. In class, you can act as if you're interested by keeping your eyes on the professor or on the visual aids being used, bending your body slightly forward as if you're hanging onto every word, or nodding occasionally to indicate that you're understanding and/or agreeing with what your professor is saying. Your professor might even pick up on this body language and conclude that you're a good student who's very interested in class. Consequently, your professor will probably look at you more often. With this increased eye contact, your brain will be even further stimulated. It's really no surprise that most students who use these techniques learn material faster and remember it longer.

Scheduling your meals.   Try to always schedule meals so that you finish at least thirty minutes before your next class or exam. Do you remember the rule you learned about not swimming for at least thirty minutes after eating? The swimming guideline exists because your body automatically sends more blood to your stomach to aid in the first stage of digestion. This may leave too little oxygen-bearing blood for leg muscles to operate effectively, leading to cramping and possibly drowning. It's useful to apply this rule to attending classes and taking exams whenever you can, for a similar reason. When part of your blood supply is diverted to the stomach, there is less blood, meaning less oxygen, going to your brain. That interferes with your learning new information and with your ability to retrieve that information at a later time.

 Working with your body's natural rhythms. Individuals have different daily rhythmic patterns, but at about 6 A.M. many adults experience a major rise in the molecules that chemically regulate attention. For them, the level of these molecules usually remains high through the morning and then decreases during the rest of the day. If this is your pattern, it's best for you to use your mornings to do whatever you absolutely need to do well. Then try to use your afternoons and evenings for tasks that require less precision and for tasks you'd enjoy at any time of day. Your interest in the more enjoyable tasks will help you maintain focus.

Time to Reflect

Make a check mark in the appropriate box to indicate your usual pattern of alertness during each of the time segments in a twenty-four-hour period:

Time of Day	Very Alert	Mostly Alert	Mostly Not Alert	Asleep
6–8 A.M.				
8–10 A.M.				
10 A.M.–noon				
Noon–2 P.M.				
2–4 P.M.				
4–6 P.M.				
6–8 P.M.				
8–10 P.M.				
10 P.M.–midnight				
Midnight–2 A.M.				
2–4 A.M.				
4–6 A.M.				

What are the best times for you to take classes?

What are the best times for you to study?

Note: If you didn't check "very alert" in more than one space, consider reflecting on your lifestyle: Are you getting enough sleep? Are you eating nutritious foods and exercising? Are you reasonably satisfied with your present situation? Are you maintaining a positive attitude? You might need to make some adjustments. Your college's health center and counseling center can help.

The traditional pattern of morning alertness may not describe your pattern at all. Most teenagers, for example, tend to be most awake and alert late in the evening. If you're a young adult, you may be at a point in your life when you're switching from one pattern to another. Whatever your pattern might be, you'll want to figure out your body's natural rhythms and develop ways to use them to your advantage.

case study 3.1

Consider Takumi . . .

Takumi signed up for a very rigorous curriculum during the first **semester** because he wanted to become a doctor. He took biology with lab, chemistry with lab, English, history, and precalculus. That added up to seventeen semester credit hours. He'd breezed through high school with little time spent in study and had expected to breeze through college, too. Takumi was thrilled that he had registered early enough to get all morning classes with early labs. That way he could work in the afternoons, so he could afford to go out on dates. This is what his first semester schedule had looked like:

Takumi's Class Schedule

Course	Monday	Tuesday	Wednesday	Thursday	Friday
Chemistry	8–8:50		8–8:50		8–8:50
Biology	9–9:50		9–9:50		9–9:50
Precalculus		8–9:15		8–9:15	
History	10–10:50		10–10:50		10–10:50
English		11–12:15		11–12:15	
Chemistry lab	11–2				
Biology lab			12–3		

All through high school, Takumi's classes had started at 9 A.M. and ended at 4 P.M. But he was convinced that he'd have no trouble getting to classes on time. He knew Mondays would be grueling, but the other available lab times had him on campus until 5 P.M. That didn't sound at all pleasant. As it turned out, Takumi usually did make it to his 8 A.M. classes on time—barely on time, but without breakfast and sometimes without a shower. Since he wasn't always wide awake, he sometimes slouched in the back row. On Tuesdays and Thursdays he had one hour and forty-five minutes between precalculus and English, so Takumi often used that time to eat a full breakfast.

Takumi would be taking his first exams in biology, chemistry, history and precalculus during the fourth, fifth, and sixth weeks. His English class required papers for his writing portfolio, and so far he'd turned them all in on time and was doing well. Takumi studied his lecture notes and read his textbooks during the third week. His longest study time was late at night after supper and his favorite TV shows. But he started having trouble making it to his 8 A.M. classes; when he did make it, he was so tired that he slouched and couldn't concentrate. He earned a B– on the biology exam, but he got D's on the other three exams. Takumi knew he had to get at least a B+ average to get into medical school. He was devastated.

3.1 (continued)

 If you were Takumi, what would you do to salvage the semester?

_____

_____

_____

Takumi made an appointment to see his biology instructor. He told her about his difficulties in his other courses and how overwhelmed he felt. She asked him questions about when he studied and how he studied, and she even looked at his lecture notes. Then she asked him if he was really willing to make sacrifices for the next two months to succeed. She told him that she would give him advice that would not be comfortable for him to follow, but that he needed to trust this advice until the end of the term to see if it would work for him.

Takumi's instructor recommended going to sleep by 10:30 P.M., waking up by 6:30 A.M., and eating a light breakfast before his 8 A.M. classes — even if only a granola bar and a carton of milk—

on Sundays through Thursdays. This shift in his sleeping schedule would be difficult, but concentrating in 8 A.M. classes required Takumi to shift his study time to much earlier in the evenings and to his optimum alert time every weekend.

She asked him to talk to his chemistry lab instructor to see if he could start attending another section that started later in the day. That required Takumi to negotiate a change in work hours with a coworker and his supervisor. But he managed to make arrangements. That gave him time for lunch and a short study session before work every day. He even decided to make lunch his major meal of the day during the week, so that he'd be more alert during his evening study times.

Takumi did have some difficulty switching to this early time schedule. But he managed to make the schedule work for the rest of that semester in order to pull up his grades. He earned an A– in biology and a C in history. He managed to bring up all of his other grades to B's. He continued with his biology major, but in future semesters he avoided 8 A.M. classes and never took more than two classes without a break between them.

Apply This Now

1. Have you ever taken an evening class or worked an evening shift? If so, describe your level of alertness and the way your body felt, comparing them with your alertness and how you feel in day classes or daytime work shifts.

   _____

   _____

2. Have you ever taken 8 A.M. classes or had some other regular early morning commitment? Describe that regular commitment and your usual level of concentration.

   _____

   _____

3. When you find your level of concentration lagging in class, what strategies do you use to help you concentrate better?

   _____

   _____

semester: Length of the period in which courses are offered in colleges and universities that break the nine-month academic year into two main parts.

Effectively Manage Stress in Your Life

▓ *What Is Managing Stress All About?*

College students tend to push themselves to new limits, experimenting with novel experiences, attempting to accomplish new goals, and deciding whether to redefine who they are. Testing your limits to learn more about yourself is the way you continually define and redefine your individuality. You will probably continue this process throughout your life. But every year, some students push themselves too far, too fast, and sometimes in the wrong directions. They end up causing themselves, and sometimes others, serious setbacks, worry, heartache, and/or injury.

Maintaining positive mental health is a matter of finding balance between harnessing the beneficial stress you feel and finding ways to release negative stress so it doesn't overwhelm you. Managing stress doesn't mean banishing stress from your life; it means harnessing it to accomplish your goals.

▓ *Understand the Difference Between Good and Bad Stress*

Stress can be good or bad for you, depending on how it affects you. Some **stressors** can actually be good, as long as you use them to keep working toward your goals. These good stressors may include getting up on time, being responsible with your money, remembering to stay in contact with family members, attending each and every class if at all possible, knowing that tests and papers are coming due, and knowing that you have to learn enough to reach your academic goals. Like most students, you probably have to maintain certain grades

$\overline{\text{Point}}$ *to* PONDER

▓ Managing stress doesn't mean banishing stress from your life; it means harnessing it to accomplish your goals.

Time to Reflect

1. What do you consider to be the good stressors in your life?

_____

_____

2. Why are they good?

_____

_____

3. What are your bad stressors?

_____

_____

4. What about them or your response to them makes them bad?

_____

_____

5. What strategies might you use in order to minimize or eliminate this week's bad stressors?

_____

_____

Note: Don't forget that your college's counseling center can assist you in coping with the stress in your life.

to be allowed to continue in school or keep your scholarship or other financial assistance. Feeling good stress about these necessary duties will keep you doing what you need to.

To the extent possible, try to avoid bad stress—the stress that keeps you from focusing on your academic and career goals. Bad stressors, both physical and emotional, get in the way of learning. They can monopolize your thoughts or cause such strong emotional reactions that you can't concentrate on what the instructor, tutor, discussion leader, or textbook is trying to teach you. A wide variety of potential bad stressors lie in wait for you every day: inadequate sleep or nutrition, arguments with loved ones, the illness of someone you care about, your own illness, going to class unprepared, financial difficulties, and just plain feeling hungry. You obviously can't avoid all bad stress, but you can adjust your behaviors and habits to minimize some of them.

▓ The Importance of Positive Thinking

Another self-inflicted bad stressor that you may experience every now and then is negative self-talk, that small voice in your head that causes you to question your ability to succeed. In Chapter 1 we discussed how much more you're able to accomplish and how much better you feel emotionally and physically when you maintain a positive, can-do attitude. Sometimes that can be difficult, especially when you engage in negative self-talk at times of high stress.

The simple act of faith in oneself and in one's goals fails everyone at times. But there are ways to combat these feelings. Some people use meditation or prayer. Others think about a positive event in their lives. Still others engage in physical exercise so that their brains release endorphins, and/or they can use their exercise time to put their brains into a state of meditation while their bodies are busy. If you have exercise equipment handy, that's great. But it isn't necessary. Taking a walk, sweeping the porch, washing the car, or doing any vigorous activity for fifteen to thirty minutes can greatly reduce the anxiety you feel. Exercise causes your brain to release endorphins that make you feel better. As an added bonus, regular exercise keeps you healthy in other important ways and makes you feel better about your body. You and your classmates can probably think of other constructive, positive ways to make your attitude more positive through even the most stressful situations.

▓ Monitor Your Reactions to Stress

It's useful to monitor your reactions to stressors in your life. When you experience stress as bad, do you tend to shift your focus to an unimportant task in order to avoid facing, for example, an important deadline? Do you focus all of your attention on what's wrong and how it affects you? Or do you tackle the stressor head on and do what you can to relieve the bad stress you feel? What's important is to learn to recognize your natural reactions to stressful events. That way you can begin to develop healthier methods of coping with and managing the stress in your life.

Point *to* **PONDER**

Stress can be good for you or bad for you, depending on how it affects you.

---

stressors: Circumstances or situations in your life that cause you to experience anxiety and/or stress, such as a fender-bender or tomorrow's test.

exercise break 3.2

1. In the space below, list three strategies you use to create and maintain positive thoughts and feelings.

_____

_____

_____

2. Form a group with three or four of your classmates, and share your strategies with one another. Write down any of their strategies that you might want to try in the future.

_____

_____

_____

case study 3.2

Consider Sarita . . .

Sarita had been an average high school student, but she hated to study. She couldn't make herself concentrate long enough to read a social studies chapter. She got sleepy while she was trying to finish her literature assignments late at night. She tried taking a modern foreign language, but she failed because she couldn't remember all the irregular verbs.

Sarita received a scholarship for the paralegal certification program at the local community college. She was both excited and scared about this opportunity. She knew she would have to spend a lot of time studying outside of class.

Sarita's first class met on Monday evenings. On the first Monday, the instructor had the students study the entire **syllabus** so they would understand what he expected them to accomplish during the term. Then he talked about his **office hours** and how the textbook was organized. He also announced a free Saturday morning study-skills workshop for all students, sponsored by the Paralegal Students Association and the college's Study Skills Enhancement Center.

Sarita felt overwhelmed by the assigned reading and papers she'd have to write. She hadn't

bought the textbook yet, but it looked thick and wordy. She was keenly aware of her tendency to react to stress by avoiding the activities associated with it.

 If you were Sarita, what would you do?

_____

_____

Even though Sarita's natural reaction was to avoid dealing with the stress, she worked up enough courage to go to the front of the room after class and sign up for the study-skills workshop. On Saturday morning she joined thirty other students at the workshop. It was being run by officers of the Paralegal Students Association and a Study Skills Enhancement Center staff member. After initial introductions and a short description about what to expect, they handed out the self-scoring version of the Myers-Briggs Type Indicator (MBTI®). The MBTI® confirmed that Sarita would enjoy and benefit from studying as part of a group, that her usual tendency

3.2 (continued)

was to learn the "big picture" better than the details, that she was likely to put undue pressure on herself when she didn't learn a concept as quickly as she thought she should, and that she liked to study subjects that had definite rules, like math formulas. The workshop involved mini-sessions that focused on how Sarita could use her strengths and work effectively in a study group.

The leaders gave Sarita practical suggestions about different study methods. The ones she found most useful included (1) studying alone on any one topic for no more than thirty minutes, (2) joining a study group that met at least once a week, (3) studying between some of her classes

and on her work breaks, (4) giving herself realistic deadlines, and (5) carrying index cards in her purse so she could study details just about any-where. The only costs were 79 cents for a package of three-by-five index cards and a couple of dol-lars for some colored markers.

Because Sarita wanted to succeed and was aware of her tendency to avoid stressful situations, she took charge and learned to use her strengths for a positive outcome, a C+ in literature, and A's and B's in her paralegal courses. These strategies proved to be so helpful to Sarita that she contin-ued to use them throughout college. She now works for a law firm, goes to college part-time in the evenings, and still employs those same strate-gies to study for her prelaw bachelor's degree.

Apply This Now

1. What are the three worst college stressors for you?

_____

_____

2. With whom on your campus might you consult for help?

_____

_____

3. With one or two of your classmates, discuss how Sarita's problems are similar to and differ-ent from yours. Would any of Sarita's new study strategies work for you? Why?

_____

_____

_____

syllabus: Written contract provided by the in-structor at the beginning of the term to explain goals, objectives, strategies, texts, assignments, and how to contact the instructor.

◆ ◆ ◆

office hours: A period of time each week when an instructor is available in her or his of-fice to meet with students. Office hours are often listed on the syllabus.

◆ ◆ ◆

procrastination: Putting off or delaying an activity until a few hours or days prior to the due date.

▓ *Overcome the Temptation to Procrastinate*

One of the most stress-producing activities that college students often engage in is **procrastination**. Why do you procrastinate? Sometimes you have other things to do that are more fun. You might make a decision to do what's more appealing at the moment. You can do the work by giving up the opportunity for fun, or you can go ahead without thinking about the time-management consequences. The latter can lead to trouble if you don't allow enough time to complete your work.

Another reason students procrastinate is that they don't want to face the assignment because they're afraid they don't know how to start. As mentioned earlier in the chapter, some people try

© *Vivian Scott Hixson*

I was going to do my research paper today, but then when I realized that the
research paper would take three days, and the weekend was only two days,
I decided to go to the beach instead."

to cope with the stress of a difficult task by shifting their focus to an unimportant task. The individual who does this is trying to avoid the stress of thinking about an important deadline or the stress of starting an important project. This tactic can create academic disaster, as well as monumental stress when the assignment deadline is just ahead. If instead the student just took the first little step toward completion, if only to do fifteen minutes of planning, the little act of taking charge might help overcome the initial fears of inadequacy.

exercise break 3.3

1. **In the space below, quickly jot down the first five or six major reasons you tend to procrastinate.**

_____

_____

_____

_____

_____

_____

2. **Now go back and select the most likely reason that you procrastinate. Write a specific plan to lessen your likelihood of procrastinating for this reason.**

_____

_____

_____

How can you break the cycle of procrastination? Various individuals use different strategies. One of the following might work for you. One way to stop procrastinating is to promise yourself a reward after you've accomplished the necessary task. The reward could be spending time on an activity you really enjoy, such as calling a friend, watching TV, or taking a walk. It could be the purchase of something you've been wanting, perhaps new shoes, a book you've wanted to read, or dinner in a restaurant. Or it could just be a mental pat on the back, telling yourself you're a better, smarter person for getting the dreary tasks out of the way.

 Another way to keep yourself from procrastinating is to use the buddy system. The way this works is to set up a task to be accomplished together with one or more other people so that finishing it requires everyone's efforts. Your sense of responsibility to the other individuals can keep you on track to do your part.

 Thinking about how much you care for another person can motivate you to complete tasks that will please that person. Sometimes the tasks you have to accomplish will lighten someone else's load. People you care about could be proud of your accomplishments simply because they care about you. For instance, your parents, grandparents, other relatives, and friends take great pleasure when you tell them you've reached a goal that's important to you. Thinking of their pleasure can spur you on to complete even the most difficult or unpleasant chore.

Take It Away!

The purpose of this chapter has been to help you learn strategies that you can use to focus your efforts for academic success. In particular, you've learned strategies to

- ***Enhance your ability to concentrate.*** When you study it's important to be aware of your body's rhythms. To keep your studying effective, take a break every now and then, and don't eat right before you have to remain alert. You can trick your brain into being alert with exercise, good posture, and eye contact that mimics alertness.

- ***Find ways to avoid or lessen bad stress in your life, and use good stress to your advantage.*** Remember that managing stress doesn't mean banishing all stress from your life. It means harnessing stress to accomplish your goals. Try to remain positive as you cope with anxiety-provoking situations, and learn what your natural reactions to stressors are so that you can learn the most appropriate ways to deal with them. Work to lessen your tendency to procrastinate, which will get rid of potential bad stress in the future.

In Chapter 4 you'll learn ways to make better use of your time, and you'll begin to understand how working in groups can help you overcome some of the hurdles to academic success. You'll also analyze how, when, where, and under what conditions you currently study so that you can make changes to make the most of your individual study time.

Questions for Critical Thought

1. Brain research indicates that we're unable to effectively concentrate on one type of activity for more than twenty to ninety minutes. How long do you think your concentration cycle lasts?
   a. How do you currently structure your study time to accommodate your brain's need for change?
   b. What other ways to accommodate your brain might you consider trying?

2. What are the best times of the day for you to study and take classes? Do you currently plan your activities to take advantage of your daily body rhythms?

3. In what ways have you tried to trick your brain into learning more? Which other ones might you consider trying?

4. Explain in your own words what is meant by the term *good stress*. What are you accomplishing in your life that you would not accomplish without good stress?

5. If you're like most of us, you tend to procrastinate.
   a. What types of tasks do you tend to procrastinate on most?
   b. How do you make yourself accomplish these tasks?

6. Look back at the Points to Ponder that appear in this chapter.
   a. Which Point to Ponder surprised you the most?
   b. How does knowing this help you better prepare for academic success?

7. How can an understanding of the concepts presented in this chapter help you outside of the college and classroom environment? Which strategies are particularly relevant to success in your career and personal life?

Web Site

Visit the *Overcoming the Hurdles to Academic Success* web site for a chapter outline, review exercises, additional case studies, links to other online resources, and a practice test.

References

King, J. (1995). "Enhancing Student Learning." *Presentation* at Texas A&M University, April.

Sylwester, R. (1995). *A Celebration of Neurons: An Educator's Guide to the Human Brain.* Alexandria, VA: Association for Supervision and Curriculum Development. (ASCD, 1250 N Pitt St., Alexandria, VA 22314).

create
Effective
study Habits

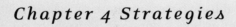

Chapter 4 Strategies

1 As you design a weekly schedule, estimate the amount of time you need every day to take care of yourself, your home, and others.

2 Try to distribute any extra hours where you think you need them most.

3 If everything doesn't fit, reduce the time on an activity so you can reach your most important and most immediate goals.

4 Alternatively, delay or modify some of your goals.

5 You may need to modify your timeline for reaching your goals.

6 Use your planner to record all important upcoming dates and deadlines (such as exams, quizzes, and term papers) as soon as you find out about them.

7 Write everything in your planner in pencil, as some of your professors will adjust their schedules.

8 Look at your planner often, at least at the beginning of each week, updating it whenever there's a change or something to add.

9 If you've been assigned a term paper or other major project, write some intermediate deadlines in your planner.

10 Before you begin a study session, have specific and achievable goals in mind.

11 Try to break your study time into fifteen- to thirty-minute chunks. Give yourself a break of one to five minutes before going on to a new chunk of study time.

12 Each time you take a study break, take stock of what you just accomplished. If you're pleased with your progress, give yourself a mental pat on the back.

13 If you're not pleased with your progress in the study session, assess why you didn't get as far as you had expected, and try to make adjustments.

14 Schedule regular study-group meetings to take a project through its various phases.

15 Keep your study group small, with five members at most.

16 Study-group members have to be clear about their expectations at the first meeting.

17 Rotate the role of group leader, so no one can dominate or ignore what other members say.

18 At each study-group meeting, have someone take notes about decisions on assigned tasks, on a rotating basis.

19 Start working as a study group as soon as you have a well-defined and relatively short assignment to work on.

20 Before an exam, study-group members can consider potential exam questions, and/or each can take responsibility for outlining or summarizing a major concept, theory, or event.

Effective Time Management

In the last two chapters you learned about the type of learner you are, and you became better acquainted with some tools for becoming an active learner. You also learned strategies for increasing your capacity to concentrate, manage stress, and think more critically when solving problems. This chapter will focus on ways to improve your study habits to become a more successful college student. You'll need to honestly examine how, where, and with whom you study now, whether it's working well for you, and if you need to more effectively manage the ways you spend your time.

The Importance of Managing Your Time

When you were in high school, you probably had very little control over your school day. You probably started and ended school at the exact same times each day. Most likely, you attended the same classes each day during a semester and had lunch at exactly the same time.

Perhaps you've been out of high school for a while, working at a part-time or full-time job. If so, it's not likely that your employer allows you to decide how you spend your work hours. It's much more likely that your supervisor not only plans your activities for you but also checks now and then to make sure you're on task. This type of routine in no way prepares someone for the hours of unplanned time between college classes.

You may have heard the saying "If you need to have something done right and on time, ask a busy person to do it." This advice works because busy people have learned to manage their time. They can squeeze in more activities than those who haven't mastered this skill. Luckily, anyone can learn the skill of time management. But it takes practice, honest self-assessment, and diligence.

Being an efficient time manager doesn't mean that you're ruled by the clock and don't have time for fun. It means that you've taken charge of how you use your time. You can schedule some fun and still meet your obligations as a student, friend, worker, and family member.

Are you making a true commitment to yourself as a student? Are you willing to put in the amount of effort it's going to take to get the grades you want? Do you know what it's going to take? As discussed in Chapter 2, a good rule of

Time to Reflect

Look back at the academic goals you set for this term in Chapter 1.

1. How many courses are you still planning to complete? List each of the courses. Next to each, write in the grade you expect to earn.

_____

_____

_____

_____

_____

2. How can effective time management help you earn these grades?

_____

_____

_____

thumb is to set aside two hours for study outside of class for every hour in class. If you're a part-time student taking one standard three-hour course that meets for 150 minutes each week, this means that you should set aside 300 minutes—an additional five hours—per week to study for that course. A part-time student taking two three-hour classes needs to set aside ten hours per week to study. Later on, you may decide to modify this 2-to-1 ratio, but don't make changes until you know the amount of time that is right for you. In some classes you might need more time, while in others you'll need less.

Even though most professors recommend this ratio, the majority of first-year students admit that they don't study this much. That's why it's not surprising that most students' predictions about their first term's grades turn out to be overly optimistic. Students who don't study the recommended number of hours usually end up with disappointing grades.

exercise break 4.1

For each course you listed in the previous Time to Reflect exercise, write down the number of study hours you think you'll need each week in order to earn the grade you expect. Now add up these out-of-class study hours.

_____

In order to schedule this number of study hours, what activity or activities might you have to give up or curtail?

_____

_____

Point *to* ponder

Even though professors recommend studying two hours outside of class for every class hour, most first-year students say they aren't studying this much. Not surprisingly, most students' first-semester grades are lower than they expect.

Suppose you're taking the minimum number of credit hours to be a full-time student, usually a twelve-hour course load. Your total in-class and out-of-class time commitment is thirty hours per week. Some full-time students take as many as sixteen credit hours a semester. For a sixteen-hour credit load, the class and study time total is forty hours a week, equivalent to a standard full-time job!

Allow Time for Your Health and Well-Being

As you begin to design a weekly schedule, be sure to estimate the amount of time you need every day to take care of yourself. Include time you need for sleeping, getting started in the morning, traveling, eating, cleaning, shopping, exercising, and winding down at night. Don't forget to add in some time each day for relaxation, a hobby, being alone, and/or being with your loved ones.

Once you've estimated the time it takes to accomplish your academic goals and meet your basic physical and emotional needs, can you fit it all in? With only 24 hours a day and seven days a week, your week totals only 168 hours. If everything fits, how many hours do you have left? Try to distribute any extra hours where you think you need them the most. If everything doesn't fit, can you realistically cut back on some activity to be able to reach your most important and most immediate goals? Alternatively, which goals can you delay or modify? Once you've figured out how you'll use your time, you're ready to plan a schedule.

Check How You Spend Your Time

It's a good idea to start planning by seeing how you're already managing your time. For an accurate look, keep track of your activities for one week. (See the first Question for Critical Thought to get started right away.)

EXERCISE BREAK 4.2

1. Briefly jot down how you spent the day yesterday.

_____

_____

_____

_____

_____

2. Spend a few minutes describing to a person who sits next to you in class how you spent the day, and listen while that person describes his or her day to you. Do either of you regret any wasted time or time doing something you don't think was worthwhile? If so, what changes could you suggest for each other?

_____

_____

3. If you and/or the person sitting next to you think you spent your time well, what time management hints could you share to help others?

_____

_____

For an example of a detailed time schedule for a successful student, examine Leticia's Monday schedule in Box 4.1. Leticia is a second-year math major who shares an apartment with another student.

BOX 4.1.   **Leticia's Monday Schedule**

12 midnight: sleep	12 noon: linear algebra lab
12:30 A.M.: sleep	12:30 P.M.: linear algebra lab
1 A.M.: sleep	1 P.M.: linear algebra lab
1:30 A.M.: sleep	1:30 P.M.: linear algebra lab
2 A.M.: sleep	2 P.M.: study break with friends
2:30 A.M.: sleep	2:30 P.M.: calculus study group
3 A.M.: sleep	3 P.M.: calculus study group
3:30 A.M.: sleep	3:30 P.M.: drive home
4 A.M.: sleep	4 P.M.: Rosie O'Donnell Show
4:30 A.M.: sleep	4:30 P.M.: Rosie O'Donnell Show
5 A.M.: sleep	5 P.M.: continue reading English literature assignment
5:30 A.M.: sleep	5:30 P.M.: talk on phone
6 A.M.: sleep	6 P.M.: prepare dinner with roommate
6:30 A.M.: up/shower/dressing	6:30 P.M.: dinner/clean up/TV news
7 A.M.: breakfast/review history notes	7 P.M.: watch TV
7:30 A.M.: drive to school	7:30 P.M.: continue reading for English literature
8 A.M.: history class	8 P.M.: start reading next calculus chapter
8:30 A.M.: history class	8:30 P.M.: start reading next history chapter
9 A.M.: coffee with friends	9 P.M.: e-mail friends
9:30 A.M.: review linear algebra notes	9:30 P.M.: surf the net
10 A.M.: linear algebra	10 P.M.: prepare for bed
10:30 A.M.: linear algebra	10:30 P.M.: pleasure reading
11 A.M.: lunch with friends	11 P.M.: sleep
11:30 A.M.: lunch with friends	11:30 P.M.: sleep

Leticia spends seven-and-a-half hours in academic pursuits, with two of these hours in classes and another two hours in a lab. Her Tuesday classes are intermediate calculus and English literature. Because she needs to prepare for these classes, she spends most of her individual and group study time on these subjects. Leticia almost completed her English literature assignment over the weekend, so she needs only one hour on Monday to finish. She won't be in her history and linear algebra classes until Wednesday, so she's only just started on those new assignments.

Leticia spends only a half hour at a time on any of her subjects. She's learned that her mind wanders if she tries to work for more than thirty minutes on any one topic. Even though she's a serious student, in just this one day she intersperses a number of short breaks—visiting with friends, watching TV, talking on the phone, playing on the computer, and reading for relaxation.

This particular schedule works well for Leticia. She's learned what she requires for sleep, chores, attending all classes, relaxation, and studying to earn mostly B grades, enough to keep her **Pell Grant** and her scholarship.

We've provided a calendar broken into thirty-minute chunks at the end of this chapter for your use over the next week. As you record your activities, write in just enough detail for the entry to make sense to you when you review it another time. Be sure to record your time usage every day, maybe each evening before going to bed.

▨ *Make Adjustments to Reality*

Before assessing how they spend their time, some students complain that they just don't have enough hours in the day or days in the week. They can't finish their assignments, go to class regularly, and still have time for friends and family. But after examining what they've written down for a week, most students discover that they can make some adjustments to use their time more efficiently. Granted, if you're attending school, raising a family, and working full-time, you're likely to have to give up some activities or cut down the amount of time you spend on them.

 Your time constraints may make it unrealistic for you to reach your academic goals within the time limits you've set for yourself. You may need to modify some of your academic goals or your timeline.

Time to Reflect

Take out your list of goals from Chapter 1. Rank them in order of importance. Do you realistically have time to accomplish all of them?

If the answer is no, which ones can wait or can be modified? (If you have a significant other, the two of you may need to make the decision together.)

case study 4.1

Consider Isaac . . .

Isaac is thirty-four and has a full-time job with regular hours. He and his wife Becky, who also has a full-time job, have two young children, a dog, and a house with a yard. Isaac is back in college part-time, taking classes on Monday through Wednesday evenings, after **stopping out** for nine years. He studies, spends time with the children, and does his share of housework and yard work.

Isaac and Becky were worried that he wouldn't have time to also be an attentive husband. They wanted their marriage to continue to be strong. They had so little time together, and they spent that time on necessary, serious decision making. There didn't seem to be enough time for enjoying each other's companionship. All this seriousness made their time together stressful.

 If you were Isaac or Becky, how might you suggest solving this problem?

_____

_____

_____

Isaac and Becky found a solution. They hired a babysitter to allow them to have regular Thursday evening dates of two or three hours. This is the only way, and the only time, they've found to have uninterrupted time alone together. It costs them a little money they'd rather not spend, but they believe the time together is worth it. They want a lasting marriage, and finding time to be alone together is as important an investment for their future as Isaac's college studies.

■ *Plan Ahead*

Many of your professors will let you know about major assignments at the beginning of the term, even though some assignments won't be due for many weeks. In order to complete all the intermediate steps of a major project on time, you need to plan how to use those weeks. It's best to write everything in one place so you can refer to it and update it as necessary. For this reason, many college bookstores sell semester-length calendars, or **academic planners**.

For years, first-year students have complained to us that we're treating them like babies when we require them to purchase and use academic planners. Many new students don't realize that we're treating them like the professionals they're preparing to be. Many professionals use calendars—sometimes electronic calendars—to keep track of appointments, special events, and the dates when they have to complete certain tasks.

Use your planner! Record all important upcoming dates and deadlines (such as exams, quizzes, and term papers) as soon as you find out about them. *Write everything in pencil,* as some of your professors will adjust their schedules. Look at your planner often, at least at the beginning of each week. Be sure to update it whenever there's a change or something to add.

If you've been assigned a term paper or other major project, you'll want to write down some intermediate deadlines. For example, schedule times to go to the

Pell Grant: Federal program that awards funds to students based on financial need. Not a loan program; a student who fulfills Pell requirements doesn't have to pay any money back.

◆ ◆ ◆

stopping out: Taking some time away from college for one or more semesters.

◆ ◆ ◆

academic planner: Calendar with spaces to write test dates, deadlines, and important appointments; important academic dates and other college-related information are usually included.

Apply This Now

1. Like Isaac, you probably have had to make some sacrifices in order to pursue your college education. List some of the major sacrifices you've made.

_____

_____

_____

_____

2. Do you feel you're either sacrificing the wrong things or sacrificing too much right now? If so, what adjustments might you want to make?

_____

_____

_____

_____

library to start research and also times to write the first draft. Write down the times and places for study-group and review sessions before exams. Be sure to write down your exam dates! This planner may become so useful and reliable that you'll want to add other important events, such as birthdays, social plans, and doctor appointments. Many professionals do this in order to keep up with their personal appointments and obligations. *Reminder:* Be sure to write *everything* in pencil, because all events and appointments—except maybe birthdays—can change.

© *Vivian Scott Hixson*

exercise Break 4.3

1. Take out the syllabus for one of your courses. Which course is it?

_____

2. In order, using a pencil, write down all the important dates and events (quiz, test, presentation, paper due, etc.) for this course. Include everything, even the final exam.

Date	Event	Date	Event

3. Now think about realistic deadlines to prompt you to undertake some activity to be ready for each event—such as when you need to start reading and/or reviewing textbook chapters and lecture notes, or when to start research. Fill in the spaces below with some examples.

Date	Event	Date	Event

▓ *Organize Your Study Time*

As much time as you'll need to study outside of class, you'll need a plan to fit it all in. Remember, you'll do best if you study regularly at your most productive study times.

Scheduling study sessions.   Don't forget to start out with the expectation of studying two hours outside of class for each hour of class time.

Assigned reading.   It's always best to do reading assignments when they are suggested by the instructor or the course syllabus. Most instructors want you to read any and all assigned chapters of the textbook *before* you attend the lecture on those chapters. This works well for some students. But it can be difficult for others for any number of reasons. If you fall into the latter group, you should at least try to get a feel for the major content of those chapters prior to attending lectures. Chapter 7 will help you develop effective reading strategies. Be sure to schedule reading time into your planner.

Managing your study time in each session.   Before you begin a study session, it's helpful to have particular goals in mind. Make sure the goals you establish for a study session are specific and achievable. If it works for you, try to break your study time into fifteen- to thirty-minute chunks. Give yourself a break of one to five minutes before tackling the next chunk. As long as you take regular breaks, you'll probably be able to study effectively for two hours or more in the right environment without feeling fatigued or becoming distracted.

Time to Reflect

Read back over the last paragraph. Now think about the information in Chapter 3 on how to keep your brain alert. How can the information on keeping your brain alert help you organize your study time better?

_____

_____

Create the Right Study Environment

Choosing the right study environment is crucial for optimal learning. This section will help you consider ways to create a study environment that will help you overcome some of your hurdles to academic success. Maybe by now you've experimented enough to know the ways in which you learn best and the ways that don't work for you. Your right study environment may be quite different from someone else's right study environment. An honest assessment of which study conditions work best for you is an important first step.

Your Attitude

Do your best to start each session with a positive attitude. You'll be more successful if you feel confident you can do the work. And you can trick your brain into thinking you're interested in studying by using the techniques described in Chapter 3 to enhance your in-class concentration.

Your Study Space

Some students like to study in their bedrooms, in their own space. Others prefer the student center, the family dining room, an empty classroom, the library, or the computer center. When the weather is nice, some study outdoors. The important thing about the right study space is that it allows you to concentrate, save time, and learn well. Where do you accomplish the most?

Your Distractions

Students often study with the TV or music playing. They say they can't concentrate when it's quiet or when they are distracted by street noises or other people in rooms around them. For others, a quiet place with few distractions is ideal. If you need relative peace and quiet, you might have to wait for the right time to get it. Turn off the TV or radio if it's distracting you. If people around you are making a lot of noise, try to negotiate for more quiet or look for another time and/or place to study. But if you study better with a particular kind of noise or music in the background, try to find a way to include that noise or music.

Many students who are also working parents study after their children are in bed and/or early in the morning. Another good study time is when the children are playing at their friends' houses or taking naps. It's always a good idea to be prepared for the occasional unexpected few minutes of quiet time; keep a book, notebook, or note cards handy. You'll be surprised by how much you can accomplish in just a few minutes while standing in a grocery line.

Point *to* ponder

■ Each time you take a study break, describe what you just accomplished, and give yourself a mental pat on the back.

Your Body

You want to be comfortable without signaling your brain that you're ready to sleep. Move around so that you don't remain in the same position too long. Wear clothes that are comfortable for the temperature of the room. Most importantly, if you can find any other time to study, avoid studying when you're tired. (Review the ideas in Chapter 2 on learning styles and Chapter 3 on ways to keep your brain alert.)

Assess Your Study Results

Each time you take a break, take stock of what you just accomplished. If you're pleased with your progress toward your study goal, tell yourself; give yourself a mental pat on the back. You deserve it! If not, don't beat yourself up about it. Instead, assess why you didn't get as far as you had expected, and try to make adjustments. Were you too ambitious about what could be done in fifteen to thirty minutes? Were you studying in the wrong place or time? Do you need help from your professor, a tutor, or your study group?

EXERCISE BREAK 4.4

1. Describe below what you consider to be the right, or ideal, study environment for you.

_____

_____

_____

2. In what ways does this right environment differ from your usual study environment?

_____

_____

_____

3. Try making changes for the next week to come closer to what you think is the right study environment for you. Then ask yourself if you think these changes have helped you study more effectively.

Participate in Study Groups

Our experience is that group learning is very effective for most students. That is, group study helps most students learn more quickly and more thoroughly, and remember the material better. More and more professors are experimenting with group learning strategies in their courses. In some instances working with a group is voluntary, and in others it is required. Most often, instructors create groups of three to five students to solve complex problems, to work on case study projects, or to write and present term projects.

Perhaps when you've worked on a project with other students, only one or two of you did most of the work. If so, you may have little or no enthusiasm for group work in college. But most college-level group learning projects have safeguards built into the process. For instance, they often require all group members to make an honest, and confidential, assessment of the contributions that they themselves and other group members made to the project.

Group learning is *active learning* by its very nature. Students tend to work harder in groups. Mature students feel a sense of responsibility to the group, and immature students know that the group can and will turn on them if they don't carry their share of the load. A successful group schedules regular meetings to take the project through its various phases rather than waiting to throw something together at the last minute.

The group must plan, research, discuss, and write. Some members might be good at certain tasks, such as drawing graphs or charts, making models, leading group discussions, revising, or creating handouts and transparencies. Although everyone takes on specific tasks, you'll all learn from one another. Furthermore, group members often learn important interpersonal skills in such areas as communications and negotiation. These skills are of tremendous value in the professional world.

Many study groups also decide to study for other classes they're taking together. We've observed some freshman teams that were so successful that they continued to register for classes together and study together for years.

Exercise Break 4.5

In a group of three or four students, brainstorm what you consider to be the necessary ground rules for all group members in order to

1. Protect everyone from potential freeloading by some members;

2. Keep one or two members from taking over;

3. Set a realistic schedule of meetings; and

4. Stay on schedule.

_____

_____

_____

_____

_____

_____

Although some of your classes may require group work, most probably will not. If your instructors don't require group work, we urge you to consider forming study groups on your own. Keep a group to a small size, with five members at most. With a larger group, it's difficult to coordinate schedules, and some members might be reluctant to speak out.

So how do you form a group? It takes a tiny bit of courage to ask a couple of classmates to study with you unless you're friends already. Most people will like the idea and be glad someone asked. The worst that can happen is that someone will decline. That person isn't sending you a message that you're not worthy, only that she or he prefers studying alone. It's not nearly as devastating as being turned down for a date. You just ask someone else.

Choosing the right people for a study group is very important. Sometimes it's easy to spot people in your classes who would be good study-group members. They're the students who are engaged in the course. They get to class on time, pay attention, hand in assignments on time, and usually can answer a question when asked. Of course, the personalities of individuals in the group play a role in its success. You'll want to work with people who are generally enthusiastic and responsible. Members with a sense of when to take charge, take a back seat, or compromise are gifted with interpersonal intelligence. They're naturals for group work.

▨ *Roles and Responsibilities*

It's *very important* for everyone in the group to understand and take seriously their and others' responsibilities to the group. You'll all have to be clear about your expectations at the first meeting. It might be useful for your group to rotate the role of group discussion leader. That way no one can be accused of trying to take over or of ignoring what some members say. Some groups have someone take notes about decisions on assigned tasks, also on a rotating basis.

▨ *Get Started*

It's best to start working as a group as soon as you have a well-defined and relatively short assignment to work on, such as a problem set or review sheet. Meet at a mutually convenient time in an easily reached neutral place. As a group you must decide how to attack the assignment and divide up the work. Then decide on the time and place for the second meeting. At this second meeting, you can discuss whether you think you've all done enough for the professor to consider the assignment complete.

By starting with a relatively minor and definitely limited project, you'll have a chance to see how well you work together. You haven't risked wasting much time or invested too much unreciprocated effort if some members don't do their part. And you will see if there are personality conflicts among members. Even if problems arise, some members of the group will probably want to continue. You might try to bring in others to replace the ones who aren't working out. And when a group *does* work well, you'll all have a much better output for your efforts.

case study 4.2

Consider John . . .

John was a wrestler in high school. In wrestling and in his classes, he had always tried to do his personal best. He was competitive by nature and prided himself on doing better than most of his classmates.

In John's first college class on Monday morning, the instructor handed out the first assignment, due in two weeks, and divided the class into study teams of four students each. She explained her reasons for giving team assignments and the penalties for students who did not uphold their responsibilities to the other members of the team. She gave the students ten minutes at the end of class to meet their team members and decide on a time and place for their first team meeting.

John's team held a short meeting on Wednesday right after class. John was worried that they might not get along and that some members of the team might not want to do their share of the work. Being skeptical about relying on others, John pushed for an early draft, even though all the other members seemed serious about the assignment. After some discussion, they divided the assignment into four approximately equal parts. They shared their phone numbers and agreed to call if they ran into problems. All group members promised to have their selected parts completed in time for an early Monday morning meeting, one hour before class, with copies for all the members of the team.

 If you were John, what would you do to prepare for the next group meeting?

_____

_____

On Monday morning, John showed up ten minutes early with his four copies. He was confident that he'd done a good job. Two other members showed up on time, and they began sharing and explaining their answers. They were worried about the fourth member, and they finally decided to divide up his questions. John was surprised that the two members who prepared answers had done such a thorough job. He was also surprised that one of them answered her part quite differently from, and much better than, the way he would have.

After class, the fourth member apologized for not making it to the group meeting. His daughter had been sick, and he hadn't had time to work on the questions over the weekend. But he wanted them to share their answers and said he would work on his part of the assignment before Wednesday.

 If you were John or one of the others who showed up on time with the work completed, what would you say to the fourth member?

_____

_____

John and the other members conferred with the instructor about what to do. They decided to meet again on the following Wednesday night. At that time, they'd see how well the fourth member answered his set of questions. If the answers seemed thorough, they'd share their answers with him. After all, he had their phone numbers and could have alerted them about his problem. The penalties had been clearly communicated ahead of time; and the fourth member of the team had a lot of catching up to do if he didn't want to fail his first group assignment.

Apply This Now

We've all been surprised from time to time by an innovative way someone else has solved a problem or completed a task. And at least once we've all surprised others in this way.

1. Think of a time when you've learned about an innovative solution to a problem. Briefly describe it.

   _____

   _____

   _____

 2. In a group of two or three students, share your experiences. How do they reinforce the potential value to you of working in groups?

   _____

   _____

   _____

▧ *Work Together as a Group*

Once you all feel that you've assembled a hard-working and productive group, you can work on some assignments with more at stake, such as studying for exams or preparing major assignments. To study for an exam, group members can **brainstorm** potential exam questions, and/or each can take responsibility for outlining or summarizing some major concept, theory, or important event. Each can volunteer for coming up with examples or applications of specific concepts. You'll need to agree on how to divide the work into chunks and who will take responsibility for each chunk. You'll also need to agree on how often you'll meet.

Take It Away!

The purpose of this chapter is to help you study more effectively. In it, you've learned strategies to

- *Take charge of your time.* Don't forget to use a planner to help you plan all of your important activities, including study time.

- *Think about how, when, where, and under what conditions you can make the most of your individual study time.* With a bit of experimentation with different study environments and an honest assessment of what makes you efficient, you'll make the most of your study time.

- *Make study groups work for you and the other group members.* You all need to agree on your expectations for individual group members and the rules you need to follow.

   The primary purpose of this chapter is to help you create effective study habits to increase your chances of overcoming the

brainstorm: An idea-generating technique in which all ideas are recorded and no judgment is made about the value of any of the suggestions.

hurdles to academic success. In addition to mastering these strategies, it's extremely important for you to use some of the academic support resources on your campus. In Chapter 5 you'll learn about the types of resources and support services that most colleges and universities provide to help their students succeed.

Questions for Critical Thought

1. Copy the one-week calendar at the end of this chapter to record your use of time each day for the next week. After you've filled it out, answer the following questions.
   a. How much time did you spend in classes? In study? Was this what you had expected? If not, how might the difference affect your grades?
   b. How much time did you spend reaching your other, nonacademic goals? Was this what you had expected? If not, how might the unexpected difference in the amount of time affect your ability to meet these goals?
   c. Were you surprised to learn how much time, or how little time, you spent on some of your activities? If so, which one(s), and how did it (they) differ from your expectations? Do you think you might make some adjustments in your goals or your use of time as a result?
   d. Do you think you might want to modify any of your strategies for meeting your goals as a result of learning how you currently spend your time? How might you do that?
   e. Consider using the calendar on page 66—or an abbreviated version—as a way to organize your time for every class day of the semester. You can write down every regular commitment, including classes, labs, work, study, meals, exercise, and sleep. Then post the calendar to remind yourself of the time commitments you've made in order to reach your goals.

2. Have you ever used an academic planner to write down your assignments? If so, did it help you organize your time and plan ahead?

3. Why do you think some students resist using a study planner or calendar to write down their assignments and other important events?

4. Look back at your answers to Exercise Break 4.4 describing your ideal individual study space and your ideal ways of studying.
   a. How close is your ideal to your actual?
   b. If it's not close, what can you do to improve it?
   c. What would be entailed in making changes?

5. Describe your ideal group study space and your ideal ways of studying in a group.
   a. How close is your ideal to your actual?
   b. If it's not close, what can you and your study group do to improve it?
   c. What problems might any members of your study group have with your suggestions? How might all of you be able to resolve these problems?

6. Write down three to five rules that you consider extremely important for members of a study group to abide by.

7. If you've worked in a study group, what did you think was useful about it? What aspects of the experience weren't so useful? What might you be able to do in the future to make group study more useful?

8. Look back at the Points to Ponder that appear in this chapter.
   a. Which Point to Ponder surprised you the most?
   b. How does knowing this help you better prepare for academic success?

9. How can an understanding of concepts presented in this chapter help you outside of the college and classroom environment? Which strategies discussed in the chapter are particularly relevant to success in your career and personal life?

Web Site

Visit the *Overcoming the Hurdles to Academic Success* web site for a chapter outline, review exercises, additional case studies, links to other online resources, and a practice test.

Reference

Light, R. J. (2001). *Making the Most of College: Students Speak their Minds*. Cambridge, MA: Harvard University Press.

Calendar Page

Photocopy the calendar on page 66 so that you have seven pages. At approximately the same time(s) each day, fill in each of the previous half-hour spaces with the activity that used up more of that time than any other activity. Continue until all pages are filled in for seven consecutive days. For some activities of a personal nature, it isn't necessary to be explicit. Such times could be designated with such terms as "personal time," "leisure," "recreation," or "hygiene." The purpose is for you to see how well you're spending your time. You may decide to change your priorities, delete or shorten some of your activities while spending more time on others, or just rearrange your activities.

Day of week: _____	Date: _____
12 midnight	12 noon
12:30 A.M.	12:30 P.M.
1 A.M.	1 P.M.
1:30 A.M.	1:30 P.M.
2 A.M.	2 P.M.
2:30 A.M.	2:30 P.M.
3 A.M.	3 P.M.
3:30 A.M.	3:30 P.M.
4 A.M.	4 P.M.
4:30 A.M.	4:30 P.M.
5 A.M.	5 P.M.
5:30 A.M.	5:30 P.M.
6 A.M.	6 P.M.
6:30 A.M.	6:30 P.M.
7 A.M.	7 P.M.
7:30 A.M.	7:30 P.M.
8 A.M.	8 P.M.
8:30 A.M.	8:30 P.M.
9 A.M.	9 P.M.
9:30 A.M.	9:30 P.M.
10 A.M.	10 P.M.
10:30 A.M.	10:30 P.M.
11 A.M.	11 P.M.
11:30 A.M.	11:30 P.M.

5

utilize academic support services

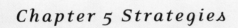

Chapter 5 Strategies

1 In your first couple of meetings with an academic advisor, be prepared to answer basic questions about your academic and career goals.

2 If you don't know where your advisor's office is, ask at the office that coordinates advising to help you find it or to direct you to another academic advisor.

3 Check for the dates of advising and early registration in your college's catalog, schedule of classes, student newspaper, or other source that publishes academic deadlines.

4 Preparing for meetings with your academic advisor will make them more productive. Make an appointment, and plan to show up at least five minutes early.

5 If you're meeting with your advisor to discuss what to take next term, have a list of courses in mind. If you're meeting to

discuss questions or concerns, write them down.

6 One good way to adapt to the teaching/learning style used by a professor is to "translate" from her or his style to your own.

7 Try adapting to a professor's teaching/learning style by working in a study group with students who are more comfortable with her teaching methods than you are.

8 If you know you'll have to miss class: (1) approach the professor *before* the class, (2) apologize for having to miss it, and (3) ask for recommendations for catching up.

9 If you're shy about visiting your professor during office hours, bring a study group member or a friend from the class with you.

10 Don't ask the following types of questions, unless the instructor has *clearly* made the offer before: (1) Will this be on the test? (2) Is this important? (3) I had to miss a class. Did you go over anything important? *Never* ask (4) May I borrow your lecture notes; I have to miss class?

11 If a teaching assistant is helping the instructor, you should be as respectful to the teaching assistant as you would be to any other instructor.

12 Your college's tutoring services can help you understand a concept, theory, application, or other important part of a course.

13 Bring your textbook, pencils and paper, class notes, and any particular assignment or study questions that you're having trouble understanding to a tutoring session. If you're planning on working with a writing tutor, take the latest draft of your paper.

14 If you can't find the tutoring assistance you need through campus resources, you might want to hire a private tutor. A private tutor can be very expensive.

15 If your school offers workshops to help you improve your study skills, consider signing up for one, even if the workshop covers some strategies you've already learned.

16 If you have a documented disability, contact the individual or office that will advocate for you as soon as you can.

The last two chapters focused on ways you can become more successful in college by strengthening your academic skills and success strategies. If you've applied the strategies described there, you're already managing your time, and you're studying more effectively alone and with others. This chapter refocuses you from skills to the academic support services your college offers.

By academic support services we mean all the resources the campus provides to help you plan your **curriculum,** register for classes, and successfully complete your courses. You've probably already received advising assistance. **Academic advising,** or **academic counseling,** is available to you throughout your college career. The resource you'll use most often is also the most important—the faculty who teach your classes. This chapter describes what instructors expect of their students and what students can expect from their instructors. Most campuses also provide tutors and others to help you learn outside of class. Other standard campus resources are networked computer labs and services for students with disabilities and other special needs. Some campuses provide special help to minority students, women, athletes, military veterans, and/or parents of young children.

Your instructors are available to you on a regular schedule at no extra cost. On most campuses, many or all of the other services described in this chapter are free of charge to enrolled students, and you can take advantage of them as many times as you want. None of these services are really free, however. Some funding source or sources make these services possible; your tuition and fees, donations and grants, and/or state and local taxes probably help pay for them.

Your campus, if at all typical, provides a wealth of services, but *you're responsible for seeking them out.* Your student handbook, catalog, or other publication might mention these services, but students often don't even know where or how to look them up. You may not wish to use all of your college's academic services. Most students don't. But it's important to find out what's offered. You or someone you care about just might need some of them someday.

Academic Advisor

Before you registered for your first class, you were probably required to meet with someone called an academic advisor or academic counselor. This person might have been a professional advisor with an office in a central advising center. You may have met with a faculty member who teaches and advises. Or perhaps you met with an experienced college student, sometimes called a peer advisor, who was specially trained to help other students schedule their beginning courses.

    In your first couple of meetings with an academic advisor, you'll want to be prepared to answer some basic questions about your academic and career goals. Have you already decided upon particular academic and career goals, or have you narrowed them down to a few options? Are you ready to commit to a major or program of study? If not, don't be too concerned. For the first year or more, many students don't know what major they want to pursue or what kinds of jobs interest them. Many others who begin college believing they've already made that decision will change their minds at least once. Don't forget that your college's career center can help you make informed career decisions. If you're confused about what to major in or what career to pursue, career counselors at the center have the tools and expertise to help.

Some colleges and universities stipulate a time by which you have to choose a major. The time is usually a major milestone, such as the beginning of

curriculum: The concepts, theories, information, and/or skills to be learned in a course or from a program of study.

◆ ◆ ◆

academic advising (academic counseling): A service provided to help you choose appropriate courses and/or academic program(s) in order to help you progress toward academic goals and, sometimes, career goals.

Time to Reflect

Surely many people have advised you in your life—parents, teachers, high school counselors, friends, and others. Think of a recent time that you sought out someone's advice.

1. Who advised you?

_____

2. What may have qualified that person to advise you, and what do you think was his or her motivation to help you?

_____

_____

3. Was the advice valuable?

_____

4. Why?

_____

_____

exercise Break 5.1

1. With one or two other students, describe your most recent experiences with an academic advisor. Include (a) what you discussed, (b) where your meeting took place, (c) the major outcome of the meeting, and (d) how you felt about the interaction.

_____
_____
_____

_____

2. In what ways were the experiences of the other group members similar to your experiences?

_____
_____

_____

3. In what ways were they different?

_____

4. Do you feel good about the way academic advising is provided on your campus? Why?

_____
_____

the sophomore or junior year. Or it may be spelled out in terms of the number of credit hours completed. Some other colleges and universities do the opposite. They don't allow their students to make a declaration of major until they've reached a milestone or completed a certain number of credits. Your advisor will know how soon you need to make this decision. If you're concerned, be sure to ask.

Time to Reflect

Once again, as you did in Chapter 4, review your academic goals.

1. Explain as you would to an academic advisor why you selected each of these goals.

_____
_____
_____
_____

_____

2. Suppose your advisor asked you how certain you were about wanting to reach each goal. Write a percentage from 0 percent to 100 percent next to each goal.

▣ *Initial Contact: Placement into Courses*

You may have been required to take placement exams as part of the initial advising process. If so, these exams have been designed to find out the level of course work that's right for you. The goal is to help you start out at a level that sufficiently challenges you but doesn't overwhelm you. Your academic advisor relies on the results of your placement tests to recommend some of your beginning courses.

Accurate placement allows you to complete your studies as quickly as possible. But it also ensures that your courses won't be hurdles set so high as to prevent academic success. If your placement indicates that your skills are not yet at a level for you to succeed, or if you have not yet met the college's minimum competencies, you may be advised to take **developmental courses**.

Colleges most commonly require students to take placement exams in mathematics, reading, and writing. It's also common to require tests in foreign languages for students who plan to continue taking foreign-language courses. That's because not all high schools teach math, writing, languages, and other subjects the same way or with the same results.

Some colleges rely on nationally standardized tests for initial course placement. Colleges that require their own tests have decided that nationally standardized tests can't tell them accurately how well their students are prepared for curricular requirements. Most are paper and pencil tests, although more schools are switching to computerized placement exams. Some are oral exams, most likely for placement into a modern foreign language. Others can be performance exams, most likely for placement for voice or musical instrument performance.

Placement information also can help your academic advisor identify certain subjects for which you seem to have advanced preparation and/or special talents. But you may need to tell your advisor about any advanced preparation you've accomplished. If you register before your scores are posted for Advanced Placement (AP) courses, you should inform your advisor about your AP work.

Your initial contact with an academic advisor may not be in the advisor's usual office. Or the advisor who met with you may no longer be assigned to you. This is likely if your first meeting is during an **orientation** session a few weeks or months before classes start. Usually you'll meet in the advisor's regular office for subsequent meetings. If you don't know where your advisor's office is, you might have to do a little research to find it. You can ask at the office that coordinates advising to help you find the same advisor or to direct you to another academic advisor.

▣ *Additional Contacts*

developmental courses: Classes that start out at your current skill level and help you develop your skills until you are ready for your college's core curriculum and beginning major courses.

◆ ◆ ◆

orientation: A program to help you make a successful transition to college, often including advising, registration, and opportunities to meet other new students and learn about campus.

Some colleges and universities require students to see the same advisor for each additional contact. Such a relationship can be very valuable because it allows you to become more comfortable talking over your goals and dreams. Formal assignment of a particular advisor is especially likely in schools with faculty advisors. Sometimes students' relationships with advisors don't work out. If this happens to you, go to the office where advising assignments are made to request someone else.

At other colleges you can work with any available advisor at any time. This method has the advantage of greater convenience and timeliness. Most colleges that use this arrangement have a centrally located advising center where advisors meet with students. It's usually possible for you to set up appointments with a particular advisor you like working with in an advising center.

▩ *Multiple Roles*

By now you probably know that your advisor's primary roles are to help you decide on a major and to guide you as you work toward fulfilling the requirements of your major. But your advisor can also help you with numerous other decisions during your college career.

Advising for the next term.   You might need to meet with your academic advisor only once each term, or not at all, to talk about the courses you plan to take. Check for the dates of advising and **early registration** in your college's catalog, schedule of classes, student newspaper, or other source that publishes academic deadlines. At most colleges, it's best to participate in early registration. By doing so, you're much more likely to get the courses you especially want at times you prefer and taught by faculty members you prefer. If you wait to register until just before classes start, usually referred to as "regular registration," the courses you want may be closed, or filled to capacity. The sections that are open may not be at your preferred times. Similarly, the professors you would like the most may not have any openings left in their sections.

EXERCISE BREAK 5.2

Visit your academic advising office. In the spaces below, write down the building and office number and the phone number. Has one individual been assigned to you? If so, write down his or her name. What are the office hours during which you could meet with your advisor?

Advising office building and office number: _____

Phone number: _____

Assigned advisor (if any): _____

Office hours:

Monday: _____

Tuesday: _____

Wednesday: _____

Thursday: _____

Friday: _____

ACADEMIC ADVISOR

VS Hixson

© *Vivian Scott Hixson*

"I started out in English, and then I went into gerontology, and then for two semesters I was into biology, but what I really want is a physics major. Is there any way I can do that and graduate next semester?"

Copyright © Houghton Mifflin Company. All rights reserved.

Point *to* ponder

■ At most colleges, it's best to participate in early registration so that the courses you want will not be closed.

early registration: Period of time during which students can register for courses for the following term, usually weeks to months before the term will begin.

Some colleges and universities use a wait-list system to help students who want to get into classes that are already full. With a wait-list system, students can ask to be placed on the list for a particular course and section. If a seat becomes available, they may enroll in the class. Check to see if your college offers this option.

Declaring your major. The advisor's role is to help you (1) decide on the major or concentration you want to declare to fulfill your career goals, and (2) figure out which courses you should take and in what order you should take them. Making academic choices narrows down the types of academic experiences you'll have. But making an academic choice also allows you to concentrate better, learn a subject in more depth, gain expertise, focus your studies, and interact with others who share similar interests and goals. You don't have to decide on a major or concentration right away. Most colleges have enough general education (or core curriculum) course requirements to fill two or more terms. Some colleges don't allow their students to declare majors until they've completed one-third or even one-half of their undergraduate courses.

Other reasons to meet with your advisor. Beyond discussing your choice of major and scheduling your courses, you may wish to meet with an academic advisor for a number of other reasons. The most typical reasons students meet with advisors are:

Time to Reflect

1. Have you chosen a major (or multiple majors) yet? _____ If not, skip to (2) below.

   a. If so, what is it (are they)?

   _____

   b. Why did you choose it (them)?

   _____

   _____

2. If not, have you narrowed it down to a few possibilities or a general area (such as science or communications)? If so, what area(s)? What about this area (these areas) of study interests you the most?

   _____

   _____

3. If you really don't know what interests you, you're more typical than you think. What resources might you seek out to help you decide?

   _____

   _____

1. **Dropping a class.** Most institutions allow students to drop classes up to a published cutoff date. You should not make a habit of doing this, because it can be quite expensive. Very few schools give a full refund after the first few days of the term. Also, dropping a class means that you'll take that much longer to reach your goals. Usually, you'll want to drop a course only if (a) you're in academic trouble in that class, *and* (b) you're convinced that it's not possible for you to improve enough by the end of the term. Your academic advisor and the instructor of the course can help you sort through the possibilities.

2. **Withdrawing** from school altogether. You may have a crisis that requires more attention than you can give it while staying in school. Examples we've seen include surgery that can't be postponed; serious or long-term illness, such as mononucleosis; serious illness or death of a loved one; and family financial crisis. We've also worked with students whose employers transferred them to distant locations, who have accepted new jobs that conflict with their academic schedules, and whose jobs suddenly required more out-of-town travel during the term. A number of these students later returned to college—either the one from which they withdrew or a different one. Leaving college doesn't need to be final. Someone who really wants to earn a college degree will find the right time, place, and financial resources to continue.

3. Seeking academic and personal support. Some students and their advisors develop a close working relationship. If this is true for you, you may feel comfortable enough to talk about issues regarding career choices or graduate schools. Or you might need to learn to whom to turn for personal

case study 5.1

Consider Su Hong . . .

Su Hong was offered a very good scholarship to a private university that was less than two hours from his home, so he decided to go there. He was interested in several different subjects, mostly in math, science, and music. This made it difficult for him to decide on a major, so he didn't declare one when he completed his application.

 If, like Su Hong, you were having a difficult time deciding what major to pursue, what would you do?

_____

_____

During his college orientation program the summer before starting college, Su Hong met with Mr. Presas, his academic advisor. Mr. Presas had copies of Su Hong's high school transcript, standardized test scores, and placement test scores. Mr. Presas told Su Hong that he was designated as an "exploratory student," the classification the university gave to students still exploring their options. He explained that *most* beginning students chose to be exploratory rather than immediately choosing a major from one of the twenty-seven undergraduate program options.

Together they built a schedule that allowed Su Hong to take English, biology, music theory, piano, and precalculus, all courses to help him explore his interests and/or meet general education requirements.

Mr. Presas continued to be Su Hong's advisor for three semesters, until Su Hong decided to focus on music performance and music composition studies. He enjoyed math and science, but he felt most creative and most at home in music studies. When he declared his major, he was reassigned to a new advisor, Ms. Rahn, who worked only with music majors. Su Hong still visited Mr. Presas from time to time to say hello and talk over his career goals. Mr. Presas was one of his references when he applied for part-time work.

Once Su Hong declared his major, Ms. Rahn helped him schedule the rest of his curriculum. Like his music professors, she advised him on choosing and applying to graduate programs to continue his music composition studies. With their advice and help, Su Hong graduated in less than five years and was awarded a teaching assistantship in a well-respected graduate program. He is now making steady progress toward a doctorate in musical arts. One of his compositions won an award, and another has been played by the university's symphony orchestra.

counseling. Your academic advisor can refer you to a professional on campus or in your community to help you work through personal problems.

▪ *Your Role as an Advisee*

Preparing for meetings with your academic advisor will make them more productive. It's best to make an appointment. Otherwise you run the risk of a long wait or being turned away. Plan to show up at least five minutes early, in case you are delayed along the way. Take some course work to study, in case your advisor is delayed. An advisor's time tends to be tightly scheduled; you don't want to miss your appointment or risk having your advisor think you're not serious or reliable.

dropping a class: Withdrawing from a single course while continuing enrollment in others.

♦ ♦ ♦

withdrawing: Formally ending your enrollment in all courses in which you have been enrolled in a term.

Apply This Now

You may not yet be ready to declare a major. But consider a situation in your life in which you've made a choice that narrowed your options, such as buying a computer, choosing to live in a particular school district, or entering a relationship with one person and letting others go.

1. What did you gain and what did you lose by making this choice?

_____

_____

2. Did this turn out to be the right choice? Why?

_____

_____

3. If it was not the right choice, how did you reverse your decision, or how might you do so?

_____

_____

 If you're meeting with your advisor to discuss what to take next term, have a list of courses in mind. If you're meeting to discuss questions or concerns, write them down so you won't forget to ask everything you originally wanted to. If you think you might be nervous, rehearse how you're going to express your thoughts. Anything you don't know or don't understand is worth asking about. After all, you're asking about your education and future career opportunities. You don't want avoidable mistakes or missed opportunities to cost you extra time or money.

Classroom Instructors or Professors

Unless you're on an athletic team or work on campus, you're likely to spend more time in the presence of your instructors than with any other college employees. Your instructors are important to your success in learning. Very few students can efficiently and effectively learn college-level material on their own. Because instructors also have responsibility for assigning grades, some students think of their relationship as adversarial. Other students are afraid to talk with instructors, fearing the instructors will be able to figure out how little they actually know. But most instructors don't like assigning grades any more than students like being graded. And they expect students to struggle with challenging course work. Instructors take great satisfaction from helping students learn and achieve their college and career goals.

■ Instructors' Classrooms

Different instructors run their classrooms in different ways. Some use their favorite learning styles. Others teach the way their own college professors taught them. Some only lecture, using a chalkboard, marker board (also called a white board or dry erase board), and/or overhead projector. New technologies allow professors to integrate a number of different audio and visual aids in one presentation. These include slides, documents projected using a document camera, computer-generated images, Web pages, and recordings. Other professors involve their students in class and/or small-group discussions. Still others offer hands-on laboratory or field experiences.

If your learning style differs from the style used by any of your professors, you'll have to adapt. One good way to adapt is to translate from the instructor's style to your own. For example, suppose the professor uses bodily–kinesthetic ways to teach—perhaps field trips and experiments—and your preferred learning style is musical. You'll do the best you can in performing classroom and field tasks, but then you might study the concepts while listening to music. You might even make up songs with lyrics that explain the concepts and their relationships to one another. Another good way to adapt is to work in a study group with students who are more comfortable with the professor's teaching methods. In fact, you can teach group members songs that explain course content, and they'll show you why or how the experiment is supposed to illustrate it.

Some of your courses are likely to meet in classrooms, lecture halls, and labs of various kinds that may not resemble your old high school classrooms. This may make it difficult for you to decide where to sit and how to concentrate. In larger classrooms and in lecture halls, you might have to remind yourself that you're in a class, not a performance designed to entertain an audience.

case study 5.2

Consider Nour . . .

Nour was a chemistry major. She especially loved labs and had always been good at math. She found it easier than most students to do the abstract thinking that math and chemistry required. As a result of her well-developed kinesthetic intelligence, science labs always made sense to her.

In her second semester, along with her math and science courses, Nour was taking required core curriculum courses in government and art history. She'd been pretty good in her art courses in high school, which consisted mostly of drawing and painting. But she'd never been an especially good visual or audio learner. Both the government and art professors used lectures, film clips, and written documents to teach. The art instructor used lectures and what seemed like a million slides. At the end of almost all of these class sessions, Nour felt that her head was aching from all the audio and visual information she couldn't easily assimilate. She studied her texts

regularly and even went to the library to study the art slides. But when she tried answering the questions at the end of the first few chapters, she knew she wouldn't do well on the tests without more help.

 If you were Nour, where and how would you seek help?

_____

_____

Nour went to see her art instructor to explain her confusion. The art instructor was an artist herself. She suggested that Nour focus more attention on the parts of the chapters and lectures that covered how the artists made their paints and other materials and how they applied them. Then Nour should imagine herself as the individual artist in the act of creation. That would let her use her natural abilities to remember which

5.2 (continued)

particular artist created which work, and in which period of history.

This study technique worked so well for Nour that she approached her government professor, hoping for similar advice. This professor, however, just told her to work harder and study her lecture notes more often. But she'd already tried that!

When Nour complained about this advice to some of her friends in the class, several commiserated with her. One, who was also a logical–mathematical learner, said he arranged the theories of government in chronological order of their evolution. Then he connected the name of a country, an important date, and important leaders with each theory. He suggested that Nour could draw the shape of the country or some other useful symbol next to each theory. Another friend, an art major, said she used her computer as soon as she could after class to copy her lecture notes, using different colors of type for different categories of concepts she needed to remember. Nour combined both suggestions. Almost immediately she noticed how much easier it was to answer the end-of-chapter questions and to remember the answers for tests.

Apply This Now

1. Are you having difficulty translating your instructors' preferred teaching styles into your preferred learning styles? _____

2. If so, to whom could you go for help?

   _____

   _____

3. If you've managed to work out these differences successfully, what strategies do you use that might be helpful for others?

   _____

   _____

Point *to* PONDER

Colleges and universities are finding it necessary to educate first-year students about classroom etiquette. Some students don't seem to know how to pay attention, sit still, and leave other students alone.

You may be surprised to learn that colleges and universities are finding it necessary to educate first-year students about classroom etiquette. Some students don't seem to know how to pay attention, sit still, leave other students alone, and/or turn off pagers and cell phones. One professor had to stop a couple who were displaying physical affection in the last row of a two-hundred-seat lecture hall! Instructors can become angry or extremely disappointed when students' behavior interferes with the learning of others. On many campuses, an instructor has the right to ask a disruptive student to leave class, perhaps for the day or even for the entire term. (It's not like high school: Students aren't sent to the principal's office or given detention.) Particularly disruptive students may be required to withdraw from a class and forfeit their tuition.

Some professors give pop quizzes or periodically call upon students by name to answer questions. This may seem like cruel and unusual punishment to you. But professors put their students on the spot like this to motivate them to prepare for class. Your best defense is to do just that. To adequately prepare, do your reading and complete other assignments on time.

▨ *Syllabus*

■ **The syllabus is the course contract. It binds both the students and the professor.**

The syllabus is the contract the instructor hands out on the first day of class. It is a great academic resource. This contract not only lets you know what's expected of you; it also binds the professor. As such it is a *very important* document. If you can, keep your syllabus with your course notes.

The course syllabus is likely to contain most of the following pieces of information:

1. Title of course, course and section numbers, and meeting times and place;

2. How and when to contact the instructor, including the instructor's name (and maybe title), office hours, building and office number, email address, and phone number;

3. Course goals and objectives;

4. Title(s) and author(s) of required and suggested text(s);

5. Reading assignments, usually for at least the portion of the course before the first exam, and possibly for the entire term;

Time to Reflect

1. Have you been in a situation in which students were annoying, rude, or disrespectful in a college course? _____

2. If so, how did that make you feel?

_____

_____

3. What did the professor do in this situation?

_____

_____

4. Was it an effective strategy? _____

5. Have you ever been called on by an instructor when you were unprepared? If so, how did that make you feel?

_____

_____

6. Did you do more after that to better prepare? If so, how?

_____

_____

7. If not, did you change your behavior in any other way? If so, how?

_____

_____

6. Other requirements for meeting course objectives, such as lectures, labs, descriptions of tests, and major assignments (e.g., research papers and oral presentations);

7. Tentative dates of exams during the term;

8. Date and time of the final exam;

9. Description of test types; and

10. The professor's grading and/or attendance policy.

One of the most important parts of a syllabus is the professor's grading policy. Some professors select an absolute standard of competency. Their policy statements tell you the points or percentages given to assignments, tests, and attendance and how these add up to the final grade. Other instructors grade on a curve. Their policies tell you which percentage of students in the class will earn certain grades. The syllabus may also include the professor's policy on dealing with academic dishonesty, such as cheating and **plagiarism**. Keep your syllabus where you can easily refer to it. If you lose your syllabus, obtain another copy.

If you miss class, you need to find out what the professor covered that day. One excellent resource is a lecture outline provided by the professor—if the professor regularly makes these available to all students. Some professors hand them out; others post them on the course web page. Of course, this will tell you only what major topics were covered that day, without any details. But it will provide structure to let you know which are the most important topics. If you know in advance that you'll have to miss class for a legitimate reason, it's always best to (1) approach the professor *before* you miss class, (2) *apologize* for having to miss it, and (3) ask for recommendations for catching up. It's possible that the professor teaches another section of the course and will allow you to sit in on it.

exercise Break 5.3

Study the syllabus for *this* course.

1. In the spaces below, list any of the ten items listed above that do not appear on the syllabus.

_____

_____

2. Create a group of two or three people. If you've listed any items missing from the course syllabus, check to see if those in your group have found them somewhere in the syllabus. If you're still unable to find them, list them below.

_____

_____

3. Now explain why that type of information would have been useful on the course syllabus. Are there any other forms of useful information not listed above that are included on the syllabus? If so, describe them briefly.

_____

_____

Another excellent resource is another student in the class. It's much easier to ask to borrow class notes if you're already in a study group or have a friend in the class. But even if you don't know anyone in the class really well, you're likely to sit near a few students regularly. Perhaps one of these students will allow you to borrow one day's notes or will allow you to pay to photocopy them.

exercise break 5.4

1. In the spaces below, jot down the names of some of the people you can turn to for lecture notes if you have to miss class.

People in My Classes

Support Person/Phone Number	Course(s) We Take Together

2. Make a few copies of this list, and post a copy in your kitchen cupboard or on the refrigerator. Keep other copies in a notebook and the place where you study most. That way, you'll know on whom you can call for help if the need should arise.

Point to ponder

Professors like their students to stop in during office hours to ask questions. All questions concerning the content of lectures, readings, and other assignments are legitimate.

plagiarism: Representing someone else's work as your own or using it without citing the author.

Office Hours

Nearly all instructors—especially full-time faculty—hold office hours, specific periods of time for meeting with students in their offices. Usually, instructors list their office hours on the course syllabus. Office hours may also be posted on or next to the instructor's office door. Professors want their students to stop in when they have questions. All questions concerning lectures, readings, and other course work are legitimate. If you're shy about going alone to visit your professor during office hours, ask a study-group member or a friend from the class to accompany you. You're likely to discover that your professor is a polite and caring person who wants to help you learn. And you may also discover that your professor becomes one of your best academic resources.

Whether you are in the instructor's classroom, office, or anywhere else, asking the following types of questions will usually irritate a professor, unless the professor has clearly made the offer before: (1) Will this be on the test? (2) Is this concept, theory, fact, or assignment important? (3) I had to miss a class. Did you go over anything important? *Never* ask (4) May I borrow your lecture notes because I have to miss class?

Study Assistance

The types of services that fall into the category of study assistance include the services of teaching assistants, tutoring, study-skills training, and programs for students with disabilities. Study assistance is provided on most campuses because the college or university is convinced that its positive effect on student success is well worth the cost. In fact, sometimes this extra help is considered so important for your success that you may be blocked from registering for

Exercise Break 5.5

In order to prepare to visit your professor during office hours, complete the following exercise. You'll learn where your professor's office is, and you'll interact with the professor at a time of relatively low stress. Having done this, it will be much easier for you to make a second or third visit when an important test is coming up or an assignment is due. And your professor will probably start thinking of you as someone who really wants to learn, not someone looking for a quick fix to earn more points.

   Ask yourself the following three questions about one of your classes that has already met this week, and write your answers in the spaces provided below.

1. Is there something in the syllabus that isn't clear to me? If so, what?

_____

_____

2. What points did the professor make this week that I'm confused about?

_____

_____

3. What parts of the book have I read this week that don't make much sense to me?

_____

_____

_____

_____

4. Visit the professor during an office hour, or use email, to ask about questions 1–3 above. Describe the outcome(s).

_____

_____

_____

classes if you don't make use of it. One common example is mandatory tutoring for students whose grades have dropped below a minimum standard.

Teaching Assistants

Some colleges and universities hire and train graduate students to help with teaching. Although on some campuses these graduate students are referred to as instructional assistants or some other equivalent title, we prefer to use the term **teaching assistant,** or TA, because of its widespread use at most colleges and universities.

Different TAs may have very different responsibilities. These may include taking attendance, distributing and collecting course materials, grading assignments and/or exams, holding separate discussion sections to help students understand the material and/or to go over problem sets, helping run lab sections, conducting review sessions for exams, and possibly giving instruction in the class. No matter how the TA is helping the instructor, you should be as respectful to the TA as you would be to any other instructor. The TA is trying to help you learn and can be a great resource for you.

Tutoring and Study-Skills Training

Tutoring.   From time to time, everyone can use a little extra help in order to understand a concept, theory, application, or other important part of a course. Even if a professor has gone over something several times in class, you may still be confused. Maybe you've even gone over it with your study group, and you're still scratching your head. That's when a tutor might be the answer.

More and more colleges and universities provide at least a limited number of hours of low-cost or free tutoring, often in a tutoring or learning assistance center. The college subsidizes the cost of tutoring because campus leaders know you aren't likely to get all the help you need if you're on a typical student budget and have to pay for tutoring. A prestigious private university in California, for example, gives students eight free hours of tutoring per semester. A state university in South Texas offers unlimited free hours of tutoring, sometimes one-on-one and at other times in groups. A community college in California is experimenting with requiring students to pay a nominal fee each semester to receive tutoring services. This college is assuming that students who pay for tutoring services will use them and take them more seriously. At numerous colleges and universities, individual departments—such as accounting, chemistry, and mathematics—hire departmental tutors.

How to learn about your institution's tutoring services.   Sometimes professors or tutors make announcements in classes. Otherwise, you might find these services advertised in your college newspaper. If you can't get information from these sources, ask your advisor, someone in the student affairs office, student government leaders, or a librarian.

How to prepare for a tutoring session.   You'll definitely want to take your textbook, pencils and paper, class notes, and any assignment or study questions that you're having trouble understanding. It's very helpful if you can pinpoint the part of the

teaching assistant: An upper-level or graduate student who has teaching responsibilities, either as an assistant to a professor or with the sole responsibility for teaching a class.

exercise break 5.6

1. Are you currently taking, or do you anticipate taking, any subjects for which you might seek tutoring? If so, what are they?

_____

2. What tutoring resources are available on your campus? Where are they located? What are their hours of operation?

_____

_____

3. What other sources of academic support might you seek if you need help?

_____

_____

lecture, section of the textbook, and/or portion of the assignment that you find confusing. If you're planning to work with a writing tutor, take the latest draft of your paper. Such information will help the tutor interpret your current level of understanding. If you build from the foundation of what you already know, the tutor will be more successful in assisting you.

 Private tutoring.   If you can't find the tutoring assistance you need through campus resources, you might decide to hire a private tutor. Your instructor might be able to refer you to someone. Some tutors advertise in the college newspaper or on bulletin boards, and sometimes an office on campus or student government will offer a tutor referral service. But beware: A private tutor can be very expensive.

 Study-skills training.   If your school offers workshops to help you improve your study skills, consider signing up for one. Even if a workshop covers strategies you've already learned, the repetition can be helpful. Being reminded of how and when to apply the strategies may jog your memory and give you an additional incentive to try them. If a workshop instructor explains techniques you haven't heard before, all the better. The more study skills techniques you learn, the more likely that you'll find some that work for your own style of learning.

If your campus has a center that offers tutoring services, study-skills assistance is likely to be offered in the same place. Just ask. If they don't offer this service, they'll know where on campus to send you.

▪ *Programs for Students with Special Learning Needs*

The Americans with Disabilities Act has been responsible for changes in facilities, attitudes, and services on U.S. campuses during the past decade. College students with physical and learning disabilities can expect facilities and the delivery of the curriculum to give them equivalent access to a college educa-

Point *to* **ponder**

■ As with everything else in college, it's your responsibility to alert college officials to any disabilities you have, provide documentation, and seek assistance you need.

tion. As with everything else in college, it's your responsibility to alert college officials to any disabilities you have, provide documentation, and seek any assistance you need.

If you have a **documented disability** that requires accommodations, your institution will provide an advocate to help you meet your needs. Advocates can advise you and your instructors about ways to help you learn. Numerous types of accommodations can help you be more successful, depending on the nature of your documented disability. These include books on tape, someone to take notes or interpret for you in class, computer programs that magnify words and other images or say the words out loud, and/or special testing conditions.

 If you have a documented disability, contact the individual or office that will advocate for you as soon as you can. This is often called the office for students with disabilities or the special populations office. Even if you think that everything is going well right now, you should at least introduce yourself. If you don't know how to connect with the right person, ask someone in the admissions office, the student affairs office, or the advising center. If you think you have a disability, but it hasn't been documented, the advocate at the college may be able to refer you to someone who offers appropriate testing and diagnostic services.

Take It Away!

The purpose of this chapter has been to help you realize the importance of utilizing the academic support services offered on your campus. Some of the services and resources we've discussed include:

- Advisors to help you plan your curriculum.
  Be sure to find out how, where, and when to contact your advisor. You'll probably want to find out when the next early registration period is and make an advising appointment before it starts.

- Classroom instructors, and what to expect from them inside and outside of class.
  Study your syllabus and write down exam dates and other deadlines in your academic planner. Be sure to visit your instructors during their office hours.

- Teaching assistants, tutors, and study-skills assistants.
  Find out whether your courses offer discussion sessions, and take advantage of tutoring and skills-enhancement opportunities available on campus.

- Staff in the office for students with disabilities.
  If you have a documented disability, take your documentation to the office for students with disabilities. It's important to discuss services with an advocate as soon as you can.

documented disability: A recognized disability accompanied by official medical records and/or documents that verify it.

Questions for Critical Thought

1. Which of the academic resources mentioned in this chapter are available on your campus? Where would you go on campus to find them?

2. Which of your instructors have you met with in their offices?
   a. Why did you meet with the instructor?
   b. Did you accomplish what you expected?
   c. What was your impression of each of your instructor's attitude about your meeting?

3. Of the classes you are enrolled in this term, which is your favorite?
   a. Which instructional strategies (such as lecture, lab, discussion, etc.) does the instructor of that class use most often?
   b. Why is this your favorite class?
   c. Of the classes that are *not* your favorites, why aren't they? How can you make them more appealing to you?

4. Have you ever worked with a tutor? Under what circumstances? How valuable would you say this experience was for you?

5. Have you ever tutored anyone, either in a school subject or in how to do something else? If so, how did you know whether you and the person(s) you tutored were more successful after working with you?

 6. Form a team with two or three of your classmates. Divide up the list of support services from Box 5.1 at end of the chapter, p. 88. Each of you should then do whatever research is required to fill in the missing information. Your college's student handbook, catalog, student newspaper, and other printed or Web-based materials might be good places to start. After each of you has done this research, report back so that everyone can have this information handy.

7. Look back at the Points to Ponder that appear in this chapter.
   a. Which Point to Ponder surprised you the most?
   b. How does knowing this help you to better prepare for academic success?

8. How can an understanding of concepts presented in this chapter help you outside of the college and classroom environment? Which strategies discussed in the chapter are particularly relevant to success in your career and personal life?

Web Site

Visit the *Overcoming the Hurdles to Academic Success* web site for a chapter outline, review exercises, additional case studies, links to other online resources and a practice test.

Reference

Light, Richard J. (2001). *Making the most of college: Students speak their minds.* Cambridge, MA: Harvard University Press.

BOX 5.1. **Support Services on Your Campus**

Type of Service	Title of Office/ Person Responsible	Building/ Room	Phone Number
Academic advising			
Athletics			
Campus activities			
Career services			
Catalog			
Check cashing/bill paying			
Child care			
Commuter students			
Computer labs (general use)			
Concert/athletic ticket sales			
Counseling			
Disabilities			
Financial aid			
Housing			
Library			
Minority/multicultural affairs			
Registration			
Schedule of classes			
Student clubs			
Student employment			
Student government			
Student handbook/code of conduct			
Student health			
Student ID			
Student newspaper			
Study skills			
Transcripts			
Tutoring			
Veterans affairs			
Yearbook			

master strategies for success

6

Take Notes to Maximize Learning

1 One of the easiest ways to organize your notes is to use separate notebooks for each course.

2 Many students like taking notes on loose-leaf paper and then placing the pages in the appropriate three-ring binder.

3 To avoid misplacing notes that you take on loose-leaf paper, be sure to place the name of the class and the date at the top right- or left-hand corner of each page.

4 Always take plenty of paper and at least two or three working pens and/or pencils to class.

5 Be sure to ask questions during class lectures and group discussions.

6 One of the more practical strategies to consider integrating into your note-taking approach is the use of abbreviations and shorthand.

7 To increase the usefulness of note-taking, it's especially important to anticipate the type of information that will be presented in a class session.

8 Many students believe that recording lectures is one of the best ways to ensure that they'll learn and remember important concepts discussed in class.

9 If you already know something, don't write it down in your notes just for the sake of writing it down.

10 Most instructors don't appreciate questions that appear to reflect a lack of interest in the material being presented.

11 Using different colored pens, pencils, or highlighters to underline important material is one of the most effective strategies for drawing attention to information.

12 You can use different colors of ink for different types of information when taking notes. For example, definitions may be in red, formulas in purple, and factual information in blue.

13 Another way to emphasize important material presented in class is to place large asterisks, arrows, or circles in your notes around important information.

14 Using a variety of writing styles when taking notes can also help you emphasize important information presented in class.

15 Verbal clues given by an instructor are clear indicators that he or she considers the information to be relatively important.

16 When an instructor pauses during a lecture or when an instructor repeats the same concept several times, you should emphasize that information in your notes.

17 It's important to pick up on nonverbal cues that instructors often convey during lectures that can give you hints regarding the information they consider especially important.

18 One way to increase the amount of material you're able to record is to take notes without paying attention to grammar, spelling, punctuation, and capitalization.

19 There are many advantages to writing your notes on only one side of the paper, not the least of which is to increase your ability to organize them.

20 You'll undoubtedly reap many benefits from developing a systematic approach for reviewing your notes regularly.

As you think back to your high school days, whether you graduated recently or many years ago, you'll probably agree that you learned many things that have been helpful to you in your life. One of the skills that is rarely taught in high school, however, despite its importance in college and in life beyond school, is note-taking. The purpose of this chapter is to provide you with useful note-taking skills, specific strategies, and effective techniques to help ensure your academic success.

Few people doubt the importance of taking good notes in college. However, you might be surprised to discover that taking good notes is important in many professional occupations as well. The image often portrayed in the media of notes being taken only by secretaries and administrative assistants is a far cry from reality. In fact, it's difficult to think of a career that doesn't require at least some sort of note-taking occasionally. Learning effective note-taking strategies can come in handy—not only as a valuable study aid while you're in college, but also as a useful resource that you're likely to use well beyond college.

In Chapter 2 we introduced you to various learning styles. Just as there are many different learning styles, there are a variety of approaches for taking notes. In fact, there are probably as many different note-taking approaches as there are note-takers. **Educational psychologists** agree, however, that certain methods of taking notes and several specific note-taking strategies tend to be particularly useful, especially when they're used consistently. As we introduce you to a few of the note-taking strategies popular among college students, it will be important

educational psychologists: Trained professionals who specialize in researching the teaching and learning process and applying concepts from psychology to it.

for you to try out each of them to determine which techniques will be most effective for you.

Remember the Ground Rules

In Chapter 1 we introduced four important ground rules to keep in mind as you learn about and begin using the more than two hundred strategies for academic success in this book. Before we embark on a discussion of specific strategies you can use to enhance the effectiveness of your note-taking it's a good idea to review the ground rules. The information in Box 6.1 will help you to see how the ground rules apply to note-taking strategies.

Specific Strategies for Note-Taking Success

Regardless of exactly how you take notes, using several specific strategies can play an important role in ensuring academic success. The discussion on the

Point *to* **ponder**

The best note-taking strategy is the one that produces the best results for you.

BOX 6.1. **Apply the Ground Rules to Note-Taking Strategies**

1. Learn a variety of note-taking strategies.	For us to claim that there's only one note-taking strategy you should use would be shortsighted. Perhaps the best way to figure out which techniques work best for you is to try out different note-taking strategies in the same class. For example, if you're in a history class, you might try using one note-taking approach one week and a different approach the following week. You'll quickly learn which approach seems to fit best with your particular learning style. In this chapter, we'll consider specific strategies and approaches for note-taking.
2. Give each note-taking strategy a try.	What might at first seem like a note-taking technique that won't work for you might end up being very effective after all. If you don't like a particular strategy after trying it once or twice, move on to another one. Eventually you'll discover the two or three that work best for you. Then, depending on the particular class you're in, you'll have several specific strategies from which to choose.
3. Evaluate the success of each note-taking strategy.	Determining which aspects of each note-taking strategy work best for you means figuring out much more than which techniques you're comfortable using. Ultimately, the best note-taking strategy is the one that produces the best results for you. You'll need to evaluate the usefulness of each approach in helping you remember and organize information presented in classes so that you can remember and successfully apply what you've learned when taking tests.
4. Master the note-taking strategies.	Once you've selected the note-taking strategies that you plan to use on a regular basis, you'll want to continue to practice each one over time to master its use. You'll benefit by learning some of the more intricate aspects of each approach and by finding out how to best use each note-taking strategy to maximize your academic performance. It will be important for you to check your success with various note-taking strategies over time.

exercise break 6.1

Write a brief description of the note-taking strategies you usually use. Answering these questions will help you get a sense of just how useful your current approach is.

1. How easy is it for you to describe the method of note-taking that you regularly use?

_____

2. Did you learn the strategies you commonly use for taking notes in a workshop or class, or from a teacher, friend, or classmate? Or did you develop the strategies on your own?

_____

3. Read your response to question (1). How well is the method of note-taking that you regularly use working for you?

_____

How do you know?

_____

_____

next several pages includes a brief presentation of many tools of the trade. You probably already integrate some of these strategies into your overall note-taking approach. Others may be new tools for you to consider using in the future. As you read the list, remember to critically evaluate how helpful each strategy is likely to be for you.

Following the presentation of the note-taking strategies, we discuss four overall approaches to note-taking that you might want to consider using in college. Whereas strategies are individual note-taking techniques, the four approaches are more general styles of note-taking that are commonly used.

■ Get Organized

It may sound almost too obvious to mention, but you'd be surprised how many students forget to put into place a well-organized system of note-taking. We can't emphasize enough how important it is to organize your notes. When you realize that in any given quarter or semester you're likely to record notes for 45 to 270 class sessions (depending on the number of courses you're enrolled in), it doesn't take too long to recognize the need for organization.

One of the easiest ways to organize your notes is to use separate notebooks for each course. If you use separate notebooks, make sure to take the right ones to your classes. Some students prefer to use only one notebook for all of their classes. If you decide to do this, be sure the notebook includes different sections for each course. Many students like taking notes on loose-leaf paper and then placing those pages in the appropriate three-ring binder. In fact, many instructors distribute handouts that are already three-hole punched for easy placement into three-ring binders. Of course, one of the potential pitfalls of taking notes on loose-leaf paper is the dramatically increased chance of losing or misplacing pages of notes.

Point *to* ponder

We can't emphasize enough how important it is to organize your notes.

To avoid misplacing notes that you take on loose-leaf paper, be sure to place the name of the class and the date at the top right- or left-hand corner of each page. You may prefer spiral-bound notebooks with pockets for handouts and homework, or perhaps you prefer using file folders or another method of organization. It will be important to figure out which method of organization is going to work best for you.

Always take plenty of paper and at least two or three working pens and/or pencils to class. The last thing that you want is for your only pen to run out of ink or your last pencil to become too dull to use. One of the benefits of having a backpack, purse, fanny pack, or other type of carrying case is that you can store backup supplies, just in case.

Actively Listen

Another important tip to keep in mind when taking notes involves putting into practice many of the active-learning strategies discussed in Chapter 2. Be sure to ask questions during class lectures and group discussions. When an instructor asks you and your classmates for your opinions, don't hesitate to speak up. Write down your questions, or make notes about material you find confusing, so that you can question your instructor later. The more involved you are with the material being presented, the more likely you'll be to remember and fully integrate it into your life.

Abbreviate

One of the more practical strategies to consider integrating into your note-taking approach is the use of abbreviations and shorthand. This doesn't mean that you have to learn how to write in actual shorthand, although many students who know how to take shorthand often comment about its usefulness in college and the workplace. But it does suggest at least some benefits associated with learning how to use abbreviations and what is sometimes referred to as "slang shorthand."

Point to ponder

The more involved you are in the material being presented, the more likely you'll be to remember and fully integrate it into your life.

exercise break 6.2

1. Think about the ways you currently organize your notes. What do you like best about this method?

_____

_____

2. Briefly talk with several of your classmates to find out how they keep their notes organized. What are some of the different ways they organize their notes?

_____

_____

_____

3. How might you incorporate some of the ways your classmates organize their notes into your system of organization?

_____

_____

Suppose, for instance, that you're taking a psychology class in which several terms are introduced during the first week or two of classes. And suppose your professor tells you that many of these terms are such an integral part of the field of psychology that you're likely to come across them many times during the course. They might be terms like *theory, classical conditioning, operant conditioning, perception,* and *motivation.* Because there's a good chance these terms will appear in your notes throughout the semester, you might benefit from adopting some sort of shorthand or abbreviation style for the words. *Th* might be the abbreviation for theory, *CC* for classical conditioning, *OC* for operant conditioning, *Pcptn* for perception, and *MOT* for motivation.

Once you've established a set of abbreviations for often-used terms in a class or a discipline, you can use them to record any reference to such terms in the future. Consider the time and effort involved in writing an important concept presented in lecture such as the following: "Classical conditioning and operant conditioning represent two theories of learning that have implications for perception and motivation." Using the personal shorthand from the previous paragraph, this sentence can be represented as: "CC & OC rep. 2 Th of Learning ⇒ Pcptn & MOT." (Did you notice the use of an additional abbreviation? That's right, *rep.* stands for represents.) It might look like gibberish or some sort of spy code to someone else, but if it's a system you've developed, it will make perfect sense to you. And that's what counts! These kinds of shorthand systems often come in handy outside of the course or discipline for which you've developed them. Sometimes, they even come in handy outside of the college environment altogether.

case study 6.1

Consider Darlene . . .

Darlene is vice president of research and development for a major engineering firm in southern California. She was recently promoted to this position after several successful years as a senior mechanical engineer with the company.

When she was in college, like all engineering majors, Darlene was required to enroll in and successfully complete several upper-division math courses. After the first semester of college, Darlene and several of her friends got together one weekend to see if they could identify some ways to study more effectively. That's when Darlene realized that it might be a good idea to develop a system of abbreviating common mathematical terms when taking notes.

 Think about some of the common mathematical terms that you use, such as less than, greater than, increase, and decrease. Write down as many abbreviations you can think of to represent common mathematical terms.

You probably thought of several useful abbreviations for common mathematical terms. Darlene did, too! The abbreviations she developed are shown in Box 6.2. There was no doubt that these abbreviations came in handy hundreds of times (or should we say 100s of X?) for Darlene and her friends who adopted the same system. When she completed her undergraduate studies, Darlene discovered that many of the abbreviations she originally developed for math classes continued to be useful. For example, she regularly uses them in her professional life when writing brief notes to herself, when working on rough drafts of business proposals, and even when taking notes during professional conferences.

BOX 6.2.   **Darlene's Abbreviations: An Example of How It's Done**

<	less than
>	greater than
fn	function
rhs	right-hand side
lhs	left-hand side
~	just about (or approximately)
=	equals (or equivalent)
Δ	change
Θ	theory
Σ	sum
⇒	implies
∧	increase
∨	decrease
w/	with

■ *Anticipate*

To increase the usefulness of note-taking, it's especially important to anticipate the type of information that will be presented in a class session. There are
a variety of ways you can do this. For example, you might try regularly completing the scheduled reading material before the class session for which it is
assigned. Many professors spend a few minutes at the beginning of the semester explaining the importance of reading the assigned material prior to coming
to class each day. And your intentions at the beginning of the term may be to
do just that. But as the weeks go by and you begin to experience some of the
stressors of college life, good intentions sometimes turn into wishful thinking.
At the very least, be sure to skim the assigned reading material and pick up on
the important topics prior to the class session. (We discuss textbook reading
strategies in more detail in Chapter 7.)

Another way to anticipate what information will be presented in class is to
talk with other students who are taking the same course. This approach may be
useful only if the professor teaches multiple sections of the same course *and*
you're enrolled in one of the sections that's taught later in the day or later in
the week. At many community and technical colleges, it's common for the
same instructor to teach several sections of the same course. The least you can
do is check into the possibility. Even a quick question to a friend or classmate

Apply This Now

By this point in the term, you've probably noticed several terms and/or phrases that each of your instructors uses on a fairly regular basis.

1. Ponder for a moment what some of the terms and/or phrases your instructor for *this* course uses on a regular basis. Then list them in the left column below.

_____ _____

_____ _____

_____ _____

_____ _____

_____ _____

_____ _____

2. Now consider abbreviations that you might use for each of the terms and/or phrases you've listed. For example, if one of the terms is *study skills,* you might consider using the abbreviation *SSs* to represent that phrase in your notes. Any time you encounter *SSs* in your notes for this class, you would know that the abbreviation stands for study skills. After considering possible abbreviations for the terms listed in the left column, place the corresponding abbreviations in the right column above.

3. Compare your list with the lists generated by two or three of your classmates. Jot down some of the additional abbreviations they've come up with that you find particularly useful.

Time to Reflect

Think back to the most recent day that you attended classes. Were you able to read all of the assigned readings prior to attending class? _____ If so, how did you make sure your reading was completed on time?

_____

_____

If you weren't able to complete your reading assignments before class, why not?

_____

If you were able to complete your reading assignments, in what ways did this allow you to successfully anticipate some of the information presented in class?

_____

What can you do in the future to ensure that you're able to complete your assigned readings prior to class?

_____

Perhaps a review of the time and stress management principles discussed in Chapters 3 and 4 could provide useful suggestions for incorporating a regular reading schedule into your weekly plans.

such as "What did Dr. Rodriguez talk about today in economics?" can help you prepare for class. On days that you have tests, however, make sure that you don't engage in any sort of cheating by asking students in earlier class sections specific questions about the precise content of an exam. Doing so could very well constitute cheating, which you'll want to avoid at all costs.

◼ *To Record or Not to Record? That Is the Question*

A note-taking strategy that some college students find especially effective is the use of audio recorders. Over the years, we've worked with hundreds of students who believe that recording lectures is one of the best ways to ensure that they'll learn and remember important concepts discussed in class. But we've come across some fairly convincing arguments that have given us concern about potential problems associated with recording lectures. If you're considering the use of a recorder in your classes, you owe it to yourself to take a look at some of the pros and cons of recording lectures that appear in Box 6.3.

◼ *Be Selective*

One of the best pieces of advice regarding lecture notes can be summed up in one sentence: If you already know something, don't write it down in your notes just for the sake of writing it down. For example, suppose your American history professor mentions that the date of the Pearl Harbor bombing was December 7, 1941. If you—like many people—already have that date firmly implanted in your mind, there's no need to write it down in your notes. You don't want to miss the next important concept presented in class because you're writing down something you already know.

◼ *Ask the Right Questions*

You can ask many kinds of legitimate questions during class. Questions that most instructors find particularly appropriate include (1) asking for clarification, (2) asking how lecture information relates to particular current events or

Time to Reflect

Think back to a class you recently attended. There were probably a number of times you could have asked relevant questions to learn more about the information being presented, but didn't.

1. Why might you have been reluctant to ask questions during the class?

_____

_____

2. How might you overcome your reluctance to ask these kinds of questions in the future?

_____

_____

_____

3. In one of your classes during the next two weeks, try to ask at least one relevant question. As you do, think critically about the benefits of interacting with your instructors this way.

BOX 6.3.   **The Pros and Cons of Recording Lectures**

Pros	**Cons**
1. You can go back and listen to portions of the class that you may have missed because of distractions.	1. You may be less likely to pay attention to what the professor is saying because you know that you can listen to it when it's convenient to do so.
2. You can study for tests by listening to recorded lectures in their entirety a second or third time.	2. You introduce yet another step in the learning process that may take extra time.
3. You can ensure that every word spoken by a professor in class is recorded for later review.	3. You may become accustomed to relying on recorded lectures and then have an instructor who discourages you from recording in class or who refuses to allow it altogether. If this happens, you may be at a loss for a backup system of note-taking. (If you decide to record your lectures, be sure to ask each of your instructors for permission to do so *beforehand*.)
4. You can go back and listen for verbal cues about the type of information that's especially important to review for a test.	4. Your recording device may have technical problems at times. Even the best audio recorders have been known to work improperly from time to time.
5. You can listen to the original lecture and watch for important nonverbal communication displayed by an instructor.	5. You may distract your classmates and instructor when you switch tapes during a lecture.
6. If you have an auditory learning style, recording a lecture and subsequently playing it back can be an effective way to reprocess information.	6. You might miss important information your instructor is conveying while you're attending to some of the more technical aspects of recording lectures, such as switching your tapes or trying to make sure the device is properly recording. (That's why if you decide to record your class lectures, you might want to consider taking a complete set of notes as well.)

issues, and (3) asking about relationships between material being presented in class and information found in the textbook. On the other hand, you'll never want to ask, "Is this going to be on the test?" Even though this may seem like a reasonable question to you, it may sound as if you're in the class only to get the grade. Whether that's true or not, most instructors don't appreciate questions that appear to reflect a lack of interest in the material being presented.

▪ *Emphasize the Important*

After reading this chapter, you may or may not make significant adjustments in the way you currently take notes. In either case, be sure to develop a system

Vivian S Hixson

© *Vivian Scott Hixson*

"I'm going to have to miss class next week. You won't be doing anything important, will you?"

Point *to* ponder

Creating a standardized system for identifying the most important information will be a helpful strategy for focusing your study time later.

for emphasizing the important material presented in class. Some information—for whatever reason—will almost always stand out as especially critical during a lecture. Creating a standardized system for identifying the most important information will be a helpful strategy for focusing your study time later.

Some of the better academic performers in our classes over the years are routinely equipped with at least two different colored pencils, pens, or highlighters. When the instructor gives some sort of verbal or nonverbal cue to indicate the special importance attached to a concept, a pen or highlighter can come in handy. Using different colored pens, pencils, or highlighters to underline important material is the one of the most effective strategies for drawing attention to information. Using a similar strategy, some students we've worked with have used different colors of ink for different types of information. For example, definitions may be in red, formulas in purple, and factual information in blue. Other students prefer a simpler approach, such as placing large asterisks, arrows, or circles in their notes around material that's emphasized during class.

Another strategy that some students find especially useful for emphasizing important lecture material is to use a variety of writing styles when taking notes. For example, major concepts and principles might be written in capital letters, with details of those concepts and principles presented in regular printing. Although it may seem as if such a strategy may be more labor-intensive than it's worth, you ought to try it. Many students find this strategy to be incredibly useful for recording and remembering important content of lectures.

Watch for Clues

Every now and then professors will communicate hints—both verbally and nonverbally—that may help you recognize what's especially important. The verbal cues are fairly obvious most of the time. It's quite common for instructors to now and then say such things as "The main point I'm trying to get across is . . . ," "Something you'll want to be sure to remember is . . . ," and "A very important concept is. . . ." Such statements are clear indicators that the information about to follow is considered relatively important and is probably worth special emphasis in your notes. You might even be lucky enough to have a professor say something as straightforward as "You're going to want to make sure you know this for the test."

Other verbal cues can be equally helpful in determining the information that your professor deems especially worthy of your time and attention. Pausing during a lecture to make sure students have ample time to write down information is a way instructors communicate the importance of particular material. Repeating concepts several times during a lecture and the ever-so-popular "Are there any questions about this?" also are good indicators that the information being presented is likely to show up on a test.

It's equally important to pick up on nonverbal cues that instructors often convey during lectures. It's always surprising to look at a student's notes after a class and discover that the student failed to write down anything that was written on the board. If only a few terms or ideas appear on the board during an entire lecture, chances are that you'll see those ideas again, maybe on a test.

Other nonverbal cues to watch for include the following:

- Hand-waving or other emphatic types of gestures that an instructor makes while discussing a concept or principle;

- Eye movements and increased eye contact during a lecture;

- Outlines of material that the professor makes available to you;

Exercise Break 6.3

In addition to the verbal and nonverbal clues we've discussed, there are a host of other signals that professors use to communicate the importance of concepts.

1. List some additional clues you've observed the instructor of *this* class use to relay the message that information being presented is important.

_____

_____

2. Think about other classes you're currently enrolled in and those you've taken in the past. What clues, both verbal and nonverbal, have you witnessed other instructors give to indicate the importance of information?

_____

_____

_____

3. Discuss with two or three of your classmates your responses to the first two questions. List any additional clues you may want to watch for in the future.

_____

_____

_____

- Information the professor has somehow drawn attention to on a handout or overhead transparency;

- Information included in a review of material from a previous class session;

- Material that appears in both the book and class; and

- Information covered in end-of-chapter questions that the instructor assigns as homework or as review questions.

Speed Write

Speedwriting is a term that's often used to refer to the pace you ought to consider using when taking notes. No matter how many abbreviations or shorthand strategies you work into your note-taking approach, it's doubtful that you'll be able to write down every single word spoken in class. Besides, who would want to write down *everything*?

One way to increase the amount of material you're able to record is to take notes without paying attention to grammar, spelling, punctuation, and capitalization. Remember that taking notes is very different from writing for someone else to read. You can leave out unnecessary words, write incomplete sentences, and delete conjunctions and some verbs altogether. Your job is to record the important information in a way that will be useful to you. Of course, you don't want to forget that your notes have to be decipherable enough for you to read them.

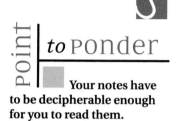

Point *to* PONDER

Your notes have to be decipherable enough for you to read them.

Write on Only One Side of the Paper

There are many advantages to writing your notes on only one side of the paper. Many students we've worked with over the years have discovered—sometimes the hard way—that writing their notes on only one side of their paper makes them much easier to decipher later on. This is especially true if the pen or highlighters bleed through the paper onto the back side. If you write on only one side of the paper, you won't have to worry about the problems that bleeding ink can cause.

Another advantage to writing on only one side of the paper is that you'll be able to spread your notes out on a table or desk without having to worry that some of them are out of sight. Spreading your notes out when it's time to study can be an effective study strategy—especially for visual and kinesthetic learners.

Review

With the many time pressures that students face, it's no wonder that most students take a second look at their notes only a day or two before a test—if at all! Working, attending to family responsibilities, reading textbooks, writing papers, maintaining friendships, and a host of other obligations require your time. It's difficult to find time to review notes just for the sake of review. But you'll undoubtedly reap many benefits from developing a systematic approach for reviewing your notes regularly.

case study 6.2

Consider Braden . . .

Braden was attending the local community college in hope of later transferring to a four-year university. He had graduated from high school one year earlier and was attending college while working part-time. Because he had struggled with many of his classes in high school, especially classes that required a lot of homework, Braden followed the advice he received from one of his instructors and set up an appointment to meet with a tutor in the college's learning assistance center.

After a brief discussion, the tutor discovered that Braden rarely reviewed his course notes because of what Braden referred to as "an extremely busy schedule." He just didn't have time to do things like review lecture notes or reread important concepts in the textbook.

Time Out If a friend of yours was in the same situation as Braden, what suggestions would you offer to help increase her or his chances of academic success?

_____

_____

_____

You're probably aware that there are many strategies Braden might have considered to improve his study-skills. One of the first things the tutor recommended was for Braden to develop a weekly time management calendar to help him analyze how he was spending his time. As he began to work out his weekly schedule, Braden started thinking about effective ways to spend a few hours each week preparing for upcoming tests. That's when he realized the value of taking his notes with him to work each day so that he could review them during breaks. In addition, he realized how useful it would be to get to each class five minutes early to review the notes from the previous session. He also began scheduling a couple of hours each Saturday afternoon for lecture-note review. Saturday afternoons were particularly appropriate for him because he was never scheduled for work on Saturdays and didn't have any other standing commitments on that day of the week.

When Braden's friends asked him why he spent so much time simply looking over notes, Braden talked about the time he saved in the long run that he would otherwise have to devote to cramming for tests. And, as we discuss in Chapter 9, cramming for tests rarely leads to any long-term benefits.

Apply This Now

List the times of the day (or days of the week) you might be able to set aside to review your course notes on a regular basis.

_____

_____

_____

Now take a look at the weekly schedule you developed in Chapter 4. Hopefully you've been using your weekly schedule for several weeks now! Consider altering your weekly schedule (if needed) to allow for regular reviews of your course notes.

Four Note-Taking Approaches

Keep in mind that you can use a variety of note-taking strategies regardless of the overall approach you use for taking notes. In the pages that follow, we describe and illustrate four distinct approaches or note-taking styles that some of our most successful students have used over the years. We present these four approaches as examples of the myriad approaches available to you. They are by no means the only ones that students use. But they'll give you a good idea of the types of overall note-taking approaches used in college.

■ *Approach 1*

This particular note-taking approach involves listing important concepts, terms, or events discussed in class on the left side of the page and listing definitions, examples, and elaboration of those terms and events on the right side of the page. The information that eventually appears on the right side of the page may be filled in after class when you have ample time to learn more about the concepts. A student's notes prepared in this style for a lecture in a general health class on the topic of alternative medicine might look something like Figure 6.1.

■ *Approach 2*

This note-taking approach, often referred to as the outline method of note-taking, entails just that: keeping notes organized in an outline form. The out-

Figure 6.1
Approach 1

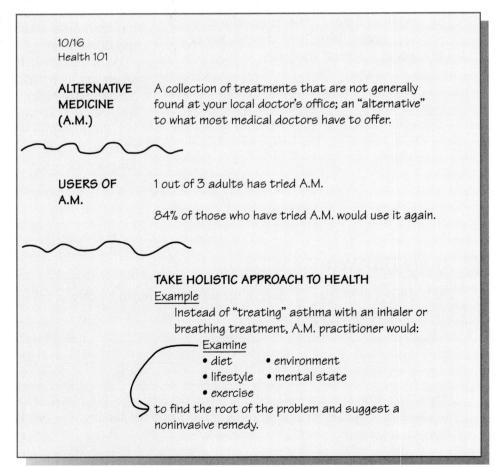

10/16
Health 101

ALTERNATIVE   A collection of treatments that are not generally
MEDICINE   found at your local doctor's office; an "alternative"
(A.M.)   to what most medical doctors have to offer.

USERS OF   1 out of 3 adults has tried A.M.
A.M.
    84% of those who have tried A.M. would use it again.

TAKE HOLISTIC APPROACH TO HEALTH
Example
    Instead of "treating" asthma with an inhaler or
    breathing treatment, A.M. practitioner would:
    Examine
    • diet   • environment
    • lifestyle   • mental state
    • exercise
to find the root of the problem and suggest a
noninvasive remedy.

line method seems especially useful for classes in which the instructor tends to present information in an orderly manner. Although the precise content of an outline will differ from lecture to lecture, the format used in the outline method of note-taking is relatively consistent, as shown below:

- Topic
  - Major Point
    - Subpoint
      - Details
        - Details

There's one very important difference between traditional outlining and the outline method of note-taking: Avoid placing Roman numerals and letters in your outline while you're in the process of taking notes. You don't want to spend time and effort in classes being concerned about whether you should place an A. or a 1. next to a particular concept. The lecture on alternative medicine illustrated in Approach 1 might look something like Figure 6.2 when employing the outline method.

▨ Approach 3

This approach to note-taking involves the creation of concept maps while listening to lectures and discussions. A concept map is created when you visually represent the relationship between various principles you're learning about. During a lecture, a professor might present information about two or three major topics. Those major topics are represented in a concept map by drawing

Figure 6.2
Approach 2

10/16
Health 101

- **ALTERNATIVE MEDICINE**
  - Definition—collection of txs not generally found at local dr's office; "alternative" to what most MDs offer

  - Users
    - Frequency—33% adults have tried
    - Feedback—84% would use again

  - Holistic Approach (body can heal itself)
    - Ex—For asthma, instead of an inhaler or breathing treatment, would examine
      - diet
      - lifestyle
      - exercise
      - environment
      - mental status
    - Tx Recommendation
      - Noninvasive
      - Focus on root of problem

a large circle around their names, with several smaller circles or boxes attached to them.

Although students with various learning styles use this note-taking approach, it's especially compatible with students who have more of a visual learning style. As you can probably guess, completing concept maps to summarize important lecture material is more of a visually oriented exercise than the first two note-taking approaches. An example of how the concept-mapping approach might have been used when taking notes on the alternative medicine lecture is shown in Figure 6.3.

■ *Approach 4*

This particular note-taking approach is rapidly becoming one of the most popular styles of note-taking on college campuses. It involves using any of the previously discussed approaches, or perhaps some other approach with which you are familiar, and—when taking the notes—writing only on the right-hand

Figure 6.3   Approach 3

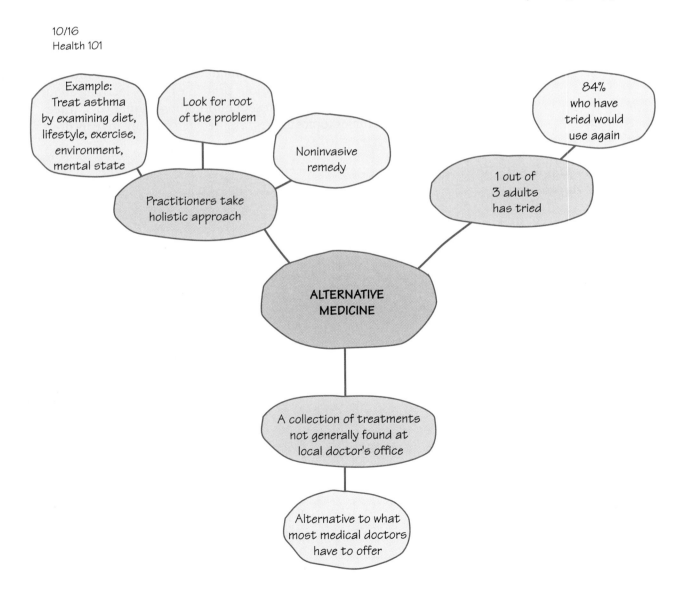

side of the page. In other words, instead of writing your lecture notes across the entire sheet of paper, you record notes on the right two-thirds of the page. This leaves ample room in an extended left-hand margin to add special notes and reminders.

As this approach has gained in popularity, paper companies have started printing and selling paper with an extended left-hand margin. You might want to check with the staff of your college bookstore or a local stationery store to find out if you can purchase such paper locally.

Both during the lecture and at appropriate times following it, you can use the extra-wide left-hand margin for special notes. Some students use the left-hand margin to indicate material the instructor emphasized as especially important, to note ideas they don't understand, to indicate comments they disagree with and want to discuss with the instructor later, and/or to cross-reference textbook material.

The expanded margin also can be a handy place to record nonverbal cues and other hints for studying purposes as well as to indicate when a handout was distributed or a special announcement was made in class. Some students use it for writing key words that indicate the major topics they'll need to study later.

An example of how this particular note-taking approach might have been used during the lecture on alternative medicine appears in Figure 6.4.

Figure 6.4
Approach 4

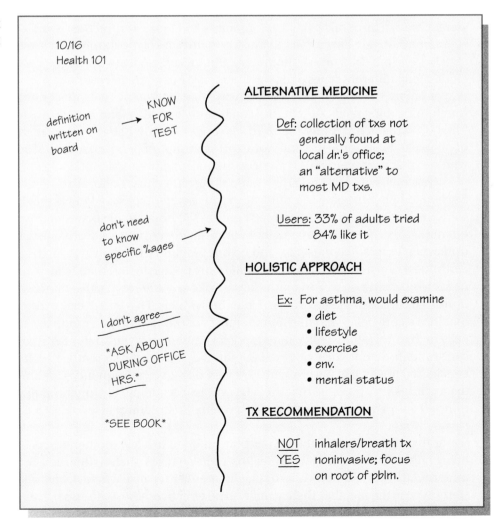

Regardless of the note-taking approach you decide to use, be sure to incorporate as many of the specific note-taking strategies we've presented in this chapter as you possibly can. The many students with whom we've interacted over the years who consistently use an organized and thoughtful system of note-taking tend to be the most successful students of all.

exercise break 6.4

Throughout the chapter we've introduced you to a number of different note-taking strategies. We've also discussed four different general note-taking approaches used by college students. Now it's time to use these principles firsthand to critically evaluate their effectiveness for you.

The following text comes from a social psychology professor's lecture on the topic of stereotypes. As you read the material, take notes as if you were listening to the professor's lecture firsthand. Even better, if you have a study partner or classmate who can help you with this exercise, ask that person to read the material to you as if she or he were your professor. As you take notes, try to use as many of the note-taking strategies presented in the chapter as you possibly can.

One concept that many social psychologists have studied over the years is the concept of stereotypes. [instructor pauses, then writes the word *stereotype* on the board] Although many of you have probably heard that phrase before, let's begin by taking a look at a brief definition. A stereotype is a cognitive representation or impression of a social group . . . that people form . . . by associating particular characteristics . . . and emotions . . . with the group. Notice that the definition doesn't say that the stereotype is true or false. [instructor pauses and looks around the room]

You may already have a bias against the word *stereotype* simply because most people consider stereotypes to be bad or discriminatory. But this may not always be the case. Stereotypes actually include many different types of characteristics. We're going to cover two of those characteristics in particular before moving on to talk about ways that stereotypes can affect human behavior and functioning. First of all, stereotypes can be either positive or negative. [instructor pauses, then writes "+ or –" on the board under the word *stereotype*] Negative stereotypes are those that consider a group of people to be in some way inferior to other groups of people because of some characteristic, whether that characteristic is physical, mental, or emotional. But don't be fooled into thinking that a positive stereotype is necessarily a good thing either. Just as negative stereotypes are beliefs that lump a group together in some inferior way, positive stereotypes are beliefs that lump a group together in some superior way. [instructor briefly pauses] So how can positive stereotypes have negative consequences? [instructor pauses and looks around the room to see if anyone wants to answer the question; when several seconds pass and no one responds, the instructor sighs and looks down, then continues] Consider the stereotype that many people foster: that Asian Americans are straight-A students who *always* do well in math classes. Like any stereotype, this particular one makes key assumptions that can be damaging to particular individuals. This is especially true when the stereotype includes a core belief that may put members of the stereotyped group at risk because of unrealistically high expectations. All Asian American students are *not* straight-A students, and all Asian American students do not *always* do well in math. An unrealistic stereotype such as this, although considered positive in nature, can have very negative consequences for individuals it affects. In this instance, it's very possible that the relatively low academically functioning Asian American will experience feelings of despair and low self-esteem. [instructor pauses, takes a drink of water, and then clears throat]

Another dimension of stereotypes that I alluded to a few moments ago is the concept of stereotypes being either accurate or inaccurate. [instructor pauses, then writes the words *accurate* and *inaccurate* underneath "+ or –" on the board] The first thing to realize when we talk about the accuracy of a stereotype is the fact that there usually is no effective, across-the-board method for measuring the accuracy or inaccuracy of most stereotypes. For example, if I operate from a stereotype that fosters the belief that most non-English-speaking-persons living in the United States are illegal aliens, it's difficult for me to know for sure if that stereotype is accurate or inaccurate without gathering lots and lots of data from the federal government. At the same time, however, social psychologists have made great strides in recent years to more accurately determine the validity of particular stereotypes. In fact, it's because of much of that research that we're now able to lend empirical support to many of the stereotypes regarding gender differences, such as the fact that men tend to be more physically aggressive than women, that women tend to be more nonverbally expressive and nonverbally sensitive than men, and that as leaders women tend to be more democratic and men more autocratic. [instructor pauses and looks around the room to make sure students are paying attention]

Notice that as I presented these stereotypes for which research evidence does exist to support such beliefs I did *not* say that these gender differences existed for *all* women or *all* men. This is a *very important* concept. [instructor pauses, slightly raising voice] I want you to remember this: One way that *any* stereotype is inaccurate is when it is viewed as applying to *every* member of a group. It is an error for anyone to assume that an individual member of a group possesses all of that group's stereotypical qualities! Did you get that? This is *very* important. [instructor pauses, makes eye contact with students, and looks slowly around the room] Stereotypes, even if they tend to be supported by research, do *not* apply to every member of a group. That's why it's so important to critically question all stereotypes and to ensure that you don't treat people you know solely on even the most well-researched and well-validated stereotypical beliefs you may hold.

After completing the note-taking portion of this exercise, answer the following questions.

1. Which note-taking *strategies* presented in the chapter did you find most useful when completing this exercise?

_____

_____

2. Which of the four note-taking *approaches* presented toward the end of the chapter does your note-taking style most closely resemble?

_____

_____

3. Are there any reasons why you might consider trying a different note-taking approach in the future? If so, what are those reasons?

_____

_____

Take It Away!

In this chapter, we've focused on several note-taking strategies and four general note-taking approaches you can use to maximize your learning potential. In particular, we've encouraged you to:

- Learn a variety of note-taking strategies.

  The best way to figure out which note-taking strategies will work best for you is to try out several different strategies in your various classes. Remember that what at first might seem like a useless technique could become a very efficient strategy for you in the long run.

- Try out as many of the strategies as possible when taking notes, and implement those that work for you.

  __ Use an organized system.

  __ Actively listen to and engage in lectures and class discussions.

  __ Abbreviate whenever possible.

  __ Anticipate the information likely to be presented in class.

  __ Consider recording lectures to enhance your memory of information.

  __ Be selective in what you write down.

  __ Ask appropriate questions during class to ensure quality notes.

  __ Emphasize important information.

  __ Watch for verbal and nonverbal clues.

  __ Write on only one side of the paper.

  __ Write without worrying about grammar and spelling.

  __ Review your notes on a regular basis.

- Try out each of the four general note-taking approaches presented at the end of the chapter before settling on the approach or approaches that work(s) best for you.

- Master the note-taking strategies that are most effective for you by practicing them again and again.

  In Chapter 7 we turn our attention to the importance of reading in the learning process. We focus on several strategies you can use to read textbooks with finesse as you continue to ensure your academic success.

Questions for Critical Thought

1. What note-taking strategies and approaches do you believe will be especially useful to you? What is it about these particular strategies that you find most appealing?

2. Why is it important to evaluate the success of different note-taking strategies and approaches? How can you evaluate the effectiveness of the different note-taking strategies and approaches you use?

3. Among the various reasons why it's a good idea to review your notes on a regular basis rather than wait until right before a test, which reason do you think is most persuasive? Why?

4. Repeat Exercise 6.4 using a completely different note-taking approach. For example, if you used Approach 1 when you completed the exercise the first time around, use one of the other approaches. After doing so, critically evaluate the pros and cons of each note-taking approach you used from *your* perspective.

5. Look back at the Points to Ponder that appear in this chapter.
   a. Which Point to Ponder surprised you the most?
   b. How does knowing this help you better prepare for academic success?

6. How can an understanding of concepts presented in this chapter help you outside of the college and classroom environment? Which strategies discussed in the chapter are particularly relevant to success in your career and personal life?

Web Site

Visit the *Overcoming the Hurdles to Academic Success* web site for a chapter outline, review exercises, additional case studies, links to other online resources, and a practice test.

References

Lebauer, R. S. (2000). *Learn to listen, listen to learn: Active listening and note-taking.* Upper Saddle River, NJ: Prentice-Hall.

Messano, M. A. (2000). *Smart notebook: A guide to effective note-taking.* Dubuque, IA: Kendall/Hunt.

7

Read textbooks with Finesse

Chapter 7 Strategies

1 Equip yourself with useful reading materials, and use them effectively.

2 Highlighters of different colors can be used to draw your attention to the different kinds of information encountered in a textbook.

3 Memory of concepts presented in a book is enhanced when a highlighter or pen is used to underline important material rather than highlighting directly on top of it.

4 Be selective in emphasizing important concepts and principles that you'll want to study at a later time.

5 Find a quiet, peaceful, uncluttered, and comfortable atmosphere in which to read.

6 When reading textbooks, it's important to eliminate distractions, such as loud noises or tempting alternatives to reading.

7 You should use a dictionary whenever you come across a word or term you don't know in a book.

8 It's usually more effective to read in brief fifteen- to twenty-minute chunks of time (with at least a three- to five-minute break between each reading session) than to read in longer chunks of time.

9 Study guides and student manuals are often useful textbook supplements that can enhance learning of new material.

10 You should consider surveying any book that you're taking a look at for the first time.

11 When previewing a chapter, look at such features as the chapter title, headings, pictures, graphs, charts, boldfaced words, marginal notes, and material that's set off in figures or boxes.

12 You should have a series of questions that guide your reading of textbook material.

13 If you approach reading in a positive way, you'll be much more likely to enjoy the

reading process and remember what you read.

14 Finding ways to make reading material more "alive" and more relevant to your own life experiences will help you remember what you read.

15 Don't hesitate to make marginal notes in the books you purchase for your classes.

16 If you purchase a used textbook, don't assume that the material highlighted by the previous owner is necessarily the most important information to study.

17 Answer any questions you generate during the Q stage of SQ3R as you read assigned chapters.

18 It may be useful to have someone quiz you now and then on some of the essential ideas included in a reading assignment you've recently completed.

19 Be sure to read at your own pace.

20 After reading an assignment, you should be able to recite (or recall) the main concepts you've read.

21 The more times you review reading material, the more likely you'll be to integrate the information into your learning process.

The Importance of Reading to the Learning Process

When many students relax during their free time, they often find it enjoyable to read. Usually such reading consists of flipping through the pages of a favorite magazine or becoming engrossed in the latest mystery or suspense novel. If you wrote marginal notes or underlined parts of a magazine or novel as you read, most people would consider your behavior odd. If you had done this in your high school textbooks, you probably would have been disciplined by your teachers! But when you're reading a textbook or studying notes for an examination in college, you'll want to remain as active as you possibly can. This chapter describes several textbook-reading strategies that will help you achieve academic success by teaching you ways to ensure that you're actively engaged in the reading process.

One of the most overlooked study skills among college students is textbook reading. Like note-taking strategies, students rarely receive much instruction on ways to read a textbook most effectively. Maybe it's because professors think students have learned such skills before college. One thing is certain: A well-organized, effective textbook-reading strategy can make all the difference in gaining a comprehensive understanding of important material. And, like effective note-taking strategies, textbook-reading skills often come in handy outside of college.

If you think about it, students spend many hours each week reading textbooks for their classes. Most professors claim that for every hour spent in class, students should be spending two or three hours outside of class engaged in a variety of class-related activities, such as meeting in study groups, attending review sessions, engaging in library research, writing papers, and so on. But reading is the one out-of-class activity that can take up the most time. Many students consider reading to be the most daunting learning task of all; yet nearly all instructors expect it to be completed *on time.*

Point *to* PONDER

A well-organized, effective textbook-reading strategy can make all the difference in the world when it comes to gaining a comprehensive understanding of material.

Time to Reflect

Think back to the discussion in Chapter 2 about learning styles. How do you think that a clearer understanding of your preferred learning style(s) can help you maximize the effectiveness of your textbook reading?

_____

_____

_____

Subtract the time spent handing back tests, reviewing material from a previous class session, and answering student questions about previous lecture material. What you have left is a limited amount of time available for presentation and discussion of new material. Therefore, college students are expected—far more than high school students—to complete reading assignments on their own and to come to class prepared to discuss them. The degree to which your reading is an effective study strategy depends, at least in part, on the ways you use your textbooks as tools for success.

Basic Concepts in Textbook-Reading Preparation

Before we present a particularly useful *method* of textbook reading, we first want to share six basic strategies you can use to read textbooks more effectively.

▪ *Equip Yourself with Useful Reading Materials and Use Them Effectively*

An important part of preparing to study is making sure you have the materials you'll need to get the job done. When it comes to reading, those materials include pens, pencils, highlighters, sticky notes, and other useful materials. Writing instruments come in many different shapes and colors. Highlighters might be yellow, blue, fluorescent green, or even hot pink. Highlighters of different

colors can be used to draw your attention to the different kinds of information encountered in a textbook. For example, in a history textbook you might use a yellow highlighter to draw your attention to dates, a blue highlighter to draw your attention to names of important persons, and a green highlighter to emphasize important historical events.

But much more important than the colors or sizes of pens or highlighters is the manner in which you use them. One of the common errors that college students make when using highlighters during textbook reading is to highlight important passages by completely coloring over the words. What most people

don't realize is that we're much more likely to attend to and remember important words and ideas when a highlighter or pen has been used to underline important content rather than highlighting directly on top of it.

Another common error is to over-highlight material. In other words, instead of reserving the pen or highlighter for the most important material, many students tend to highlight material that turns out to be of relatively little importance. Part of the skill involved in textbook reading is learning how to determine what is and is not worthy of emphasizing. You don't want a page in your textbook to look like you dipped it in yellow paint. Instead, be selective in emphasizing important concepts and principles that you'll want to study at a later time. At first, you might need to read a paragraph or even an entire section and then go back to underline the important material.

In many ways, taking notes as you read isn't all that different from taking notes during a lecture. You look for certain cues during a lecture or class presentation to help you figure out the especially important information. Similarly, when you read you should look for ways of determining what reading material is important enough to warrant highlighting. The good news is that you'll learn much of that process with regular practice over time. With each additional textbook-reading experience, you'll become increasingly aware of which passages are worth highlighting.

■ *Find a Quiet, Peaceful, Uncluttered, and Comfortable Atmosphere in Which to Read*

Many students claim they do their best studying with the television on or music playing in the background. Nevertheless, most students report the best recall of information when they read in a quiet, peaceful place that's well lit and comfortable. If you do your best reading and studying with background music or with the television on, you should make sure that these environmental stimuli aren't too distracting.

An uncluttered environment is especially important. As we discussed in Chapter 4, a workspace in which it's difficult to find materials and keep information organized undermines your ability to read successfully. You need ready access to paper, pens, highlighters, sticky notes, and other study materials. The more cluttered your reading and study space is with items that you don't need, the more difficult it is to engage in quality studying.

■ *Eliminate Distractions*

Eliminating distractions is perhaps most crucial for effective textbook reading and studying. How many times have you found, three or four pages into material you're reading, that you don't remember a single thing you just read? It's pretty easy to be several pages into a chapter without having actively attended in any way to the material itself. It's almost as if, now and then, we go through the *motions* of reading without paying much attention to *what* we're reading.

When reading textbooks in the hope of remembering the information you read, it's important to eliminate distractions, such as loud noises or tempting alternatives to reading. Therefore, reading in a setting that makes it easy to block out distractions increases your chances of achieving success. Clearing your mind of distracting thoughts, daily worries, and anxieties can make it a whole lot easier to focus on the material.

■ *Keep a Dictionary Close By*

Although most textbooks include a glossary of terms, you're likely to encounter a few undefined words that are new to you in at least some of your textbooks. Don't try to fudge your way through the material by guessing at the meaning of such words. It doesn't take that long to look them up in the dictionary and ensure that you understand them in that context.

point *to* PONDER

■ Most students report the best recall of information when they read in a quiet, peaceful place that's well lit and comfortable.

case study 7.1

Consider Juan . . .

Juan was a recent high school graduate who had decided to pursue a career in veterinary medicine. During his first semester in college, Juan found himself struggling in two of his courses. He seemed to perform well on tests that covered lecture material but not on questions based on the textbook. During a meeting with one of his professors, Juan shared his concerns. The professor asked him to talk about his strategies for reading textbooks. Juan mentioned that he used highlighters and always made sure that he studied in a nice, peaceful, relaxing atmosphere.

By asking Juan a few more questions about his study habits, the professor learned that Juan did most of his studying of lecture notes in the campus library, but read textbooks at the beach! Although the beach provided Juan with a "nice, peaceful atmosphere," people surfing and playing beach volleyball were a constant distraction.

 If you were Juan's professor, what suggestions would you share with him to increase the effectiveness of his textbook-reading strategy?

_____

_____

As you might imagine, Juan's professor suggested that he consider other comfortable and relaxing reading environments that might not be as distracting as the beach. Juan was resistant at first. He continued to read his textbooks and study at the beach for three more weeks. After Juan received the results of his midterm exams, however, he decided that he should probably heed his professor's advice. Midterm grades of D+ and C– were much lower than Juan expected.

Juan found a quiet cubicle in the library that seemed to work pretty well. It wasn't the greatest place to get a tan, but at least his grades improved remarkably. Juan experienced much more success during the second half of the semester as a result.

Apply This Now

If you were studying at home, where would the quietest, most peaceful location tend to be?

_____

When you need to read your textbooks at school between classes, what's your favorite place?

_____

What do you need to do to ensure that your reading and study spaces are as comfortable, uncluttered, and free from distractions as they can possibly be?

_____

_____

▨ *Chunk it Out*

One strategy you can use to increase your reading comprehension is to read in brief, fifteen- to twenty-minute chunks of time, with at least a three- to five-minute break between each reading session. As we discuss in Chapter 8, "chunking" information into more memorable bits of information can significantly increase your memory capacity. Between your study periods, trying out some of the isometric exercises discussed in Chapter 2 might be a particularly effective use of time. Taking breaks helps you avoid fatigue and increases your ability to recall information you've read.

▨ *Consider Buying and Using Study Guides or Student Manuals if They're Available*

Study guides and student manuals are usually written by textbook authors or their colleagues who are familiar with the content of the textbook. These types of supplements can be valuable resources for reading textbooks and helping you prepare for examinations.

exercise Break 7.1

Think about the place where you usually read textbooks. Evaluate that environment by answering the following questions.

1. Are you equipped with different colored pens, pencils, highlighting markers, and sticky notes?

   _____

   _____

2. Do you have a dictionary close by in case you have to look up a word or phrase?

   _____

3. Do you "chunk" your reading time, breaking it up into fifteen- or twenty-minute periods to allow increased comprehension of information?

   _____

4. What types of isometric exercises, if any, do you use to keep your brain active during the reading process?

   _____

5. What other strategies do you use to remain active while reading?

   _____

6. How effectively do you use study guides to supplement your reading activities?

   _____

7. After considering your responses to these questions, what changes might you consider to enhance the effectiveness of your study routine?

   _____

   _____

   _____

Although the content of study guides and student manuals varies from book to book, most contain such features as chapter overviews and ideas for integrating the textbook reading into your overall study plan. Probably the highlight of most study guides is the set of sample test questions for each chapter. Study guides are an excellent resource for evaluating your mastery of textbook material and gauging the degree to which you've adequately prepared for a test.

The SQ3R Approach

One technique you may find especially effective for reading college textbooks is the SQ3R method, which is considered one of the best models for reading a textbook. Hundreds of thousands of students each year find it to be a particularly useful strategy. You may learn about other textbook-reading methods from some of your instructors or classmates. If you do, you owe it to yourself to find out how you might integrate those methods into your system of reading. Many useful approaches have been developed over the years. The SQ3R method is one of the most popular.

Each of the letters referred to by the acronym *SQ3R* stands for a particular approach to reading. The letters *S-Q-R-R-R* are arranged in a particular order to remind you of the chronological approach to carrying out the reading process: survey, question, read, recite, review.

▪ *Survey*

Movie trailers (previews) of upcoming releases usually give you a pretty good idea about the plot of soon-to-be-released movies. These previews help you decide whether you want to spend your money to see certain films. They also give you a pretty good sense of what an upcoming release is about. In the same way, surveying reading material before you actually read it can help you get a much clearer sense of what to expect from a book or chapter.

You should consider surveying any book that you're taking a look at for the first time. Several parts are particularly important to preview. These include the title page, table of contents, preface, foreword, appendix, references, glossary, and index. Just a quick glance at these parts of a book can give you a fairly clear indication of what the book is about and what kinds of information you can expect to learn by reading it.

The table of contents, for example, helps you figure out the essential content and organization of the book. You may recall that in Chapter 6 we discussed the value of anticipating the content of a lecture. Similarly, having a good idea of what to expect in a book can give you an extra edge when it comes to understanding the material. A brief overview of the glossary and index will provide you with a similar overview of information.

When surveying a chapter (as opposed to an entire book), the important thing is to get a general sense of the information you're going to come across while reading it. To begin with, take a look at the chapter title and the headings in the chapter. It's also a good idea to take a look at pictures, graphs, and charts. Checking the chapter for boldfaced words, marginal notes, figures, and material set off in boxes also helps you figure out what the chapter is about. Take time to skim the first paragraph of the chapter, the section and chapter summaries, and end-of-chapter questions or exercises.

Point *to* ponder

▪ Surveying reading material before you actually read it can help you get a much clearer sense of what to expect from a book or chapter.

VS Hixson

© *Vivian Scott Hixson*

"I think I deserve some credit for this course. I mean, after all, I did buy the books."

exercise break 7.2

Take a few minutes right now to preview the content of Chapter 8 of this book. Remember to do some of the things suggested in the previous paragraph. After previewing Chapter 8, write a brief summary of the main concepts you think are going to be covered in the chapter.

_____

_____

_____

How does knowing the general content of a chapter prior to reading it help you prepare for the reading process?

_____

_____

 Question

After you complete the chapter survey process, you'll benefit by creating several questions to guide your reading. In many textbooks, including this one, there are several summary questions at the end of each chapter. Some professors may develop and distribute study questions from these. If not, you may need to generate your own list. Whatever your resource for questions, be sure to have several in mind—written in the margins or on a separate piece of paper—as you read an assignment.

You'll also want to allow for the formulation of a few new questions to guide your reading as you make your way through a chapter. During the reading process, you can ask yourself a series of questions that might make the material seem more "alive" and meaningful to you. If you have trouble figuring out

Time to Reflect

Look back at the section of this chapter on textbook-reading preparation, and answer the following questions.

1. What main messages are we trying to convey?

_____

_____

2. Why are these concepts important?

_____

_____

3. How does this material fit in with what you read in the last chapter?

_____

4. How might you be asked to remember this material on a quiz or exam?

_____

_____

what types of questions to ask as you read a chapter, you might want to ask your professor for some tips.

Read

After surveying reading material and developing a list of questions to guide your reading, you'll be prepared to engage in the actual process of reading itself. One of the first things you might want to consider is your attitude about the reading process. Many students have reported that they simply don't enjoy reading textbooks. They think of it as one of the necessary evils of college life. Such students often perform poorly on examinations that cover a great deal of reading material. As in so many other areas of life, the power of positive thinking can have a tremendous impact on the quality of your reading skills. If you approach reading in a positive way, you'll be much more likely to enjoy the process and remember what you read.

Point *to* PONDER

As in so many other areas of life, the power of positive thinking can have a tremendous impact on the quality of your reading skills.

Time to Reflect

Quickly review the major concepts presented in Chapter 6. Which of these concepts do you believe are particularly relevant to the textbook-reading process?

_____

How might you apply the concepts from Chapter 6 when reading *this* textbook?

_____

_____

_____

Just as quality note-taking requires active-listening skills, textbook reading requires a type of "active reading." Many of the concepts discussed in Chapter 6 have direct application to the reading process. Finding ways to make the material you're reading more "alive" and more relevant to your own life experiences will do wonders to help you remember the information. It also will increase your chances of finding ways to integrate it into the overall learning process.

In addition to relating what you read to your own life experiences, there are four other tips that you may want to keep in mind to ensure that your reading experience is as active as possible. These strategies are presented in Box 7.1.

BOX 7.1.   **Tips for Actively Engaging in the Reading Process**

1. Take notes in the margins of the book.

In college, your textbooks are yours to do with as you please. After all, you pay for them, right? Don't hesitate to make marginal notes in the books you purchase for your classes. Write in your books, highlight important passages, fold back pages, circle important material. Do anything that works to draw your attention to especially important or worthwhile information.

If you purchase a used textbook that's fairly well marked up, be sure not to take the prior owner's word for what's important. Don't assume that the previous owner knew which concepts were worth emphasizing. We've worked with students who thought it would be more efficient to just read what was already highlighted in a book rather than going through the entire chapter. They quickly changed their strategy after receiving the results of their first exam.

2. Answer questions as you read assigned chapters.

Don't forget about the questions generated during the Q stage of SQ3R. Be sure to refer back to your list of questions periodically to help focus your reading efforts. If the questions are well written and apply directly to the reading material, you should have few problems answering them as you go along. Also note the page numbers where you found the answers. This may come in handy later.

3. Ask a friend to give you a quick quiz on the reading material.

Many students find it helpful to have someone quiz them on some of the essential ideas now and then. This is especially useful when working in study groups. A group member who has already read the chapter can quiz you on some of the important concepts while you're still reading the chapter. It's a quick and easy way to be sure that you're remaining focused and comprehending what you're reading.

4. Read at your own pace.

It's important to remember that everyone reads at a different pace. Many students come to college with the expectation that successful students read two thousand words a minute or something way out of the ordinary like that. It's more important to comprehend and apply the information you read than it is to compete for a speed-reading championship.

exercise Break 7.3

Approaching reading with a positive attitude, engaging in active reading, taking notes in your textbooks, and reading at your own pace are just a few of the ways you can learn and remember what you read. List below any additional strategies you've used in the past to help you effectively process and remember material you read.

_____

_____

_____

_____

Ask two or three of your classmates about the strategies they use while reading textbooks. List strategies that are new to you. Consider trying them the next time you have a reading assignment.

_____

_____

_____

_____

■ *Recite*

After reading an assignment, you should literally be able to recite (or recall) most of the main concepts you've read. It's not a bad idea to engage in some sort of recitation or recall after each major section of a chapter. You might even try writing the main ideas of a section or passage in your own words. If you have more of an auditory learning style, you may try reciting the main ideas out loud.

It's also a good idea to spend a few minutes at the end of each day recalling the main ideas associated with the reading you've completed that day. Many students report that they're more likely to recall material they look at prior to going to sleep each night than information they learn at other times during the day.

■ *Review*

The final stage in the SQ3R method is review. Plainly put, the more times you review reading material, the more likely you'll be to integrate the information into your learning process. One of the best ways to engage in the review process is to imagine what you'd do if you were the professor. After reading an assignment, consider how your professor would create a test covering the material. What kinds of questions would be asked? What are the important concepts from the reading assignment?

It's always a good idea to anticipate the kinds of questions that might be on a test. It usually doesn't take too long to come up with some fairly good questions. You can do this very effectively in your study group. And it can serve a useful purpose in the review stages of the SQ3R method.

As you consider the types of information most likely to end up on a test, you can pick up on clues found throughout a chapter. These clues might include terms and concepts that appear in boldfaced type, figures and charts that present information concisely, and ideas that are included in chapter summaries. Getting a sense of what the authors of a book consider especially important will help ensure that you're reviewing the most important material.

case study 7.2

Consider Paige . . .

Paige was a twenty-nine-year-old mother of three children who had recently divorced her husband of ten years. After working primarily within the home for the prior eight years as a homemaker, Paige decided to return to school and enrolled in courses at her local community college.

During her first term, Paige enrolled in three general education courses: introductory psychology, English composition, and art history. Because she wasn't sure which degree program she would eventually enroll in, Paige figured that it made sense to start off with courses needed to fulfill the general education requirements.

By the beginning of the third week of classes, Paige was feeling overwhelmed. Juggling responsibilities at home and at her part-time job was difficult in itself, even without the added stress of going to school three evenings a week. Paige was having a particularly rough time figuring out how to fit studying into her weekly schedule. Somehow she found a way to study lecture notes each afternoon during lunch and to take care of class assignments during the weekends. She also made sure that she read all of her reading assignments each morning, but she was having problems remembering what she read. She decided to talk with some of her friends who were also attending the college to see if they had any advice for her.

 If you were Paige's friend, what advice would you offer to help her remember the textbook material she was reading each day?

In this chapter alone we have presented more than a dozen strategies that Paige could consider integrating into her textbook-reading routine. Luckily, Paige had a friend who had taken a study-skills course during the summer. That friend shared several textbook-reading strategies, including the important principles of the SQ3R method.

As Paige learned about SQ3R, she paid especially close attention to the recite and review components. Paige quickly realized that although she completed each of her textbook-reading assignments on a regular basis, she read the assigned material only once. Furthermore, she didn't take any notes while reading that she could review at a later time.

Because of her busy schedule and the idea of having even more notes to study, Paige came up with what she considered a creative solution. Each time she read one of her textbooks, Paige dictated the main concepts and important points into a microcassette recorder as a form of recitation. Then, while driving to and from work each day and immediately before going to sleep each night, Paige played the recorded messages as a form of review. The results were excellent performance on all of her exams that semester and a new technique in her arsenal of academic success strategies that could be used throughout her college career.

Apply This Now

Which academic strategies discussed in this chapter, as well as earlier in the book, could you use to enhance your ability to remember information you read?

_____

_____

Given your particular life situation, how might you go about discovering an effective way to implement the recite and review components of the SQ3R method?

_____

_____

exercise Break 7.4

1. How do you plan to remember what *SQ3R* stands for?

_____

_____

2. Which of the five steps of SQ3R were you using regularly before reading this section of the book?

_____

3. Which ones seem the *least* comfortable to you and why?

_____

_____

4. If you were the instructor of *this* class, what question about the SQ3R method would you place on an upcoming quiz or exam?

_____

_____

_____

take it away!

In this chapter we discussed the importance of reading in your learning process. In addition, we presented you with a variety of strategies you can use to read textbooks with finesse.

- Remember the six basic points of effective textbook-reading preparation:
  - __ Equip yourself with useful reading materials, and use them effectively.
  - __ Find a quiet, comfortable atmosphere in which to read.
  - __ Eliminate as many distractions as you can.
  - __ Keep a dictionary close by.
  - __ Chunk your reading into fifteen- to twenty-minute sessions.
  - __ Use study guides and student manuals to supplement your reading.

- Try using a proven, reliable method for reading, such as the SQ3R approach:
  - __ Survey, question, read, recite, review.
- To improve your capacity to read textbooks with finesse, be sure to
  - __ Take notes in the margins of the book.
  - __ Answer questions as you read the material.
  - __ Quiz yourself (or have a friend quiz you) on the reading material.
  - __ Read at your own pace.

In Chapter 8 we continue to add to the list of effective strategies you can use to increase your chances of academic success. We focus on methods you can use to enhance your memory skills—something you'll find especially relevant to college coursework.

Questions for Critical Thought

1. If you don't read textbooks effectively, how can this negatively influence your chances of achieving academic success? What can you do in order to read more effectively?

2. In what ways is taking notes while you read similar to taking notes during a lecture? In what ways is it different?

3. Of the six basic points of effective textbook-reading preparation presented in the chapter (and summarized in the Take It Away section above), which do you think you'll have the most difficult time implementing? Why? What can you do to increase your chances of implementing that particular strategy more effectively in the future?

4. What stage of the SQ3R approach do you think is the most important for you to incorporate into your reading style?

5. Look back at the Points to Ponder that appear in this chapter.
   a. Which Point to Ponder surprised you the most?
   b. How does knowing this help you better prepare for academic success?

6. How does the information presented in this chapter help you in your life outside of the classroom and college environment? Which strategies discussed in the chapter are particularly relevant to success in your career and personal life?

Web Site

Visit the *Overcoming the Hurdles to Academic Success* web site for a chapter outline, review exercises, additional case studies, links to other online resources, and a practice test.

References

Allen, S. (1997). *Making connections: Reading and understanding college textbooks.* Fort Worth, TX: Harcourt College Publishers.

Ediger, A., & Paulik, C. (1999). *Reading connections: Skills and strategies for purposeful reading.* New York: Oxford University Press.

8

enhance your memory skills

Chapter 8 Strategies

1 By eliminating distractions during study periods, you're better able to pay attention to important material you're trying to learn.

2 One of the easiest ways to increase your chances of remembering information is to study it over, and over, and over again.

3 An effective way to capitalize on existing memories when learning new material is to come up with a story to connect the new material to an old memory.

4 As you study information for a class, you might try to develop mnemonics to help you remember it more efficiently.

5 Organizing important concepts and information can have a positive effect on your memory capacity.

6 Share any memory-enhancing ideas you've found particularly useful with your friends and classmates, and ask them to share strategies they've found useful with you.

7 One of the best ways to ensure that you'll remember information presented during a lecture or in your textbook is to review your notes as soon as possible after taking them.

8 Each evening, if only for ten or fifteen minutes, review *all* of the notes you took that day. At the end of each week, review all of your notes from the week several times.

9 An effective strategy for improving memory of lecture and reading notes is to use note cards.

10 Placing your notes into a word-processing document after initially writing them provides you with at least three things simultaneously: relearning, increased organization, and greater legibility.

11 Tape recording the notes you take while reading an assignment is a useful way to review the information.

12 Comparing your notes with your classmates' notes gives you the chance to see what others in the same class consider important and may help you remember information more effectively.

How Our Memories Work

In Chapters 6 and 7 we introduced you to strategies you can use to improve the quality of your notes and the effectiveness of your textbook reading. In this chapter we introduce you to a variety of strategies you can use to enhance your memory as you attend classes, read textbooks, and study for exams. As you learn and practice these strategies, we're confident that you'll appreciate the efficiency with which you'll be able to remember new information. As a consequence, much of the information you'll be learning throughout your college experience will remain active in your memory for years to come.

Before discussing specific strategies to increase the capacity of your memory, we want you to have working knowledge of how your memory operates. One of the easiest ways to explain the way memories work is to use the analogy of a computer's operating system.

A Brief Overview

There are three stages to the memory process: (1) getting information, or encoding it, into the brain, which is analogous to computer programming; (2) storing information, which is similar to saving a file on a hard drive or floppy disk; and (3) retrieving information, which is similar to accessing a program or data on the computer (see Figure 8.1). Each of these three processes—encoding, storing, and retrieving—plays an important role in our ability to remember information we learn throughout our lives.

As you might imagine, very little of the information that our senses initially detect is stored for any significant length of time in our memories. Much of that initial information is lost, because we don't pay attention to it or consider it important enough to store in our memories, or simply because our memories are limited in the amount of information that can be stored. Some psychologists have estimated that we're bombarded with more than a thousand bits of sensory information every second. That's a whole lot more information than we can possibly deal with. As complex as our brains are, we simply don't have the hardware or software to consciously attend to that much information at one time.

POINT *to* PONDER

Some psychologists have estimated that we're bombarded with more than a thousand bits of sensory information every second.

Figure 8.1
Stages of the
Memory Process

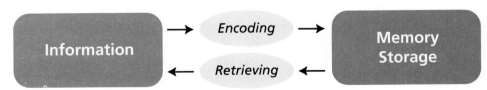

exercise break 8.1

1. Study the list of twenty words that appear in Box 8.1 (found at the end of the chapter on p. 142) for sixty seconds—no more, no less. (You'll probably want to set a timer or ask a friend or classmate to time you.)

2. After the time has elapsed, write as many of the twenty words as you remember in the space below.

_____

_____

_____

_____

_____

_____

_____

_____

3. Look again at the list of words in Box 8.1. Cross out the words you remembered accurately, and circle the words you were unable to remember. We'll return to the list later in the chapter.

Most people who complete this type of short-term memory exercise remember somewhere between five and nine words. Why is it that most of us are unable to remember a greater percentage of the words in a list of twenty after studying that list for a full minute? The answer lies in an understanding of what psychologists refer to as short-term, or working, memory.

Short-Term or Working Memory

After we're exposed to information in our environment, the information is either lost through memory decay or enters our short-term, or working, memory. As the term implies, working memory requires conscious effort on our part. The phrase *short-term* is used to describe this stage of memory because the information that gets stored in our short-term memory is limited in at least two ways.

First, information that enters short-term memory lasts from only a couple of seconds to a few minutes at most. Second, we're able to store only a small amount of information in our short-term memory at any given time; most of us are only able to remember between five and nine bits or chunks of new information when we're exposed to it. One way we can increase the storage capacity of short-term memory is to find creative ways to combine multiple bits of information into larger, cohesive chunks, a concept we return to later in the chapter.

Long-Term Memory

Of the many bits or chunks of information we're exposed to each day, only a very small portion is processed by short-term memory. An even smaller por-

point *to* ponder

■ **Unfortunately, information cannot make its way into long-term memory unless we actively engage in an active process to remember it.**

tion reaches long-term memory. Much of the information that reaches short-term memory decays before it reaches long-term memory. The one good thing about long-term memory, however, is that it has a very large storage capacity. It doesn't take long to realize how important it is to get information that you

Exercise Break 8.2

Check to see how well you remember the main ideas presented in the chapter so far by answering the following questions *without* reviewing the first few pages of the chapter.

1. How can our memory systems be likened to a computer?

_____

_____

2. According to psychologists, how many bits of sensory information are we exposed to every second?

_____

3. What is another name for *short-term memory*?

_____

4. How long does information remain in short-term memory?

_____

5. What are the two main reasons that information stored in short-term memory is limited?

_____

_____

_____

6. How many bits or chunks of information can most people store in their short-term memories?

_____

7. What are the major differences between short-term and long-term memories?

_____

_____

_____

Now go back through the first few pages of the chapter and check your answers.

1. How well did you do?

_____

_____

2. Was there a question or two that you were unable to answer correctly?

_____

3. If so, why do you think you were unable to answer those questions?

_____

_____

4. What factors contributed to your knowing the answers to those questions you answered correctly?

_____

_____

want to remember into your long-term memory. You might even say that encoding information into long-term memory is the essential goal of all studying. As with short-term memory, however, information cannot make its way into long-term memory unless we *actively* engage in a very conscious process to remember it.

Specific Memory-Enhancing Strategies

Our primary goal in this section is to focus on six specific memory-enhancing strategies that college students consistently report as especially useful. You'll probably want to review all of these strategies and consider integrating as many of them as possible into your regular study routine. Of course, you may already be using these or other strategies. Remember, the goal is to first encode new information into short-term memory and then to transfer the information into long-term memory. Each of the six strategies discussed in this section can be used to enhance your memory during both the short- and long-term memory process.

■ *Pay Attention to Important Material*

Paying attention to important material may seem like an obvious way to increase your memory capacity—and it is. There isn't anything magical or surprising about paying attention. But it's one of the best ways for improving your memory of important information. In Chapter 4 we emphasized the importance of avoiding distractions during study periods. We encouraged you to create a study environment that allows you to focus on what you're doing. By eliminating distractions during study periods, you're better able to pay attention to important material you're trying to learn. Suppose, for example, that while trying to study at home, you're constantly being interrupted by the tele-

exercise break 8.3

Many students report that they're often distracted in a number of ways during class lectures.

1. What types of distractions do you tend to experience during class?

_____

_____

2. What strategies do you use to minimize those distractions?

_____

_____

_____

3. Discuss your responses to the first two questions with one or two of your classmates. What strategies for minimizing distractions do your classmates use that you may want to use in the future?

_____

_____

_____

phone or distracted by loud music. You're probably going to have a more difficult time getting the material into short-term memory, let alone long-term memory, because of these distractions.

Repeat It (Again and Again and Again)

One of the easiest ways to increase your chances of remembering information is to study it over, and over, and over again. This isn't easy to do if you procrastinate until the night before a test. The most effective repetition occurs over a much longer period of time, with numerous breaks between studying sessions. For instance, if you know that one week from today you'll be tested on the gestational differences between mammals and other animals in a biology course, *now* is the time to begin repetitive activities, such as reviewing note cards and reading and rereading lecture notes. By repeating the studying process several times, you'll increase your chances of remembering the information over the long term.

Connect the New to the Old

Another effective memory-enhancing strategy is connecting new information to information you've been exposed to previously. Psychologists refer to the process of connecting new material to existing memories as elaboration. One of the great advantages of elaboration is that it doesn't require a lot of effort.

For example, suppose you have a fairly good memory of the early battles of the Civil War—something you may have learned years ago in a high school history class. Off the top of your head, you would probably be able to write down a fairly substantial summary of some of the early Civil War battles. If you were exposed to additional information about the Civil War in one of your college history courses, you might be able to connect this new information to your existing memory about the war. As a result, you'd be much more likely to remem-

Apply This Now

Think about some of the concepts you've been learning in this class. There have undoubtedly been numerous instances when you've been able to liken a concept to a recent experience you've had, like Logan did by connecting training his dog with the concept of reinforcement.

1. Describe one instance of elaboration you used in the past to increase your memory of a new concept or fact.

_____

_____

2. Consider a concept you've learned recently in *this* class. How could you use elaboration to enhance your memory of that concept?

_____

_____

_____

_____

case study 8.1

Consider Logan . . .

During Logan's first semester, he was one of 350 students enrolled in an introductory psychology class. Although he considered the course to be very interesting, Logan had difficulty grasping several of the concepts presented in class. With the help of the course teaching assistant, however, Logan found ways to connect some of the concepts he was learning to existing memories and personal life experiences.

One way in which Logan used elaboration had to do with his efforts to comprehend the psychological concept of reinforcement. As his professor explained in class, reinforcement involves rewarding an organism's behavior in the hope of increasing the frequency of that behavior in the future. Although the concept seemed somewhat abstract at first, Logan began to understand it much more clearly when he likened the concept of reinforcement to his recent experience trying to teach his puppy to roll over and play dead.

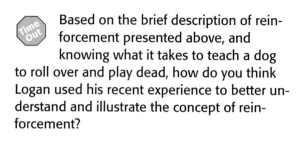 Based on the brief description of reinforcement presented above, and knowing what it takes to teach a dog to roll over and play dead, how do you think Logan used his recent experience to better understand and illustrate the concept of reinforcement?

_____

_____

_____

In order to teach his Labrador retriever puppy to roll over and play dead, Logan rewarded the puppy with a lot of praise and pats on the head each time it fell to the ground. Eventually, the puppy began to fall down on command with very little prompting by Logan. There are probably many different ways Logan could have used elaboration to connect the concept of reinforcement with his experience of training his dog. As Logan recalled this recent event in his own life, the concept of reinforcement made much more sense.

ber the new information when asked about it on a test. As you might imagine, elaboration can be an especially useful strategy for subjects and topics for which you already have some degree of familiarity and expertise.

 Another way to capitalize on existing memories is to come up with a story to connect the new material to an old memory. This works especially well if you can connect it to a memory that's personally meaningful. You might relate information you're learning to a relevant example from your own life or to an example from a favorite book, movie, or TV show. This type of elaboration can help increase your memory capacity for a wide variety of topics. Elaboration makes a connection to something already stored in long-term memory. Through this connection, you essentially create a shortcut for putting new information into long-term memory.

▦ *TSM: Try Some Mnemonics*

There are many different types of **mnemonics** that college students find useful. As the definition in the margin implies, mnemonics involve little tricks or plays on words to make remembering information easier and sometimes even fun. You've probably used at least a few mnemonics in the past to remember information.

© *Vivian Scott Hixson*

My Very Educated Mother Just Served Us Nine Pizzas
(Mnemonic for the planets, in order)

Acronyms are one of the most commonly used mnemonic devices. If you've ever taken music lessons, you may recall learning a mnemonic for the musical notes of the treble clef. The acronym FACE can be used to remember that the notes between the lines of the treble clef are, in order, F, A, C, and E.

Or perhaps you recall learning the saying "Every good boy does fine" as a way to remember the notes that are represented on the lines of the treble clef. Taking the first letter of each word in the saying, you can easily remember that the corresponding notes are, respectively, E, G, B, D, and F. This type of mnemonic involves remembering a saying of some sort in which the first letter of each word in the saying represents the first letter of some other word or denotes specific information in and of itself.

Another example of this type of mnemonic is the saying "My very educated mother just served us nine pizzas" to remember the order of the nine planets in our solar system (Mercury, Venus, Earth, Mars, Jupiter, Saturn, Uranus, Neptune, and Pluto). Like the use of acronyms, this type of mnemonic can be an amusing way to learn information and increase the likelihood of remembering important information later.

Perhaps you've used other mnemonics to remember concepts presented in a class, such as the acronym HOMES to remember the names of the Great Lakes (Huron, Ontario, Michigan, Erie, and Superior) or the saying "my dear Aunt Sally" to remember the order in which you carry out mathematical functions in an equation (multiply, divide, add, subtract). As you study information for a class, you might try to develop mnemonics to help you remember it more efficiently.

Some people use famous melodies to remember important information about the composer or about the music itself, or even about something unrelated to music. For example, if you can recall the very famous sequence of four notes that open Beethoven's Fifth Symphony, you can assign the lyric "Beethoven's Fifth, Beethoven's Fifth, . . ." to them. Remember learning your A, B, C's? Did the song you

mnemonics: Strategies or tricks you can use to improve your memory.

learned along with it help you remember them when you were younger? It was probably a very useful mnemonic that you used at a relatively young age. Mnemonics of all sorts can be used as a chunking shorthand and can also act as an effective elaboration strategy.

Organize It

Organizing important concepts and information is another strategy that can have a positive effect on your memory capacity. Suppose, for example, you have a French test coming up in a week for which you're responsible for knowing the meanings of more than a hundred French verbs and adverbs. You wouldn't want to go about the studying process from the perspective that there are a hundred separate words you need to remember. Instead, you'd probably benefit by organizing those words into meaningful groups or categories. You might group all of the regular verbs into one group, all of the irregular verbs into another group, and all of the adverbs into yet another. Although there are still a hundred or more words that you have to learn, you could study the terms in categories that might help you see meaningful relationships between them. As you might have already guessed, psychologists have found that using these types of grouping systems, sometimes referred to as chunking, significantly increases memory capacity.

Time to Reflect

Try to remember mnemonics you've used in a high school or college class to remember information. Jot them down below.

_____

_____

_____

_____

Ask two or three of your classmates what mnemonics they've used in the past to remember important information. List any that you consider especially useful or creative.

_____

_____

_____

_____

_____

Now go back to the twenty words in Box 8.1 (see page 142), and come up with a mnemonic to remember as many of the circled words you didn't initially remember as possible. Briefly describe the mnemonic you came up with in the space below.

_____

_____

_____

_____

Share the Wisdom

Share any memory-enhancing ideas you've found particularly useful with your friends and classmates. In turn, you can ask them to share any strategies they've found useful. You might even want to take a few minutes during study-group sessions to share some of the more successful strategies that each group member has used to remember the material you're discussing. When studying for an exam, share helpful hints with your classmates. Discuss specific mnemonics that you're using, and describe other strategies for remembering the information. It's a win-win situation when you and your classmates discuss ways to improve your memory of information. This is an active-learning strategy. Memory usually works best when we're actively engaged in the material we're trying to remember. That's because we're naturally more attentive when we're actively engaged.

exercise Break 8.4

1. Briefly review the six specific memory enhancing strategies presented in this section of the chapter. In the left column, use the rating scale that's shown to indicate the degree to which you've used each of these strategies in the past.

	1	2	3	4	5
	Have never used at all		Have used every now and then		Have used extensively

Past Experience   **Future Plans**

Past Experience		Future Plans
_____	Pay attention to important material	_____
_____	Repeat it (again and again and again)	_____
_____	Connect the new to the old	_____
_____	Organize it	_____
_____	TSM: Try some mnemonics	_____
_____	Share the wisdom	_____

2. Indicate those strategies you're most likely to use in the future by placing an X in the right column.

3. Which of the strategies do you plan to use most in the future?

_____

4. Why are those particular strategies especially appealing to you?

_____

_____

5. Which of the strategies do you *not* plan to use very much in the future?

_____

6. Why are those particular strategies unappealing to you?

_____

_____

Enhance Your Memory of Lecture and Reading Notes

What you do with your notes after you take them is at least as important as implementing the note-taking strategies discussed in Chapters 6 and 7. This section presents five strategies you can use to help make your lecture and reading notes more meaningful and easier to remember. Over the years we've seen each of these strategies work for many students. They're a great way to integrate note-taking into the broader context of learning and to enhance your ability to remember important information from your notes.

Review Your Notes as Soon as Possible

One of the best ways to ensure that you'll remember the information presented during a lecture or in your textbook is to review your notes as soon as possible after taking them. It's common for students to sit through a lecture, take good notes, and then not look at those notes again until the night before an exam. Doing that prevents the information from getting stored in long-term memory.

If you haven't already done so, *now* is the time to create a good habit: Each evening, if only for ten or fifteen minutes, review *all* of the notes you took that day. At the end of each week, review all of your notes from the week several additional times. When it's time to study for tests, you'll be glad your notes are that much fresher in your mind and, as a result, much easier to remember.

Prepare and Use Note Cards

One of the most common strategies for improving your memory of lecture and reading notes is to use note cards. Using note cards to enhance memory capacity is based on the flash-card concept used to help children learn arithmetic and vocabulary. Perhaps you recall learning multiplication tables or simple division with flash cards.

Most students who use note cards place an important term, concept, date, event, or formula on one side of a three-by-five-inch index card. On the other side, they write a definition, details, a translation, the meaning of the term, or elaboration of the concept. For example, a note card for a computer class might look like the one shown in Figure 8.2.

At various times throughout the year, it's common to see several students on campus reviewing their note cards in anticipation of upcoming exams. The frequent use of note cards is probably the best evidence in support of their effectiveness in increasing memory of important information.

Many students have developed interesting and useful strategies for using note cards as a way of organizing their study time. It can be helpful, for example, to use different colors of ink for different types of terms or concepts. One Spanish instructor recommends this technique to his students when they're learning English translations of Spanish words. As you can probably guess, Spanish terms appear on one side of the note card, and the English translations appear on the other side. Beyond that, the Spanish instructor also recommends using one color of ink for verbs, a different color for nouns, and yet a third color for adjectives. Some students find it useful to tape study cards to various items in their homes, such as the bathroom mirror or the refrigerator, or to tack them to bulletin boards in their rooms.

case study 8.2

Consider Choi . . .

In his second semester of college, Choi was beginning to experience some of the pressures associated with taking five classes in one term. He was having a particularly challenging time remembering the definitions of hundreds of different terms he was expected to know for his anatomy and physiology class.

For an upcoming exam, Choi was going to be tested on his knowledge of more than 250 terms. He would be expected to know the location and function of the major bones in the human body, the purpose and function of the major organs associated with the central nervous system, and the location and function of parts of the digestive system. Heeding the advice of one of his classmates, Choi tried using note cards for the first time.

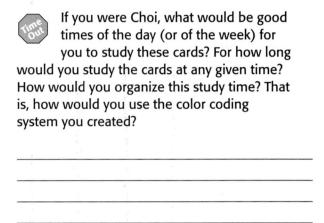 Based on the concepts presented in this chapter, how would you use note cards to prepare for an exam covering more than 250 anatomy and physiology terms?

_____

_____

_____

The strategies you came up with in response to the Time Out question would no doubt be effective for you—given your particular learning style and study routine. Choi selected three different colors of note cards to use in preparation for his exam. He used green three-by-five-inch cards for the major bones in the human body. On one side of each card he wrote the name of the bone, and he wrote its location and function in the body on the other side. He used yellow note cards for terms associated with the central nervous system. He wrote the name of a central nervous system organ on one side of each card and the location and function of each organ on the other side. Choi did the same for the information about the digestive system using blue cards.

If you were Choi, what would be good times of the day (or of the week) for you to study these cards? For how long would you study the cards at any given time? How would you organize this study time? That is, how would you use the color coding system you created?

_____

_____

_____

Throughout the week preceding the exam, Choi spent an hour or so each day reviewing his note cards. By picking out all of the cards of a particular color, Choi was able to study one set of terms at a time. When he wanted to study the various concepts all at once, he mixed up the terms by shuffling the cards together.

All week long, Choi took advantage of a few moments each day to study his note cards. When he arrived in a class a few minutes early, he took out the cards and got in a little studying time. When he rode the campus bus each morning and afternoon, he studied the cards. He even quizzed himself every now and then to make sure he was learning the terms. Sometimes he would look at the term on the front side of the card and see if he could remember the location and function of that particular organ, nerve, or bone. At other times he looked at the location and function of the organ, nerve, or bone on the back of the card to see if he could figure out the name of the organ, the part of the central nervous system, or the bone described.

When test time arrived, Choi easily remembered the information he had studied. Choi became a true believer in the use of note cards as an effective studying tool. As you can imagine, he's been using them in every one of his classes ever since.

Apply This Now

1. Have you ever used note cards to study for an exam?

2. If you answered yes, discuss the ways in which you've used note cards in the past and the degree to which using note cards has helped you achieve academic success.

3. If using note cards in the past didn't help you as much as you anticipated, did you use them as described in the chapter?

   If not, in what ways could you have used them more effectively?

4. If you answered no to Question 1, discuss your reasons for *not* using note cards in the past and any plans you have to use them in the future.

5. How might your preferred learning style affect the benefits you receive from using note cards as part of your regular study routine?

Figure 8.2
Sample Note Card
Used for Studying

Front of card

REBOOT

Back of card

A term used to refer to the process of restarting a computer.

Type Your Notes into a Word-Processing Document

Although it may at first seem like nothing more than unnecessary repetition, placing your notes into a word-processing document after initially writing them provides you with at least three things simultaneously: relearning, increased organization, and greater legibility. The most obvious benefit of placing your notes into a word processor is that it gives you the chance to relearn the material, several times over. As you type, you're likely to focus on your notes on at least a couple of different levels. First, as you read through your notes during the typing process, you're automatically reviewing the lecture material. The review occurs a second time as you take a look at the printed copy of your notes and check it for accuracy.

If you used a fair amount of shorthand or abbreviations during the actual lecture or reading period, placing the notes into a word-processing document also allows you to substitute the full spelling of terms for the abbreviations. If your particular learning style is such that you benefit from visual materials, you'll reap even more benefits from using this technique. Finally, if you're a kinesthetic learner, the very act of keying in the words will probably help you remember the concepts.

Audiotape Your Notes

In Chapter 6 we talked about the pros and cons of taping lectures. But tape recording *your* notes is different. Taping your notes involves verbally recording on a cassette tape or some other recording device the notes you've taken in class or the notes you've jotted down while reading an assignment. Tape recording your notes is a useful way to review your notes when looking down at written material might be particularly challenging or dangerous, such as when driving a car, taking a walk, or enjoying a morning jog around campus. This also is a great strategy if you're more of an auditory learner. As with word processing your notes or making up note cards, you get to review the material while you're transferring it into a new form (from written to verbal).

Establish Study Groups

Point *to* ponder

There are numerous benefits from meeting with your classmates to discuss issues and debate ideas presented in class and in the textbook.

We've emphasized the value of working in study groups in almost every chapter so far. That's because there are numerous benefits from meeting with your classmates to discuss issues and debate ideas presented in class and in the textbook. The benefits of working in study groups are perhaps most evident when reviewing lecture notes and reading notes. Even if you used all of the suggestions presented in Chapters 6 and 7, there's no guarantee that your notes would contain each and every important bit of material presented in class or in your textbook.

No one can avoid daydreaming now and then while listening to a lecture or reading a textbook. And it's doubtful that anyone can pick up on every verbal and nonverbal cue about lecture material that professors convey. That's why comparing notes with some of your classmates is such a good idea; it gives you the chance to see what others in the same class consider particularly important, and it provides you with the opportunity to look at various note-taking strategies that your classmates are using. Who knows? As a result of comparing notes with other students in the class, you might decide to try out a new note-taking strategy. Not only is this an active-learning strategy, but it's also an opportunity for a little repetition.

A Concluding Thought

The list of memory-enhancing strategies that we've shared with you in this chapter is by no means exhaustive. There are many other methods for improving your memory skills. In fact, you may have already experienced success with a variety of other techniques. We want to encourage you to keep using the strategies you've found useful in the past as you consider trying some of the new techniques described in this chapter.

The ultimate goal is to have as many options as possible for enhancing your memory. Mastering several different strategies will make it that much easier to remember important information as you continue to overcome the hurdles to academic success.

Time to Reflect

1. What memory-enhancing strategies have you used successfully in the past that were not presented in this chapter?

_____

_____

2. Select one of the strategies you listed above. Describe in detail how students who have never used that strategy would go about implementing it into their study routine. In other words, explain how to use the strategy as if you were talking with someone who has never heard about it.

_____

_____

_____

3. Share your responses to the first two questions with two or three of your classmates.

4. Did you learn any new memory-enhancing strategies from your classmates that you're thinking about using in the future?

_____

If so, briefly describe them.

_____

_____

_____

Take it away!

We began this chapter by teaching you about the ways our memories work. That discussion included information you can use to improve your memory skills.

- Encoding and storing information into our short-term memories require at least some minimal effort on our part.

- Information gets encoded into and retrieved from our long-term memories much more effectively when we use specific memory-enhancing strategies.

We then discussed a variety of strategies you can use to enhance your personal memory capacity, which included the following:

- Pay attention to important material.

- Repeat important information again and again once you've been exposed to it.

- Connect new material to existing memories from previous experiences.

- Organize the information you need to remember in a way that's efficient and meaningful.

- Use mnemonics.

- Share your memory-enhancing ideas with friends and classmates, and ask them to do the same.

Finally, we discussed specific strategies you might want to use to increase your memory of lecture and reading notes.

- Review your notes regularly and as soon as possible after taking them.

- Prepare and use note cards.

- Type your notes into a word-processing document.

- Audiotape your notes.

- Establish and meet regularly in study groups.

In Chapters 9 and 10 we focus on strategies you can use to improve your test-taking skills. We teach you ways to decrease your test anxiety and increase your chances of experiencing success when it comes to taking tests.

Questions for Critical Thought

1. If you want to remember information that's presented in class, what are three things you can do on the day of the lecture to prevent decay of the information?

2. What mnemonic devices (if any) have you used in the past week to help you remember information for a test? Why is it that most adults can still remember mnemonics they learned when they were children?

3. Why is it important to review your lecture and reading notes as soon as possible after taking them and then several additional times in the next few days? Why is this type of review more effective than only reviewing notes immediately before an exam?

4. What are three ways that engaging in study groups can help increase your memory of information you need to know for a test?

5. Look back at the Points to Ponder that appear in this chapter.
   a. Which Point to Ponder surprised you the most?
   b. How does knowing this help you better prepare for academic success?

6. How can an understanding of concepts presented in this chapter help you outside of the college and classroom environment? Which strategies discussed in the chapter are particularly relevant to success in your career and personal life?

Web Site

Visit the *Overcoming the Hurdles to Academic Success* web site for a chapter outline, review exercises, additional case studies, links to other online resources, and a practice test.

References

Herrmann, D., Raybeck, D., and Gutman, P. (1993). *Improving student memory.* Seattle, WA: Hogrefe & Huber Publishers.

Lorayne, H., & Lucas, J. (1996). *The memory book.* New York: Ballantine Books.

BOX 8.1.   **Words to Study for Sixty Seconds**

Party	Argumentative
Blue	Yodeling
Compact	Wishful
Hungry	Spectacles
Future	Decipher
Energy	Guess
Laminate	Known
Tonsils	Prospective
Interesting	Ominous
Misty	Entertainment

9

prepare for tests to expect the best

Chapter 9 Strategies

1 It's important to write down (in pencil) your quiz, test, and exam dates in an academic planner.

2 You should study for several days or even a full week before each of your exams, rather than cram the night before.

3 Meeting with the course instructor or TA can help you make sure you're aware of the competencies you'll need to have mastered by test time.

4 Review sheets and review sessions can help reduce your anxiety about what to expect on a test.

5 It's useful to ask other students who have previously taken the course what they think the content of the test is likely to be.

6 Be sure to balance your review of the lecture notes and reading material based on what you know of the test's format.

7 Taking the time to review study guides is an important part of test preparation.

8 If you're having a difficult time understanding particular concepts, you owe it to yourself to seek guidance and direction.

9 Don't procrastinate! Make sure your academic planner or calendar includes blocks of time to study for tests.

10 When answering objective test questions, it's important to realize that the wording of a question can help you eliminate possible wrong answers.

11 When answering multiple-choice questions, it's helpful to at first cover up all of the answer options so that only the question is showing.

12 Don't assume that the first apparently correct answer in a list of options is the correct response.

143

13 "All of the above" is often the incorrect answer. Don't assume every time you see "all of the above" that it's the appropriate response.

14 When answering a multiple-choice question, eliminating options that are clearly incorrect by crossing them off the list can make answering the question more manageable.

15 When answering matching questions, it's a good idea to mark off options in the right column once they've been used to answer items in the left column.

16 It's important to be fully aware of the directions of matching exercises.

17 Answering matching items in the opposite direction can be useful.

18 When answering fill-in-the-blank questions, consider the number and length of the blank spaces you're required to fill in.

19 Sometimes the grammar of a sentence can give you clues about how to answer a fill-in-the-blank question.

20 You shouldn't consider true/false questions to be trick questions.

21 Especially in true/false questions, you should watch out for words (e.g., always, never, all, and none) that often make a statement false.

22 It's useful to take the time to read true/false questions very carefully.

23 With short-answer and essay questions, it's a good idea to know your instructor's expectations regarding appropriate length of responses and the type of structure or format that's acceptable.

24 When reading an essay question, be sure you understand precisely what type of information you're being asked to provide.

25 It's helpful to pay especially close attention to key verbs when answering essay questions.

26 The first thing you should do after reading an essay question is write down your initial thoughts and reactions on scratch paper.

27 It's often useful to number your initial thoughts about an essay question in the order you want to write about them.

28 Essay responses should be simple and concise.

29 Try to find ways to cite reading and lecture material when answering essay questions.

30 Consider finishing your answers to essay questions with brief summaries.

31 Essay questions should be answered in a legible fashion.

32 Unless you're told otherwise, you should probably use a pen when answering essay questions on an in-class exam.

33 To the extent possible, you should respond to essay questions even if you're not fully prepared to answer them.

34 It's important to review your answers to essay questions before turning them in for a grade.

Evaluate Your Test Anxiety

In Chapter 8 we discussed a variety of techniques you can use to enhance your memory. There's no question that mastering those techniques can have a positive influence on your ability to remember important information. In Chapter 9 we turn our attention to specific strategies you can use to prepare to perform your absolute best on tests.

We begin with a discussion of several techniques you can use to decrease the amount of anxiety you might experience while preparing for tests. This will help you channel your stress to maximize your test-taking performance. We then present various strategies you'll want to use when you answer objective test questions, such as multiple-choice, matching, fill-in-the-blank, and true/false questions. Finally, we conclude the chapter with a discussion of strategies to consider when answering short-answer and essay questions.

If you're like many students, you sometimes struggle with high levels of anxiety when taking tests. As you may recall from Chapter 3, bad stress or anxiety interferes with your ability to do your best. The degree to which this type of stress interferes with test performance varies from person to person. So, to get a sense of just how much test anxiety you tend to experience, complete Exercise Break 9.1.

The good news about test anxiety is that it tends to decrease as you gain ad-

Exercise Break 9.1

Using the scale below, indicate the degree to which you agree or disagree with each of the following statements. Place the appropriate number next to each statement.

1	2	3	4
Strongly disagree	Disagree	Agree	Strongly agree

Test Anxiety Inventory

____ 1. I usually have trouble sleeping the night before a test.

____ 2. When I walk into a classroom to take a test, my heart begins to race as I wonder what's going to be on the test.

____ 3. My mind seems to go blank now and then during tests.

____ 4. Just the mere thought of taking a test makes me nervous.

____ 5. If I could relax a little bit when I take tests, I'm sure my performance would improve.

____ 6. I often get upset with myself after taking a test for having made stupid mistakes.

____ 7. Panicky thoughts and worries often frustrate me during tests.

____ 8. No matter how much I prepare to take a test, I never feel fully prepared.

____ 9. I often experience a dry mouth and/or sweaty hands when I take tests.

____ 10. During tests I usually find myself thinking about whether I'm going to get a lower grade than I want.

_____ **TOTAL SCORE**

Add up all of your responses. Scores above 25 indicate a fairly high level of test anxiety; scores below 15 represent relatively low levels of test anxiety; scores between 15 and 25 indicate a moderate level of test anxiety.

Follow-Up Questions

1. What does your score on the Test Anxiety Inventory reveal about your level of test anxiety?

_____

_____

2. What coping strategies have you used in the past to decrease the amount of anxiety you experience when you take tests?

_____

_____

3. Which coping strategies consistently help you when taking tests?

_____

_____

Point *to* PONDER

■ **The good news about test anxiety is that it tends to decrease over time as you gain experience taking college exams.**

ditional experience taking exams. Think back to the very first time you tried riding a bicycle. It's likely that you experienced at least some degree of anxiety. But after you practiced a lot, riding a bike probably became second nature. The experience of swerving into a tree a few times or falling down helped you learn how to accomplish the task. The same is true of test anxiety. The first few exams students take in college often produce quite a bit of anxiety, but with each additional test students usually report a dramatic decrease in anxiety. In Chapter 10, we discuss test anxiety in more detail and provide several strategies you can use to deal with anxiety during the test.

For some students, high levels of test anxiety persist even after the first couple of college exams. That's why we've outlined a variety of strategies that you might want to consider as means of decreasing your level of test anxiety and creating a low-stress approach to test taking. Even if you're one of the fortunate students who don't experience high levels of test anxiety, you'll probably find these strategies useful from time to time.

Create a Low-Stress Approach to Test Taking

■ *Plan in Advance*

Point *to* PONDER

■ **Studying a little here and a little there several days in advance of a test is much more effective than staying up all night to study for the next day's test.**

One strategy that many students find extremely useful for reducing test anxiety is to write down their quiz, test, and exam dates in an academic planner. As we discussed in Chapter 4, an academic planner can be any type of calendar or appointment book in which you record important dates and activities. If you write down the dates of all of your scheduled exams and remember to review your planner on a regular basis, you can make sure you have plenty of time to study for tests. Be sure to write in pencil, because instructors are known to reschedule tests every now and then.

You'll want to study for several days or even a full week before each of your exams. This is the opposite of what is commonly referred to as **cramming**. Research conducted by educational psychologists is very clear about the benefits of studying information over an extended period of time. "Pulling an all-nighter" in hopes of cramming every piece of information you possibly can into your brain in just a few hours doesn't allow you to re-

case study 9.1

Consider Thomas . . .

Thomas was a thirty-four-year-old electrician who after several months of career exploration decided to go back to college to become a high school math teacher. Teaching high school students had been his lifelong dream, and he was more than adequately motivated to achieve his goal.

During his first term at the local state university, Thomas experienced an extremely high level of test anxiety. A couple of days before his first exam, Thomas became so ill that he missed work. After a sleepless night, Thomas was so petrified by the thought of taking the test that he decided to withdraw from the university altogether rather than face taking the exam.

The university's withdrawal policy required Thomas to meet with a counselor prior to officially withdrawing from his classes. The university had established this policy to help students consider the ramifications of such a decision and to help them consider alternatives to withdrawing. When Thomas met with the assigned counselor, he described his recent experiences and explained that it just wasn't worth it. As much as he wanted to become a high school math teacher, Thomas couldn't bear the agony of preparing for and taking tests.

Thomas' counselor explained that high levels of test anxiety are quite common among students—especially students who have been out of school for several years. The counselor asked Thomas to consider meeting with her on a weekly basis to learn how to effectively cope with test anxiety and other sources of strain and stress. She also offered Thomas a twenty-eight-page pamphlet entitled "Coping with Test Anxiety," and she encouraged him to begin attending the test anxiety support group that met on campus each Friday at noon.

Thomas was amazed that so many resources were available to help him cope with his problem. After speaking with the counselor for two straight hours, Thomas no longer considered test anxiety to be an insurmountable obstacle. Instead, he considered it a hurdle that he was going to most definitely overcome. With his counselor's help, Thomas made arrangements to make up the exam. He decided to remain in all of his other classes as well, and he eventually went on to graduate with a degree in education. Today, Thomas is a high school math teacher and track coach at a large high school in Los Angeles. Furthermore, his own struggle with test anxiety has helped him become a better and more empathic teacher for students with math anxiety.

 If you were the counselor, what kinds of things might you say in the hope that Thomas might reconsider withdrawing from the university?

_____

_____

_____

member information effectively. Studying a little here and a little there several days in advance of a test is much more effective than staying up all night to study for the next day's test.

■ *Size Up the Test*

Just as you would want to know as much as possible about a new car before buying it, you should get to know a test as much as possible before taking it. There are numerous ways to successfully engage in the process of "sizing up the test." We discuss each of these ways in detail below.

cramming: Studying large amounts of information in a brief period of time—usually immediately before a test.

Apply This Now

1. Review your responses to follow-up question number 2 in Exercise Break 9.1. Then get together with two or three of your classmates and discuss the various strategies each of you has used in the past to reduce anxiety during tests.

_____

_____

_____

2. List any coping strategies your classmates use that you might want to try in the future.

_____

_____

_____

_____

A week or two before an exam is scheduled, try to find out all that you possibly (and ethically) can about the content of the exam. You might consider meeting with the course instructor or TA to make sure you're aware of the competencies you'll need to have mastered by test time. Professors will often prepare review sheets for a test. When they do, take advantage of such gifts and do all that you can to incorporate the review sheets into your test preparation. On large campuses where class sizes may exceed two or three hundred students, TAs may offer review sessions prior to midterms or final exams. These sessions are almost always optional, but don't be fooled by the term *optional*. Review sessions can be extremely helpful in finding out what kinds of questions are likely to appear on an exam.

Ask other students who have previously taken the course what they think the content of the test is likely to be. This can be especially helpful if you know students who previously took the course from the same professor. Although you can't be 100 percent sure that professors will include the same kind of information on their tests each and every term, at the very least you can usually

Time to Reflect

1. Reread the section in Chapter 4 on academic planners. Have you been using an academic planner this term?

_____

2. If you haven't been using an academic planner, why not?

_____

_____

3. Why do you think that most academic advisors and counselors *strongly* suggest that students use an academic planner on a regular basis?

_____

_____

BOX 9.1.   **Sizing Up the Test**

---

1. Try to find out all that you possibly (and ethically) can about the content of the exam.

2. Ask other students who've previously taken the course what they think the content of the test is likely to be.

3. Be sure to balance your review of the lecture notes and reading material based on what you know of the test's format.

4. Remember the importance of study groups.

5. Don't forget to review your textbook study guides.

6. Ask for help if you need it.

count on somewhat similar content. You'll also get a good idea of the test's structure (in other words, multiple-choice, true/false, essay, etc.).

Be sure to balance your review of the lecture notes and reading material based on what you know of the test's format. For instance, if you're aware that an upcoming exam will be based primarily on lecture, with only about 30 percent of the questions based on information in the book, then distribute your study time accordingly. In such a case, you'd probably want to spend twice as much time reviewing lecture notes as you would reviewing material from the textbook. (And, remember, by the time you're studying for a test, you should have completed—well in advance—your reading assignments.)

Don't forget to review your textbook study guides. Students with whom we've interacted over the years are often amazed by how many questions on an exam come directly from textbook study guides. It's common for professors to take a few exam questions straight out of a textbook study guide or prepare questions very similar to the types of questions that appear in the study guide. The reason for this is simple: Study guide questions are often well written and usually cover some of the most important material in the textbook. Taking the time to review study guides is something you should consider a very important part of test preparation.

Ask for help if you need it. One of the things that many students are reluctant to do is ask for help. If you're having a difficult time understanding particular concepts, you owe it to yourself to seek guidance and direction. You might be able to get the help you need by meeting with a study partner or talking with members of your study group. In some cases, however, you might have to contact the course TA or professor. If you need to meet with a TA or professor, you should set up an appointment several days prior to the test date.

Remember the importance of study groups. If your study group is functioning well, everyone will have important insights about the structure and/or content of the upcoming exam. The multiple perspectives are certain to come in handy during the final stages of test preparation. In addition, you may find it more enjoyable to study with your classmates when you prepare for a test. You're also less likely to procrastinate if study group members are relying on you to do your part.

case study 9.2

Consider Maria . . .

Maria, an eighteen-year-old first-year college student, was attending an urban community college in the Southwest. Just prior to the beginning of her second term, Maria received a letter notifying her that she was on academic probation because her grades— two C's and one D—were below a C average. The dean of enrollment services who wrote the letter encouraged Maria to visit the learning assistance center, where study-skills advisors would be able to recommend specific learning strategies to enhance her academic performance.

Because she was shy when it came to asking for help, Maria initially hesitated. She wanted to perform well in her classes, but the idea of telling a stranger that she was struggling academically was anxiety provoking. After thinking about it for a couple of weeks and after a lot of prodding from her friends, Maria finally decided to give it a try.

During her first meeting with the tutor, Maria explained some of the hurdles she encountered during the fall term. Although she had paid attention in class, read all the textbook assignments, and studied for exams well in advance, Maria wasn't performing well on tests. She told the tutor that she was often surprised at the actual content of the tests. Even though she paid attention in classes and read the assigned textbook material several times prior to an exam, Maria seemed to be studying the wrong information.

After discussing several strategies Maria might want to try in order to improve her performance on tests, the tutor suggested that she set up study groups for each of her classes. As you might imagine, Maria was extremely reluctant to form study groups. She told her tutor about the extreme shyness she suffered from and about the anxiety she was sure to experience if she were to study with fellow classmates.

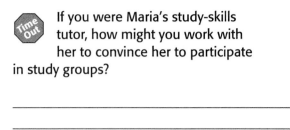 If you were Maria's study-skills tutor, how might you work with her to convince her to participate in study groups?

_____

_____

_____

Maria's tutor asked her if she had any friends in the classes she was enrolled in. Sure enough, Maria knew one other person in each of her classes. The tutor recommended that Maria gradually get used to the idea of study groups by initially studying with the one friend she had in each class. Then, later in the term, Maria and her friend could invite others to join them.

For the next couple of weeks, Maria chose not to follow her tutor's suggestion. She was too anxious about asking her friends to study with her. But after getting her first set of exams back, Maria realized that something had to change. Grades of D, D–, and C– just weren't acceptable any longer. As a result, Maria invited her one friend in each class to study with her once a week on a regular basis. To her surprise, several of her friends also were experiencing academic challenges. They welcomed the opportunity to be Maria's study partners.

One year later, although Maria had not completely overcome all of her academic challenges, she was no longer on academic probation, and she continued to benefit from study groups in each of her classes. She realized she was also less shy, which pleased her almost as much as improving her grades.

■ *Put an End to Procrastination, and Don't Wait Too Long!*

There's one strategy for decreasing test anxiety that you've probably already heard over and over. Still, it bears repeating: *Don't procrastinate.* As we discussed in Chapter 4, time management is very important to academic success. When preparing for tests, time management becomes especially relevant.

Apply This Now

1. In what ways can studying for exams with a study partner increase your chances of academic success?

_____

_____

_____

2. When was the last time you studied for an exam with a partner or study group?

_____

3. Did studying with others help you perform better on the exam than you would have performed otherwise?

_____

   If so, how?

_____

_____

4. What might have made your study-group experience even better?

_____

_____

_____

Make sure your academic planner or calendar includes blocks of time to study for tests. You don't want to wait until the last minute to do the things you need to do to perform your very best on a test.

exercise Break 9.2

1. Why is it important to avoid procrastination when preparing for exams in college?

_____

2. List things you can do to prevent procrastinating when it comes time to study for a test.

_____

_____

_____

3. Talk with two or three of your classmates about ways they avoid procrastination. List any strategies for avoiding procrastination your classmates use that you might want to try in the future.

_____

_____

_____

_____

Point *to* PONDER

■ **Make sure your academic planner or calendar includes blocks of time to study for tests.**

Another way to avoid procrastination is to remain focused on achieving your goals. In Chapter 1, you clarified the academic goals that you're currently striving to achieve. When you find yourself tempted to procrastinate, force yourself to take a look at your goals. Doing so may be the motivation you need to study instead of play—at least for the time being!

Of course, it's much easier to tell yourself that you're not going to procrastinate when it comes time to study for a test. It's another thing altogether to actually avoid procrastination. If you have a particularly difficult time with procrastination, you may want to visit your college counseling office and set up an appointment to meet with a counselor. College counselors are excellent resources for dealing with and overcoming procrastination.

Strategies for Answering Different Types of Test Questions

▨ *Objective Test Questions*

The term *objective tests* has traditionally been used to refer to tests that contain multiple-choice, matching, fill-in-the-blank, and/or true/false questions. They're called objective tests because there's usually only one right answer to each question, and that answer is one that can be objectively determined in advance.

Regardless of the type of objective question that may appear on a particular exam, you'll want to carefully consider the wording of each and every question as well as the directions for answering the questions. Often, the wording of a question can help you eliminate possible wrong answers. *Always, never, all,* and *none* are just a few examples of the terms that can help you figure out the correct answer to questions. For true/false questions, for example, these extreme words often—although not *always*—make statements false.

Suppose, for example, you must determine whether the following statement on a political science exam is true or false: "Vice presidents of the United States are always elected." If you take out the word *always,* the statement is generally true, right? Nearly all U.S. vice presidents have been elected. However, the word *always* in the statement makes it false. Some vice presidents of the United States have not been elected. President Richard Nixon appointed Gerald Ford as his second vice president after Spiro Agnew's resignation from office, and when Ford became president after Nixon's resignation, he appointed Nelson Rockefeller as vice president. So to say that vice presidents of the United States are always elected is a false statement.

Multiple-Choice Questions.   Multiple-choice questions are probably the most common type of test question, especially in classes with large numbers of students. You might want to consider the following four strategies when answering multiple-choice questions on exams.

1. Cover up all of the answer options when you first look at a question so that only the question is showing. Consider the following example from a film class:

   Which of the following motion pictures starred Johnny Depp?

   a. *Heart and Souls*

   b. *Titanic*

   c. *Edward Scissorhands*

d. *Enemy of the State*

e. None of the above

When you cover the response options while you read the item, you might come up with several possible answers. You might begin thinking about all of the movies you're aware of in which Johnny Depp starred. Then, after you've attempted to answer the question on your own, you can consider each of the options. If you had come up with a list of movies you know Johnny Depp starred in, then you might have more readily recognized (c) *Edward Scissorhands* as the correct response. In essence, this strategy can help you recall information you've studied without being tempted to select an incorrect option.

2. Read all of the options carefully before selecting your response. This can be especially important when an apparent correct answer is listed as option (a), but in actuality all of the options are correct or a better answer is listed farther down in the options list. This advice is especially useful when responses include an "all of the above" option, as illustrated in this example:

Which of the following professional football teams has won a Super Bowl?

a. New England Patriots

b. New York Jets

c. Chicago Bears

d. All of the above

If you simply look at the first option, New England Patriots, and—because you know they recently won a Super Bowl—mark (a) as the correct answer, you would be making a mistake. All of the teams listed in the response options have won a Super Bowl. Therefore, the correct answer is (d). Don't assume that the first apparently correct answer in a list of options is, in fact, the correct response. Be sure to read all of the options before marking your answer, even if you're fairly confident that one of the first two or three options is correct.

3. Another important strategy to keep in mind when taking multiple-choice exams has to do with the ever-so-popular "all of the above" option. Just because "all of the above" is listed as a response option, it's not necessarily the correct answer. Sometimes professors offer "all of the above" to challenge students to think really hard about a question. Don't assume every time you see "all of the above" that it's the appropriate response. It is often the incorrect answer. To be honest, it's often included as an option when a professor can't think of any more wrong answers to list.

4. Eliminate response options that are clearly incorrect. Even when a question is difficult to answer, there are likely to be some options you can rule out automatically. For example, suppose you were asked to answer the following question on an American history quiz:

Abraham Lincoln was the _____ president of the United States.

a. ~~third~~

b. fifteenth

c. sixteenth

d. ~~forty-second~~

Point *to* **ponder**

When answering multiple-choice questions, be sure to read all of the options before marking your answer—even if you're confident that one of the first two or three options is correct.

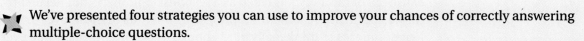

© Vivian Scott Hixson

 You don't have to be an American history expert to know that Abraham Lincoln was not the third or the forty-second president of the United States. Eliminating those two options by crossing them off the list (as shown on page 153) is one way to make the task of answering the question a bit more manageable.

exercise Break 9.3

We've presented four strategies you can use to improve your chances of correctly answering multiple-choice questions.

1. What additional strategies have you used in the past to help you answer multiple-choice questions on a test?

_____

_____

2. Get together with two or three of your classmates and talk about strategies each of you uses when answering multiple-choice questions. List below any strategies your classmates use that you might want to try when answering multiple-choice questions in the future.

_____

_____

_____

Matching Questions.   A few strategies you should consider using when answering matching items on a test are discussed below.

1. Mark off options in the right column once they've been used to answer items in the left column. (This assumes, of course, that options in the right column can be used only once in each matching section. We'll return to this issue later.) Consider this example from an introductory Spanish class:

   Match the English translations listed in the right column with the Spanish words listed in the left column.

__B__	1. la cocina	A. ~~window~~
__E__	2. la mesa	B. ~~kitchen~~
__A__	3. la ventana	C. shirt
____	4. la camisa	D. dog
____	5. el perro	E. ~~table~~

   The student completing this matching exercise increases her or his chances of coming up with the correct response to items 4 and 5 by marking off the options in the right column that have already been used to answer items 1, 2, and 3. It also saves time by eliminating the number of items to consider when answering items 4 and 5.

2. Be fully aware of the directions. This is especially important because of the tendency for directions for matching questions to vary from exam to exam. One rule that's likely to be different, as we alluded to above, has to do with whether options in the right-hand column can be used more than once to complete the matching exercise. There are times when you can use options in the right-hand column to answer more than one of the items in the left-hand column. Consider the following example from an introductory psychology class:

   Match the person in the right-hand column with the principles of learning in the left-hand column the person was responsible for developing. **You may use options in the right-hand column more than once, and you do not necessarily have to use all options in the right-hand column when completing this section.**

____	1. operant conditioning	A. Bandura
____	2. social learning theory	B. Pavlov
____	3. vicarious learning	C. Skinner
____	4. modeling	D. Thorndike
____	5. law of effect	E. Freud

   The correct answers to this matching exercise are 1–C, 2–A, 3–A, 4–A, and 5–D. As you can see, reading *and understanding* the directions is a very important strategy. In this case, if you weren't aware that you could use the names listed in the right-hand column more than once, you probably would have answered several of the questions incorrectly.

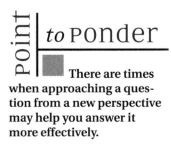

There are times when approaching a question from a new perspective may help you answer it more effectively.

3. Answer the items in the opposite direction. Rather than looking for answers to items listed in the left column, you can look for answers to the items listed in the right column. For instance, in the above example, Pavlov is known for classical conditioning and Freud for psychoanalysis. Neither is offered in (1) through (5). In essence, you're attacking

the problem from a different angle, and there are times when simply approaching a question from a new perspective may help you answer it more effectively.

Fill-in-the-Blank Questions.   You might find a couple of strategies particularly helpful when answering fill-in-the-blank questions.

1. Consider the number and length of the blank spaces that you're required to fill in. Take a look at Examples A and B below from a health exam:

   Example A: According to the textbook, three methods of birth control that have increased in popularity in the past five years include

   _____, _____,

   and _____.

   Example B: According to the textbook, the use of condoms has increased within the past five years primarily because

   _____

   _____

   _____

   Example A requires three words or short phrases. This is apparent not only because of the wording of the question but also because of the number of spaces allowed for the response. On the other hand, Example B requires a more comprehensive sentence and, as such, requires several more words than Example A.

2. Take a good look at the grammar of an item when considering possible responses. Consider the following example from a zoology exam:

   If you were on the island of Borneo and observed a small ape-like animal with long arms, you would probably be looking at an _____.

   Sometimes the grammar of the sentence can give you clues about how to answer a fill-in-the blank question. In this case, the correct response is a word that begins with a vowel. You can figure that out by the clue provided. The word *an* informs you that the correct answer (orangutan) must begin with a vowel. Of course, professors will sometimes write a fill-in-the blank question with "a(n)" at the end to take away this type of clue (indicating that the answer could start with a consonant or a vowel).

True/False Questions.   Many college students prefer true/false questions to just about any other type of test question. But many others despise such questions. Some students have a preconceived notion that true/false questions are inherently difficult to answer and that the professor is almost always trying to trick students—especially when the appropriate response seems obvious.

1. Try to avoid thinking of true/false questions, or any other exam questions for that matter, as trick questions. Professors rarely place questions on an exam for the sole purpose of tricking you. Besides, worrying about being tricked is one of the quickest ways to increase your anxiety level and distract your attention from the task at hand.

2. As you answer true/false questions, don't forget the advice offered earlier in the chapter: watch out for words (e.g., *always, never, all,* and *none*) that often make a statement false. Although such words may appear in other objective test questions, they're especially common in true/false questions and need to be considered when determining the truthfulness of a statement.

3. It's also important to take the time to read true/false questions very carefully. Make sure you take a few extra seconds when responding to true/false questions to ensure that you don't rush through them. The extra time will almost certainly improve your chances of responding successfully. Otherwise you may miss one small critical word, such as *not, meters,* or *Celsius.* That one little word can totally change the meaning of a sentence and, consequently, the correct answer.

Time to Reflect

Briefly review the material covered in the chapter so far. Then answer the following questions.

1. Which of the four types of objective test questions do you usually have the most difficult time answering on tests?

_____

2. Why do you think you struggle with that type of test question?

_____

_____

3. What strategies have you learned so far in this chapter that can help you answer that type of objective test question in the future?

_____

_____

_____

_____

■ *Short-Answer and Essay Questions*

Just as with objective test questions, several strategies are at your disposal to help increase your chances of correctly responding to short-answer and essay questions. Short-answer and essay questions are often referred to as subjective questions. This is because answers to such questions are often open to interpretation. Furthermore, although there are many similarities between short-answer and essay questions, there is one major difference between them as well. Short-answer questions usually require a sentence or two (and maybe as much as a full paragraph) to complete. Essay questions, on the other hand, usually require a much longer answer, sometimes spanning several pages. Despite this difference, there are several strategies you can use when answering such questions.

1. First and foremost, when answering short-answer and essay questions, be sure to read the directions and, if necessary, ask your instructor about the approximate response length and acceptable structure or format for each question. You might be asked to answer several different types of essay questions on a test. As mentioned above, although short-answer questions *usually* require only a few sentences and essay questions *usually* require several paragraphs, it's still important to know as much as possible about your instructor's expectations regarding appropriate length of responses and the type of structure (such as paragraph form, lists, etc.) that's acceptable.

2. When reading an essay question, be sure you understand precisely what type of information you're being asked to provide. If you're unsure, ask your professor or TA for clarification. If that feedback isn't available or useful, take a minute or two prior to answering the question to write down, directly on your answer sheet, what you think the question means. That way the person who grades your exam will at least have a sense of what you thought the question was asking.

3. Another way to make sure you know what type of information you should be providing in an essay question is to pay especially close attention to key verbs in the question. A few of the more common verbs to look for in essay questions include *analyze, compare, contrast, define, describe, discuss, evaluate, explain, illustrate, interpret, list,* and *summarize.* It may not seem that important, but being asked to *compare* two concepts is very different from being asked to *contrast* two concepts. Comparing requires you to point out *similarities,* while contrasting asks you to point out *differences.* Making sure you understand the type of response that's indicated by each of these verbs is an important prerequisite for answering essay questions effectively.

4. Immediately after reading an essay question, jot down some of your initial thoughts about the question. For example, suppose the following essay question appears on an exam in a speech and debate course: "Compare and contrast the essential elements of competitive extemporaneous and impromptu speaking." The very first thing you should do after reading the question is write down your initial thoughts and reactions on scratch paper. These thoughts shouldn't be complete answers. They should simply allow you the opportunity to begin thinking about your response. For this question, you might write something like the notes in Box 9.2.

BOX 9.2.   **Compare and Contrast Competitive Extemporaneous and Impromptu Speaking**

Similarities (Compare)	Differences (Contrast)
Both allow limited preparation time	Extemporaneous = current events Impromptu = general topics
Both require spur-of-the-moment thinking skills	Extemporaneous time limit = 10 minutes Impromptu time limit = 5 minutes

Exercise Break 9.4

1. Write a definition for each of the following verbs that often appear in essay questions.

Analyze _____

Compare _____

Contrast _____

Define _____

Describe _____

Discuss _____

Evaluate _____

Explain _____

Illustrate _____

Interpret _____

List _____

Summarize _____

2. Get together with two or three of your classmates and share your definitions. Feel free to revise your own definitions based on the definitions offered by your classmates.

3. Check the accuracy of the definitions you and your classmates generated by consulting a dictionary. Be sure to revise your definitions again if necessary.

4. It's not a bad idea to memorize the meaning of these terms. That way, when they appear on a test you'll know what you're being asked to provide in a response.

These initial thoughts are far from a complete answer, but they allow you to get some of your immediate thoughts down on paper and can serve as the basis for more complete answers that you'll generate later.

5. Number your initial thoughts in the order you want to write about them. Once you've taken a moment or two to think about your initial responses, you can develop a clear order for answering the question. Although more detailed than the few phrases you may have initially written, a list of the topics in the order you'll be writing about them is still not a complete answer. Nevertheless, preparing the list will help you make sure your final answer doesn't leave out an important point.

6. When preparing your answer to an essay question, remember that your response should be simple and concise. In other words, get right to the point. Many college students think they're better off sprucing up their

answers to essay questions by adding a lot of irrelevant information. Professors and TAs, however, devote several hours to grading essay questions. They would much rather read answers that are clear and to the point than muddle through paragraph after paragraph of useless information, searching endlessly for the correct response.

7. Throughout your answer to an essay question, try to find ways to cite reading and lecture material that you studied in preparation for the exam. Citing correct information from your book or from a class lecture helps make your answer more impressive. It also ensures that you don't leave out important information relevant to the question.

8. If you have enough time, consider finishing your answer to essay questions with brief summaries. This strategy is especially important when essay questions require answers that are several paragraphs in length. A professor or TA will probably be able to find the key terms and ideas somewhere within your answer, especially if it's well organized and based on an outline. But providing the key elements of your response in a summary statement can ensure that the person who grades your exam won't miss important points.

9. Be sure to write legibly. Although the content of an essay answer is what matters most, it certainly doesn't hurt to make the task of evaluating your answer easier by writing out your answers in an easy-to-read format. Unless you're told otherwise, you should probably use a pen when answering essay questions on an in-class exam. Simply put, ink is much easier to read than pencil. If you're concerned that you might want to rewrite or correct parts of your answer, consider using a pen with erasable ink.

10. Always write something, but be honest! It's very rare that you'd be penalized on an exam for guessing an answer to an essay question. To the extent you have time, respond even to those questions for which you're not fully

Time to Reflect

1. What are some of the hurdles you've faced in the past when you've had to answer essay questions on a test?

_____

_____

2. What strategies presented in this section of the chapter can help you overcome some of those hurdles?

_____

_____

3. What hurdles that have prevented you from answering essay questions are you still unsure how to overcome?

_____

_____

4. You might want to visit with one of your professors or contact someone in your college's study-skills or academic resource center for strategies you can use to address these challenges.

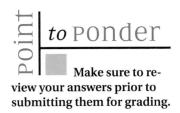

Point *to* ponder

Make sure to review your answers prior to submitting them for grading.

prepared. Even if you're unsure of the fully correct response, let the professor know that you remember at least some relevant information. Your response may not earn you full credit, but it may earn you a point or two that you wouldn't have received if you didn't answer at all.

11. Finally, as with all questions on an exam, make sure to review your answers. Doing this immediately after answering each essay question, as well as at the conclusion of the entire exam, allows you to correct careless mistakes . It also gives you one last chance to add additional information you may have initially left out of a response.

Take It Away!

The purpose of this chapter is to provide strategies you can use to increase your chances of performing your absolute best on tests. In particular, you learned the following important concepts:

- You can create a low-stress approach to test taking by planning in advance and avoiding procrastination when it comes time to study. It's also important to size up the test:

  __ Find out all that you possibly can about the content of the exam.

  __ Ask other students who have previously taken the course what they think the content of the exam is likely to be.

  __ Balance your review of lecture and reading material based on what you know of the test's format.

  __ Review your textbook study guides.

  __ Ask for help if you need it.

  __ Remember the importance of study groups.

- You also learned strategies for answering different types of test questions.

  __ It's important to thoroughly read a question to see if you can eliminate possible wrong answers.

  __ For multiple-choice questions, it's important to:

  —cover up answer options while reading the question so that you can attempt to answer the question on your own.

  —remember that the first apparently correct answer in a list of options may not be the correct response.

  —realize that "all of the above" is often an incorrect answer.

  —eliminate response options that are clearly incorrect.

  __ For matching questions, it's important to:

  —mark off options in the right column once they've been used to answer items in the left column.

  —be fully aware of the directions.

  —consider answering the matching items in the opposite direction.

___ For fill-in-the-blank questions, it's useful to:

—consider the number and length of the blank spaces that you're required to fill in.

—take a good look at the grammar of an item when considering possible responses.

___ For true/false questions, you'll want to:

—try not to think of true/false questions as trick questions.

—watch out for words that often make a statement false.

—take the time to read true/false questions very carefully.

___ For short-answer and essay questions, it's important to:

—read the directions carefully and be sure you're aware of the expected response length and format you're supposed to use.

—be sure you understand precisely what type of information you're being asked to provide.

—pay especially close attention to key verbs in the question.

—write down your initial thoughts and reactions on scratch paper immediately after reading an essay question.

—number your initial thoughts in the order you want to write about them.

—remember that your response should be simple and concise.

—find ways to cite reading and lecture material you studied.

—consider finishing your answers with a brief summary.

—write legibly.

—always write something, but be honest.

—make sure you review your answers.

In Chapter 10 we focus on additional strategies you can use on the day of a test—as well as after the test—to improve your test-taking skills. We also discuss strategies you can use when completing nontraditional kinds of tests (such as group tests, open book or open notes tests, and take-home exams). And we explain why it's important to make a personal commitment to academic honesty and integrity.

Questions for Critical Thought

1. What are some of the signs you can look for that would indicate that you're experiencing a high level of text anxiety?

2. Why is it important for you to feel comfortable meeting with your professors to discuss information you're having a difficult time understanding?

3. In addition to the suggestions discussed in the chapter, what steps can you take to plan for exams in advance?

4. Why is talking with students who have taken a class from the same professor considered a good test-taking strategy?

5. Look back at the Points to Ponder that appear in this chapter.
   a. Which Point to Ponder surprised you the most?
   b. How does knowing this help you better prepare for academic success?

6. How does the information presented in this chapter help you in your life outside of the classroom and college environment? Which strategies are particularly relevant to success in your career and personal life?

Web Site

Visit the *Overcoming the Hurdles to Academic Success* web site for a chapter outline, review exercises, additional case studies, links to other online resources, and a practice test.

References

Meyers, J. N. (2000). *The secrets of taking any test,* Second Edition. Boston: Learning Express.

Tracy, E. (2001). *The student's guide to exam success.* Buckingham, England: Open University Press.

10

take tests with confidence

1 Eating healthy foods is one of the most important things to do on test days.

2 Be sure to dress comfortably on test days so that you'll increase your chances of performing your best.

3 Remember to bring all of the materials you need to complete the test, and don't wait until the last minute to purchase materials you need.

4 You might want to post a list of materials you've needed for previous exams in a handy place (e.g., a refrigerator, bulletin board, on top of your textbooks).

5 If you have an important exam in the morning, you might want to ask a classmate or friend to call you, just in case your alarm clock isn't reliable.

6 Make sure to sit in a comfortable setting when completing an exam.

7 When taking tests, be sure to take an extra minute to read and reread all instructions so you know what's expected of you.

8 It's important to preview an entire exam's content before beginning to answer questions; you may want to answer questions that appear later in the exam before you answer earlier questions.

9 As a way of breaking down an exam into smaller chunks, you might want to view the different sections of a test as mini-quizzes.

10 If your instructor informs you that writing directly on an exam isn't allowed, ask if you may use a blank sheet of paper to make notes that will help you answer the questions correctly.

11 Go through an exam and answer "sure shots" first.

12 Taking a few seconds to make sure you fully understand a question is well worth the time and effort.

13 Asking for clarification about a question you don't understand will help ensure that you know what's being asked.

164

14 If you can narrow down the correct answer to one or two possible responses, guessing between those two options is probably worth the risk.

15 Now and then, you'll find information from one test question useful for answering another.

16 Keep aware of time limits, and make sure you leave enough time to answer the more difficult questions and those that are worth the most points.

17 Take a break—if needed—during an exam; but be sure to find out what your professor's policies are so that you don't break any classroom rules.

18 Even if you're unable to answer a question or two, you need to approach all subsequent questions with as much confidence as possible.

19 Minimize intrusive thoughts and other such distractions as much as possible when taking tests.

20 If you begin to feel anxious during a test, remember to BRACE yourself (**b**reathe regularly and deeply, **r**elax, keep a positive **a**ttitude, **c**enter yourself, and **e**xpect a change).

21 As time permits, review your responses to all test questions.

22 Be sure to check with your professor to find out any particular rules of a testing procedure, especially when you're completing nontraditional tests (e.g., open book or open notes tests, group exams, take-home tests).

23 One of the most important things to do as soon as possible after receiving a group test is to agree on assignments of tasks and duties.

24 Attaching sticky notes to key pages of your book or notes is a useful strategy when preparing for open book or open notes exams.

25 The first thing you'll want to do when working on a take-home exam is avoid procrastination.

26 Unless your instructor informs you otherwise, prepare essay questions on a take-home examination on a word processor or computer.

27 Make sure that directions for completing a take-home exam are clear before you leave the classroom.

28 As soon as you complete an exam, review your notes to see what kinds of information you failed to study as well as you should have.

29 You'll also want to spend quality time reviewing the results of your exams once they are graded and returned to you.

30 Reflecting on what went right and what went wrong with an exam can help you figure out ways to improve your test-taking performance in the future.

31 Now is the time for you to make a personal commitment to engage in the absolute highest level of academic honesty.

The Day of the Test

In Chapter 9 we discussed a variety of techniques you can use to more effectively prepare for tests. In this chapter we turn our attention to strategies you can develop to confidently approach the test-taking experience on the day of the test. We discuss a variety of things you can do during the test to maximize your chances of performing your best. The chapter includes a discussion of nontraditional test formats you may experience during college. We share a variety of strategies you can use to perform your best on group exams, open book and open notes tests, and take-home exams. We also discuss the importance of evaluating test results. We conclude the chapter with a discussion of the importance of making a personal commitment to academic honesty and integrity.

Once test day arrives, you'll want to do all you can to ensure successful performance. If you've been effectively preparing for the test-taking experience the week or two before the test, you don't want any last-minute problems on the day of the test to ruin your chances for success. The strategies discussed in this initial section of the chapter can help you take care of last-minute test preparations and reduce your overall anxiety.

■ *Eat Well*

 One of the most important things to do on test day is to eat healthy foods. You don't want to skip a meal or eat a lot of junk food and deny your body important energy. Not only will skipping meals diminish your capacity to remember information during the test, but eating poorly can also lower your body's resistance to infection. The last thing you need on the day of an exam is to come down with a cold.

■ *Dress Comfortably*

After all of the time and effort you put into the studying process, you certainly don't want your performance on an exam to be adversely affected because you're uncomfortable. Be sure to dress comfortably on test days so that you'll increase your chances of performing your best.

■ *Bring the Materials You're Going to Need*

One thing that should be at the top of your list on the day of an exam is to remember to bring all of the materials you'll need for the test. You don't want to arrive for a math exam without your calculator (if you're

Point *to* PONDER

■ Be sure to dress comfortably on test days so that you'll increase you chances of performing your best.

Time to Reflect

In Chapter 3 we discussed some of the effects of eating heavy meals prior to class. Review that discussion, and answer the following questions.

1. On the basis of the information you reviewed in Chapter 3, why should you avoid eating a heavy meal immediately before taking a test?

_____

_____

_____

2. What alternatives to eating a heavy meal prior to taking a test might you consider to make sure your stomach doesn't growl throughout it?

_____

_____

_____

allowed or required to use one). For an essay exam, take a couple of pens and pencils. On many campuses, students are expected to purchase Blue Books or Scantron® forms from the bookstore and bring them to class on test days. Be sure you know what materials you need to have. Whatever you do, don't wait until the last minute to purchase them. It might not go over well when you tell your professor, "But the bookstore was out of them," or "I didn't know I had to bring a number 2 pencil."

exercise Break 10.1

1. To the best of your ability, think back to *all* of the exams you've taken in college. List all of the materials (e.g., number 2 pencil, Scantron® form) that you've been asked to bring to class for exams.

   _____   _____

   _____   _____

   _____   _____

   _____   _____

   _____   _____

2. Get together with two or three of your classmates and ask them what materials they've had to bring to class on exam days. Add any additional materials they've had to bring to exams to the list.

3. You might want to post a list of materials you've needed for previous exams in a handy place, such as on your refrigerator, on a bulletin board, or on top of your textbooks. That way you can consult the list prior to an exam to make sure that you're bringing everything you need.

■ *Arrive Early*

Be sure to arrive at least a few minutes early for an exam. There's nothing worse than arriving after special instructions have been given and everyone has already started. You'll feel guilty for interrupting; you'll begin to wonder if you missed important instructions; and your anxiety level will increase dramatically. If you have an exam in the morning you might want to ask a classmate or friend to call you, just in case your alarm clock isn't reliable. You don't want an unexpected power outage to keep you from being on time for an important test.

■ *Get Comfortable*

Once you arrive at the classroom, make sure you do what's necessary to get as comfortable as possible. If you usually sit in a specific location, try to sit in that same chair for the exam. If that's not possible, at least make sure the air conditioner or heating unit isn't blowing directly on you and that sounds from adjacent classrooms aren't too intrusive. Take out and organize the materials you've brought with you. Do everything you can in advance of starting the test to minimize all potential distractions and maximize your chances for success.

exercise break 10.2

1. What unexpected situations have you experienced on test days that have prevented you from performing your best?

_____

_____

_____

2. Which strategies presented earlier would have helped you cope with such situations?

_____

_____

_____

3. In addition to the strategies presented thus far in the chapter, what other things can you do on the day of the test to prepare for or avoid unexpected events and ensure a successful test-taking performance overall?

_____

_____

_____

_____

_____

Reduce Anxiety During the Test

In Chapter 9, we discussed a variety of techniques you can use to reduce your anxiety as you prepare to take tests. You also might want to consider using anxiety-reducing strategies during the test itself. By using these strategies, you'll increase your chances of performing your very best.

▨ *Read All Test Instructions Thoroughly*

Some of the most common errors that we've witnessed students make on exams result from careless reading of instructions. Students often miss questions because they misread a word or two or fail to read the instructions altogether. Be sure to take an extra minute to read and *reread* all instructions so you know what's expected of you. And watch for directions to change during a test. As you begin each new section, read its instructions carefully. By reading instructions before you begin answering questions, you'll decrease anxiety by taking some guesswork out of the picture.

▨ *Preview the Entire Test Before Starting*

It's always a good idea to preview the entire exam in the first few minutes. This allows you to get a sense of what you're going to be expected to do before you actually do it. Sometimes you may want to answer questions that appear later on an exam before you answer earlier questions. Previewing an entire exam allows you to figure out the point values associated with each question, which helps you prepare mentally for particularly challenging questions. It also helps you ration your time better. The important thing is to be prepared. The fewer surprises, the better off you'll be.

case study 10.1

Consider Dr. DeLaMare . . .

Dr. DeLaMare was a physics professor at one of the nation's premiere institutions. Her introductory physics class was considered one of the toughest introductory classes offered at the university. During one term a couple of years ago, several students in Dr. DeLaMare's classes began complaining that her first two exams were "way too difficult." After meeting with several students, Dr. DeLaMare realized that students were having a particularly difficult time on the exams because they weren't taking the time to read the complex directions at the start of each section. In addition, students weren't previewing the exams in advance—mostly because they feared that they wouldn't have enough time to finish if they previewed an exam.

Time Out If you were Dr. DeLaMare, how would you emphasize the importance of reading all test instructions thoroughly and previewing the entire test prior to answering the questions?

_____

_____

_____

_____

_____

What Dr. DeLaMare decided to do was quite creative. A few days after meeting with the concerned students, on a day without an exam, Dr. DeLaMare announced a timed pop quiz that was going to cover the prior week's lecture material. After a chorus of "Oh, no!" echoed throughout the classroom, she announced that only forty-five minutes would be allotted to complete the quiz. She then distributed the four-page quiz, which included a set of directions at the beginning followed by fifteen short-answer essay questions.

About thirty-five minutes later, several students began shaking their heads and whispering, "Oh my gosh!" in a seemingly embarrassed tone. Soon thereafter, several others joined in, until eventually everyone was looking around, chuckling. The reason for the responses? Dr. DeLaMare was teaching them a lesson.

Not a single one of the forty-two students in the class had taken the time to read the instructions thoroughly prior to answering the questions on the quiz! The instructions clearly stated, "Be sure to read *all* of the test questions thoroughly before beginning this quiz!" If the students had done this, they would have read the last question prior to beginning the quiz. That question read: "15. Now that you've followed the instructions and read all of the test questions, all you need to do is write your name at the bottom of this page. The quiz is over. You don't need to answer any of the quiz questions at all!"

As you can imagine, nearly every one of the students in Dr. DeLaMare's class made sure to read all test directions thoroughly and preview all exam questions on every test they took after that. In addition to exemplifying the importance of reading directions, this case demonstrates the idea of using professors as a resource and not being intimidated by them all the time. If the students hadn't shared their concerns with Dr. DeLaMare, she never would have known about the problem or taken steps to fix it.

Apply This Now

1. On a scale of 1 to 10, with 1 indicating *never* and 10 indicating *always,* how often do you preview the entire content of an exam before answering the first question?

_____

2. On a scale of 1 to 10, with 1 indicating *never* and 10 indicating *always,* how often do you read instructions on an exam prior to answering the questions?

_____

3. What can you do to ensure you'll *always* preview exams and take the time to read *all* directions prior to answering a single question on exams in the future?

_____

_____

_____

■ *Break It Down!*

Rather than worrying about an entire exam, break the exam into smaller chunks—at least in your mind. This can be an especially useful outcome of previewing the exam. You might want to view the different sections of a test as mini-quizzes. A test that includes several sections—perhaps a multiple-choice section, a fill-in-the-blank section, and a short-answer essay section—can be thought of as three separate exercises. This can help what at first may seem like an overwhelming activity seem much more manageable.

■ *Unless You're Told Not To, Write on the Exam*

Make any and all notations you want to on a test to help you organize your thoughts, prepare your responses, and reduce your anxiety. If your professor or TA tells you that writing directly on the exam isn't allowed, ask if you may use a blank sheet of paper to make notes that will help you answer the questions correctly.

■ *Answer "Sure Shots" First*

There's one very effective strategy many students never even attempt, even though there are demonstrable benefits: Go through the exam and answer "sure shots" first. A sure shot is a question for which you're *completely* certain of the right answer. It may be an essay question or a simple true/false item. Either way, answering questions for which you absolutely know the correct answers can increase your confidence and allow you to spend the bulk of your time answering questions you're not so sure about. This is an easy strategy to integrate into your test-taking repertoire if you're already previewing exams as described earlier.

■ *Read Each Test Question Thoroughly*

We don't want to give you the impression that most professors try to trick you. But it's very common for professors to write a few questions that you're likely to miss if you answer them too quickly. Taking a few seconds to make sure you

Taking a few seconds to make sure you fully understand a question is well worth the time and effort.

fully understand a question is well worth the time and effort. Reading each test question thoroughly will help decrease your anxiety by allowing you to fully recognize what the professor is looking for in your response.

If You Don't Understand a Question, Ask for Clarification

Asking for clarification about a question will ensure that you know what's being asked. Plus, you'll probably be doing your classmates a favor. Almost always, if one student is unclear about something on a test, several others are unclear about it as well. That's why every now and then a professor interrupts a test to make an announcement about a question. Professors want all students to do their best. Sometimes clarifying a question or response option is necessary to make that happen. The chances are that, by asking for clarification about a confusing question or set of directions, you'll reduce not only your own anxiety but the anxiety of others in the class as well.

Try to Answer Every Question on an Exam

Try to answer every question that appears on an exam unless penalties for wrong answers outweigh the benefits of guessing the correct response. Professors are usually pretty clear about whether there's a penalty for guessing. If you're not sure about the scoring procedure for a particular test, just ask. If you can narrow down the correct answer to two possible responses, guessing between those two options is probably worth the risk, even with a small penalty for guessing. As discussed in Chapter 9, if you're answering essay questions, you should probably try to answer each question as well as you possibly can rather than leaving questions completely blank.

Review Other Test Questions for Clues

Now and then, you'll find information from one test question useful for answering another. This is fairly common when a test contains essay questions and multiple-choice, true/false, or matching items. You may find several clues for answering essay questions by reviewing the objective questions or vice versa.

Pace Yourself

Keep aware of time limits, and make sure you leave enough time to answer the more difficult questions and those that are worth the most points. Part of your initial previewing of the exam should involve determining which questions or sections of the exam are worth the most points. You don't want to spend too much time answering questions worth only a point or two at the expense of not answering questions worth five or ten points.

If Time Permits, Take a Break

Many students have the mistaken belief that once they begin an exam there's absolutely no opportunity to take a break. However, most professors don't mind if you need to use the restroom during a test or want to get up and stretch a bit. Be sure to find out what your professor's policies are so that you don't break any classroom rules by leaving the room for a brief break. Remember that you want to stay fresh and alert, so don't hesitate to take a break now and then if doing so will help you decrease your anxiety and perform your best.

Time to Reflect

Review the information in Chapter 3 that describes the importance of using your brain as a method of enhancing concentration while you study. Then answer the questions.

1. How does the information that you reviewed in Chapter 3 apply to taking breaks during exams?

_____

_____

2. Based on what you know about your learning style and preferred methods of studying, describe an ideal break for you to take during an exam.

_____

_____

3. Consider taking this type of a break during your next exam. Afterwards, describe how taking the break helped you do your best on the exam.

_____

_____

_____

Think Positively

Plainly put, you want to think positively throughout an exam. Even if you're unable to answer a question or two, you need to approach all subsequent questions with as much confidence as possible. View the test you're taking as an opportunity to perform your best rather than as an unusually cruel form of punishment. The importance of maintaining a positive mental attitude cannot be emphasized enough. If you're confident that you'll do well on a test, that confidence alone will increase your chances of achieving success.

Exercise Break 10.3

1. What are some things you can do to avoid negative, self-defeating thoughts during an examination?

_____

_____

2. Ask two or three of your classmates if they've used any strategies to prevent negative self-talk during exams. List any additional approaches that you might want to try in the future.

_____

_____

_____

Stay Focused

With so much going on in your life besides taking tests, it's no wonder that you may find yourself thinking about something else during an exam. It could be your date on Friday night, something you forgot to do that morning, concerns about work, or family plans. These kinds of intrusive thoughts are more common than you may realize. However, you'll want to minimize intrusive thoughts and other such distractions as much as possible when taking a test. Doing some free thinking (i.e., thinking about nonacademic things that are going on in your life) the morning before an exam may be one way to deal with such thoughts. If distractions keep you from focusing on a test, try stretching or walking around for a few minutes to refocus.

BRACE Yourself

BRACE is a mnemonic that you might find particularly effective if you're ever consumed by anxiety during a test. Each of the letters that make up the acronym refers to a different strategy, as shown in Box 10.1 (see page 174). If you begin to feel anxious during a test, remember to BRACE yourself.

Review Your Answers

As time permits, review your responses to all test questions. Just as it's important to preview an exam prior to answering questions, it also is important to review your responses prior to completing an exam. You might be surprised

Time to Reflect

Think back to the last two or three exams you've taken as you answer the following questions.

1. When you received your test results, did you find silly or careless mistakes on questions that you knew the answers to but somehow missed?

_____

2. If so, why do you think you made such mistakes?

_____

_____

_____

3. What will you do in the future to avoid making the same types of mistakes?

_____

_____

4. If you didn't make any silly mistakes on the past few exams you've taken, why do you think you've been so successful in avoiding them?

_____

_____

5. What advice would you offer to people who tend to make a lot of silly mistakes on exams?

_____

_____

BOX 10.1.   **BRACE Yourself**

B   Breathe regularly and deeply.

R   Relax by trying to clear your mind of worries and concerns.

A   Attitude: Remember the importance of a positive attitude.

C   Center yourself, and imagine positive energy flowing from the center of your body to your brain and hands.

E   Expect a change. Expect the tension and anxiety to begin to slip away slowly but surely.

---

how useful it is to spend a few extra minutes reviewing your answers before turning in an exam. You can correct a silly mistake or catch an error you made when transferring your answer from a test booklet to an answer sheet. As you review your answers, think twice before changing your responses to questions that were initially difficult to answer. Most of the time your initial responses to challenging questions are likely to be correct.

Special Kinds of Test Formats

An important part of being confident about performing well on college tests is being aware of the various types of tests you might face. Most of the tests you'll take in college will be of the traditional type (i.e., individually completed, in-class exams with no books or notes allowed). However, some of your professors may ask you to complete other kinds of tests. In this section, we describe some of the more popular nontraditional exam formats and provide useful strategies for performing your best on them.

 For all special kinds of exam formats (including group exams, open book and open notes tests, and take-home exams), be sure to check with your professor about the rules of the testing procedure. You'll need to find out whether you're allowed to access information from other sources, such as books, magazines, newspaper articles, and/or the Internet. Also be sure you're clear about the expected format of your answers. If you do all these things, you'll ensure a much more successful and satisfying testing experience.

■ *Group Exams*

Group exams are becoming a popular alternative to traditional tests. Group exams—as you've probably already figured out—involve groups of students working together to answer a set of questions. Some professors distribute a group test for completion during the same class period. Others distribute them with the expectation that group members will answer the questions together outside of class.

 One of the most important things to do as soon as possible after receiving a group test is to agree on assignments of tasks and duties. The group may decide that each member will work on a different question for a specified period of time. Then, at some later time, group members can reconvene to discuss their initial responses. Or you may decide to work together on each question rather than parceling out the questions to various group members. The important thing is to reach consensus within the group about your strategies.

A similar consensus-building process should occur during the other stages of the group examination process. You'll need to decide who will write out or word process the group's answers, which questions are going to be answered first, the kinds of resources you're going to use for answering the questions, and other procedural matters.

◼ *Open Book and Open Notes Tests*

Some of your instructors may administer tests of the open book and open notes variety. These are exams on which you're allowed to use your textbook and/or lecture notes while answering questions. At first, such exams may seem like a gift from the instructor, a guaranteed A. Because you have access to your notes and/or textbooks during the exam, you may believe that much less preparation than usual is necessary. However, such an approach to open book and open notes tests can be a costly mistake.

Professors who are preparing open book and open notes exams realize that you're going to have access to these materials during the test. As a result, they aren't very likely to ask questions that are particularly easy or have obvious answers. In fact, many students believe that open book and open notes tests are among the most difficult they've ever encountered.

Open book and open notes tests require an extra degree of organization and preparation. You probably ought to prepare for these kinds of tests by devoting even more time to the studying process than usual. Several days in advance of this kind of exam, be sure to organize the materials you're going to take to the exam.

Attaching little sticky notes to key pages in your book or notes is a useful strategy. By doing so, you'll increase your efficiency in accessing information. The last thing you want to do is waste time during the exam trying to find the page in your notes that contains important information for answering a question. The more familiar you are with the location of information in your notes and in the book, the more quickly and easily you'll find the right answers.

◼ *Take-Home Exams*

As the term implies, you complete a take-home exam away from the classroom. Instructors usually distribute take-home exams a few days—and sometimes even a full week or two—prior to the date they're due. Although take-home exams may include objective test questions, they're often composed of essay questions or complex problems to solve.

The first thing you'll want to do when working on a take-home exam is avoid procrastination. It's easy to rationalize putting off a take-home exam that isn't due for several days. You'll be in much better shape if you begin working on the exam the same day you receive it. Even if all you can do is read the exam, at least you'll begin thinking about possible answers to the questions and/or determining strategies for coming up with answers.

Unless your instructor informs you otherwise, prepare essay questions on a take-home examination on a word processor or computer. Preparing your responses in a word processing program will give you the chance to edit and improve them and ensure that they're legible and easy to read. Most professors expect answers to take-home essay questions to be well-organized and printed on a laser printer. If you don't have a good printer, check to see if you can use one at a computer lab on campus.

Finally, make sure the directions for completing the take-home exam are clear *before* you leave the classroom. This is especially important when a take-home exam is due back by the next class session. If you fail to read the directions prior to leaving the classroom, you may not find out until it's too late that one of the questions is confusing or that the directions are unclear.

You also need to make sure you have a clear understanding of the rules of the take-home examination. Some professors allow classmates to discuss their responses with one another prior to submitting them. Other professors are adamant about not allowing this kind of discussion. Some professors require answers to be submitted electronically, or in a folder or notebook, while others may want you to staple pages together and place your name on a cover page.

exercise Break 10.4

1. Select one of the three exam formats discussed in this section that you've experienced at least once in the past. Write the name of that exam format:

_____

2. Briefly describe your experience with this type of exam.

_____

_____

_____

3. If you've performed well on this type of exam in the past, summarize the reasons you've been successful.

_____

_____

_____

4. If you've had difficulty with this type of exam format in the past, summarize the problems you've experienced.

_____

_____

_____

_____

Evaluate Test Results: When Learning *Really* Happens

With so much time and energy going into test preparation, it's surprising that so few students spend any significant amount of time reviewing the test after it's over. There's considerable value in taking a look at your notes soon after completing a test to see what kinds of information you failed to study as well as you should have. You'll also want to look up answers to questions you weren't sure about. Even just ten or fifteen minutes of reviewing your notes or looking through the book can help you figure out how to change your method of test preparation in the future.

point *to* PONDER

You'll want to spend some quality time reviewing the results of your test once your instructor grades and returns it.

Similarly, you'll want to spend some quality time reviewing the results of your exam once your instructor grades it and returns it. Many students claim that the most meaningful learning experiences take place when they review the questions they missed on an exam. It's easy to get so caught up in the challenges of studying for tests that we forget what tests are really designed to do: help us determine what we've already learned and what we still need to learn.

Sometimes reviewing your graded exams can also provide useful insights about your test-taking skills. Reflecting on what went wrong and why it went wrong can help you figure out ways to improve your test-taking performance in the future. Reading through your graded exams also can help you perform your best on final exams. If you weren't able to answer questions correctly on a midterm exam, you'll want to understand why you missed them so that you can answer them correctly if the same (or similar) questions appear on the final exam.

case study 10.2

Consider Chloe . . .

Chloe's performance during her first semester of college wasn't too bad. She was earning high B's in all but one of her classes. She was struggling in her art history class. Her three exam grades were C–, C+, and C, far lower than what she had hoped they would be. Before each exam, Chloe had a fairly good understanding of the material, but her knowledge of the information wasn't translating into high grades. Two weeks before the final exam, Chloe met with her professor to see if she could do anything to perform better on the final.

As Chloe and her professor reviewed the previous exams, they found a distinct pattern: Chloe had correctly answered almost every one of the questions based on material covered in class. Out of the 120 questions based on lecture material, she had answered 115 correctly. However, of the 80 questions based on textbook material, Chloe had answered only 23 correctly.

Not until Chloe met with her professor for an in-depth analysis of previous exams did she real-

ize that lack of information from the reading assignments was the reason for her poor test performance.

 If you were Chloe, what would you do to increase your performance on the final exam in this class?

_____

_____

_____

As a result of her newfound knowledge, Chloe did what you probably thought she would. She spent considerably more time studying concepts and information from the book in preparation for the final exam. She still studied material from in-class lectures and discussions, but she almost tripled the amount of time she spent studying book material. The result was a grade of A– on the final exam and a final course grade of B.

Apply This Now

1. Why do you think it's important to review the results of your exams after they've been graded and returned?

_____

_____

2. How might reviewing the results of your exams with the course professor or TA be particularly helpful?

_____

_____

Make a Commitment to Academic Honesty

Before concluding the discussion of test-taking strategies, we want to briefly discuss the issue of academic honesty. Just as in high school or in any other educational environment, some college students are tempted to cheat on tests. Sometimes cheating can be very serious, especially when it involves such criminal offenses as stealing an exam from a professor's office. Whether a particular form of cheating is illegal or not, one thing is certain: it's *always* unethical.

Some college classes are going to be more difficult than others. You're likely to be under especially high levels of stress and anxiety to earn a high grade in those courses. But these circumstances *never* give you permission to cheat your way through an exam. All forms of cheating—whether glancing at a classmate's test, stealing the answers from a professor's office, consulting a "cheat sheet" with answers or formulas, or showing a friend your answers—are completely inappropriate.

On many campuses, students who are caught cheating on exams or engaging in other forms of academic dishonesty are immediately suspended or expelled. Each year we read reports of legal action taken against college students who've participated in some of the more severe forms of cheating. Plainly put, it's simply not worth it! Besides placing your academic standing in jeopardy or inviting legal action, cheating on a test denies you the opportunity to truly evaluate your knowledge of important information.

Almost everyone has cheated at least once in their life. Sometimes it's when you're young and want to win a competition of some sort. Sometimes it's when you get sick and tired of losing at something. But as you grow older, you learn that cheating isn't appropriate, often results in legal consequences, and lowers both your self-esteem and your confidence in your ability to succeed on your own merits.

Suppose for a moment that you're diagnosed with a medical condition that requires surgery. Probably the last person you would want to perform the operation is a doctor who cheated her or his way through medical school. Or suppose you're on your way to an exotic vacation in the Bahamas. The last person you would want flying your plane is a pilot who cheated on the pilot's certification exam. Although these examples may sound extreme, the message is the same: When you cheat on an exam, you cheat not only yourself but also the many people who will ultimately rely on your apparent knowledge and skills.

Point *to* ponder

All forms of academic cheating are completely inappropriate.

© *Vivian Scott Hixson*

"Hey, don't worry about it. We faked our way through college.
We can fake our way through this."

Each time you cheat, it becomes easier to talk yourself into cheating again. You might tell yourself that no one will be hurt if you cheat on a history or literature exam. But if you cheat then, you might be overwhelmingly tempted to cheat on a more critical exam in the future.

Now is the time for you to make a personal commitment to engage in the absolute highest level of academic honesty. We hope you'll make this commitment and hold yourself to high standards of academic integrity throughout your college career.

exercise break 10.5

Take a moment to consider the many reasons to avoid cheating, and then answer this question: Why is it important *to you* to make a commitment to maintain the highest level of academic honesty throughout your college career?

_____

_____

_____

_____

Take It Away!

This chapter focused on strategies you can use on the day of a test to perform your absolute best:

- It's important on the day of a test to

  __ eat well.

  __ arrive early.

  __ dress comfortably.

  __ get comfortable.

  __ bring the materials you'll need.

- To reduce your anxiety while completing tests, it's also important to

  __ read all test instructions thoroughly.

  __ preview the entire test before starting.

  __ break the test down into smaller parts.

  __ write on the exam (unless you're told not to).

  __ answer sure shots first.

  __ read each test question thoroughly.

  __ ask for clarification if you don't understand a question.

  __ try to answer every question on an exam (unless there are substantial penalties for wrong answers).

  __ review other test questions for clues.

  __ pace yourself.

  __ take breaks.

  __ think positively.

  __ stay focused.

  __ BRACE yourself.

  __ review your answers.

- It's important to be aware of effective strategies you can use when completing non-traditional tests. This includes the general rule of checking with your professors about any particular rules as well as the following:

  __ Group tests:

  —agree on assignments of tasks and duties.

  __ Open book and open notes tests:

  —be well organized by adequately preparing and organizing your notes.

  __ Take-home exams:

  —ask questions if you don't understand the directions or rules; don't procrastinate; and prepare your exam on a word processor or computer.

- Evaluate your test results once they're returned to you. Reviewing graded exams can provide you with useful insights about your test-taking skills and suggest ways to improve your test-taking performance in the future.

- Make a personal commitment to academic honesty and integrity. All forms of cheating—whether illegal or not—are *always* inappropriate and unethical.

In Chapter 11 we turn our attention to other skills that are important to academic success: writing papers and making presentations.

Questions for Critical Thought

1. What kinds of things can you do to make sure you're never late to an exam? What are the benefits of arriving several minutes before the start time of a test?

2. Many students believe that take-home and open notes exams are easier than traditional in-class exams. Why can this assumption be a big mistake?

3. How can you benefit from reviewing your results on a test once it has been returned? When might it be appropriate to set up an appointment to meet with a course professor or TA to review the results of your tests?

4. Look back at the Points to Ponder that appear in this chapter.
   a. Which Point to Ponder surprised you the most?
   b. How does knowing this help you better prepare for academic success?

5. How can an understanding of concepts presented in this chapter help you outside of the college and classroom environment? Which strategies discussed in the chapter are particularly relevant to success in your career and personal life?

Web Site

Visit the *Overcoming the Hurdles to Academic Success* web site for a chapter outline, review exercises, additional case studies, links to other online resources, and a practice test.

References

Newman, E. (1996). *No more test anxiety: Effective steps for taking tests.* New York: Learning Skills Publications.

Wakefield, J. F. (2001). *Educational psychology.* Boston: Houghton Mifflin.

11

prepare papers and presentations

1 As you do to improve all other important skills, you should regularly practice writing and speaking.

2 As the first step for completing an in-class writing assignment, immediately put your ideas down on scratch paper, as fast as you can.

3 As the second step, read over what you've written and begin to organize these ideas in your mind.

4 If you can't think of ideas to make a composition long enough, broaden your topic, discuss more details, give examples, or write about something else.

5 If you're assigned a major paper, your professor might indicate the appropriate style book on the assignment sheet. If not, ask.

6 If you're writing about a topic already covered, refer to that material and assume your audience knows that much, *unless* the instructor has told you to write for a different audience.

7 Be sure you have several references that support the points you're making, using all the references you cite and using them in ways that make sense.

8 You might want to mention references that contradict the point you're trying to make to let your instructor know that you've considered other viewpoints.

9 For an accurate and informative paper or presentation, use recent sources to tell about *recent* ideas of scholars and/or other experts.

10 To restate someone else's writing in your own words, try writing it as if you were trying to explain it to your parents or a friend.

11 Never write your paper directly from the author's text; instead, write from your notes.

12 If you can't think of a synonym for a particularly descriptive word or phrase that an author has used, use a thesaurus to help you find related words.

13 Sometimes, the words an author uses are so eloquent that you'll want to quote them exactly.

14 If your college offers tutoring support for writing, take a draft of your paper for help.

15 Deal with everything that causes you stress in giving speeches in the same ways you deal with the stresses of taking an exam.

16 In preparing for a public speaking assignment, consider audio visual aids for helping you communicate with your audience.

17 Create good notes to help you practice and deliver a presentation, using marginal notes to indicate when you want to use audio visual aids.

18 Organize your speech into three simple parts: an introduction, the body, and a conclusion.

19 Remember to tell your audience what you intend to say; say it as well as you can; and then remind the audience that you've said it.

20 Your most important strategy for delivering a speech is practicing it *out loud*.

21 Be sure to time yourself each time you practice giving your speech, using a clock or a timer.

22 Practice your presentation enough times to feel comfortable about it—at first all by yourself in front of the mirror, and again in front of a trusted friend, family member, or a classmate.

23 The last time you practice your speech, note how much time you spend on each section to help you to judge your speed when you present it in class.

24 Wear something dressier than usual on days you give speeches.

25 Since good stress makes you more engaged and makes your mind sharper, harness your good stress to be a better speaker.

26 Check the time during your speech to see if you're taking the amount of time you thought you would, so you can adjust if necessary.

27 Prepare something extra to say at the end of your speech, just in case you talk faster than you expected and have extra time.

28 When delivering your speech, make eye contact with the audience, allowing no more than two or three sentences before looking up and around the room.

29 Practice the way you move your eyes from your notes to the audience as you practice your speech, to avoid having your eyes flit or your head bob.

The last two chapters focused on ways to improve your performance on tests. Grades in most college courses depend—at least in part—on how students perform on tests. It was probably easy for you to see an immediate payoff from learning and using test-taking strategies. Writing papers and making presentations are also important to your grades in many classes, although they're not used as often to assess your knowledge and skills.

As you continue through college, you'll probably observe that many of your upper-level courses require you to write papers. In addition, the traditional practice of not assigning papers in lower-division courses is changing. In some

Point to Ponder

In some undergraduate courses, no tests are given. Instead, each student's entire grade depends on submitting a writing portfolio and/or making a series of oral reports to the class.

required freshman courses, as well as in other undergraduate courses, at the colleges where we teach, no tests are given. Instead, each student's entire grade for the semester depends on submitting a writing **portfolio** and/or making a series of oral reports to the class. This practice is becoming more and more common because some faculty are using "writing to learn" and "speaking to learn" strategies.

These strategies require students to describe what they're learning in their own words on paper, talk with their classmates, and/or give formal speeches. Research shows that when students explain course material in their own words, they actually learn more theories, facts, examples, and applications. In the process, students augment such academic skills as reading, writing, speaking, listening, analysis, problem solving, and synthesis. The real payoff is that students who write and talk about course material remember what they've learned for a longer time. This is very useful for taking final exams and applying knowledge in subsequent classes.

This chapter is divided into two major parts, dealing with strategies to improve your performance in (1) writing papers and (2) making presentations in class. Reading this chapter won't make you an instant success as a college writer or speaker. As with all other important skills, regular practice makes the difference. The more you write or make speeches, the more skilled and confident you'll become. This chapter contains information about the resources your college offers to help you improve your skills, as well as generally recommended strategies for you to try.

Time to Reflect

In Chapter 2 you studied active learning and critical thinking and applied them to problem solving.

1. Why would writing concepts and giving examples in your own words require you to be

   a. an active learner?

   _____

   _____

   b. a critical thinker?

   _____

   _____

   c. a problem solver?

   _____

   _____

2. In groups of two to four students, share your answers. Discuss how explaining concepts to others in your class or study group also requires you to develop and use these skills. What new ideas did you learn in the group discussion?

   _____

   _____

   _____

   _____

Write Papers for Academic Success

Writing papers for college classes is likely to be very different from most high school writing assignments. One reason for the difference is your access to an extensive variety of written materials in and through your college library (see Appendix A). This access allows you to research more sources on most topics. Another reason is that an instructor expects much more of your writing skills. You'll often be required to use the **jargon** of your field of study. You'll be expected to write your thoughts with greater clarity, precision, and organization. You may be expected to include both theory and examples to make your points. But more than that, the way you indicate that you know what you're writing about is different. Earning good grades requires you to back up your opinion with a methodically laid out logical argument and/or research from multiple sources other than encyclopedias.

▪ *Different Types of College Writing*

In college you'll write in different ways for different kinds of assignments. We've split up this section into the three major types of writing, based on what the assignment is intended to teach you.

1. In-class writing is intended to find out what you already know and/or your attitudes about a topic.

2. Writing for a freshman English composition class also concerns the content about which you write. But more than that, the relatively short writing assignments in a freshman English composition class focus on teaching you how to become a better writer.

3. Writing a major paper for a class generally involves scholarly research. Its main objectives are to teach you about researching and help you learn about a particular content area in depth.

Timed In-Class Writing. Don't be surprised if you're required to complete timed in-class writing assignments for some of your courses. Many instructors give this kind of assignment to encourage their students to do the assigned reading before coming to class. Others might have you start class this way to help focus your attention on the topic to be discussed. And you may encounter in-class writing on quizzes, tests, and exams if your instructor uses essay or short-answer questions.

 A good strategy for completing an in-class writing assignment is to put your ideas down on scratch paper as fast as you can. Don't worry about writing complete sentences. Don't think about whether you're writing them in a logical sequence or whether they're contradictory. Just spend two or three minutes jotting them down. This is often referred to as the first stage of "free writing" because it's free of rules. It's the one-person equivalent of a brainstorming session.

Once you think you've finished writing your immediate thoughts on the topic, or once your brain starts to stall, whichever comes first, read over what you've written, and begin to organize the ideas in your mind. In the process, you might choose to cross out some ideas, enhance others, and/or add to the list. You might even want to jot down numbers in front of the items you've written, in the order you want to use them.

portfolio: A carefully selected collection of one's work products, usually including only one's best work, with the purpose of showing a variety of skills and accomplishments.

♦ ♦ ♦

jargon: A term for the specialized vocabulary words of a particular discipline or field of study. These may be commonly used words, but they have very specific meanings for people in the field.

exercise Break 11.1

On separate lines below, list the courses you are enrolled in this term.

Courses and Writing Assignments

Course	Type(s) of Writing Assignment(s)

Examine the syllabus for each of these courses. Next to each course you've listed, write the kinds of writing assignments you're expected to complete. If there are no writing assignments, write "none." How do you feel about the amount and types of writing assignments required in each course?

_____

_____

Why do you think you feel this way?

_____

_____

Next write a short introduction to tell the instructor the topic(s) your essay will cover. Then start to write the thoughts you jotted down on the scratch paper, in complete sentences and in the order in which you numbered them. If your essay covers several major points, indicate when and why you are transitioning from one major point to another.

In a timed-writing situation, it's not as critical to have a conclusion as it is to make your argument(s), based on theories, specific facts, and/or your own observations about course material. But if you have some extra time, you might try writing a conclusion.

Writing for a Freshman English Composition Class.   You're likely to be required to complete one or two freshman English courses as part of the core curriculum. These are usually the most writing-intensive courses taken by first-year

Time to Reflect

Review the section in Chapter 9 on answering essay questions. Which strategies do you think would work best for you in a timed in-class writing situation?

_____

_____

college students. You may have learned a writing "formula" in high school English classes. The most popular of the formulas is generally referred to as the five-paragraph essay. In the first paragraph, you tell the reader what you'll be writing about. In the next three paragraphs, you develop three main thoughts on what you said you'd be writing about. In the fifth paragraph, you summarize what you wrote about in the second, third, and fourth paragraphs. Some college instructors might expect you to use this form in freshman composition, but many others will not.

 You're at least as likely to have an instructor who wants to break you of the habit of writing by formula. This approach expects you to choose the topic and write enough words and paragraphs to get your major points across. Usually the professor will tell you to write some minimum and/or maximum number of pages. It's not likely that your instructor will let you get by with something shorter than the typical formula paper. So don't expect to get by with writing less. If you can't think of more ideas to make your paper long enough, try broadening your topic, discussing more details, giving examples, or writing about something else.

case study 11.1

Consider Shanikwa . . .

Shanikwa was confident that she knew how to write compositions. She learned the five-paragraph essay formula in tenth grade and used it successfully from that point on. She never received a high school composition grade lower than a B. Imagine her dismay when her freshman composition instructor handed back her first essay with a D+ in red ink at the top, along with the scrawled note "too formulaic."

Shanikwa was extremely upset. She'd never in her life earned such a low grade, and she wrote this essay at least as well as she had ever written any essay. She waited anxiously for her instructor's next office hours and arrived early. As soon as the instructor arrived, she asked what the note meant and what she needed to do to write better.

The instructor explained that writing for college classes and beyond should not follow formulas. Formulas were fine to help beginning writers organize their thoughts. But college writing is beyond basic writing, and the intermediate college writer needs to learn to write as many paragraphs as it takes to fully develop enough ideas in a composition.

Then the two of them carefully looked through Shanikwa's composition. The instructor asked Shanikwa some questions about her ideas. From her answers, both Shanikwa and her instructor could clearly see other ideas emerge that would have made the paper much stronger. By including more good ideas to support what she was trying to say, she also could have made her opening and concluding paragraphs more persuasive.

 If you were Shanikwa's composition instructor, what advice would you give her?

_____

_____

Apply This Now

1. In high school or in college, were you coached to use a writing formula? _____ (If not, skip to (2) below.)

    a. If yes, were you more successful once you started using it? _____

    b. Describe it below:

    _____

    _____

2. Since starting college, have any of your instructors discussed other strategies for structuring short compositions? If so, describe one of those writing strategies. If you've tried the new strategy, describe your experience.

    _____

    _____

    _____

Major Research Papers.   If you're writing a paper outside of class, you need to be concerned about neatness, the style your professor wants you to use, and precisely naming your references.

BOX 11.1.   **Learning to Use a Word-Processing Program**

If you haven't learned how to use a word-processing program, now is the time. At some schools, this is part of the first semester's curriculum. If not, do it on your own. Find out about the availability of student computer labs on campus, and find out which word-processing program is most widely used. You'll need to set up a student account. If you have a friend who has already used the campus computer labs, ask to tag along to learn how. Or you can do this on your own with a little research. Most campuses have a computer services staff; some have a designated writing lab staffed by students and professionals whose main job is to help with writing assignments. With a little guidance and a little practice, you'll pick up most of what you need to know right away. (See Appendix B, Using Computers, for more information.)

   Computer word-processing capabilities have revolutionized the way we write. You can start brainstorming right on the screen. You can move the text around with ease to reorganize ideas. You can insert new thoughts whenever you want. Most programs have a spelling checker, a thesaurus, and a word counter. Beware of becoming too reliant on these tools. You still need to proofread to be sure your composition reads well. And you still have to check for typos. The spelling checker can't tell you when you should have keystroked the word *kind* instead of *king,* for instance, because *king* is a real word and is spelled correctly. Some word-processing programs have grammar or sentence-structure checkers. Be sure to test them first before entrusting your composition to their suggestions for changes. Most grammar checkers are not able to handle complex sentence structure.

exercise вreak 11.2

Before the next time this course meets, find out the following:

1. Where are the campus computer labs that you can use when writing papers?

_____

2. What hours are they open?

_____

3. What word-processing programs are available for your use?

_____

4. Who provides training for using these word-processing programs? Where and when?

_____

When you're writing a paper to fulfill a major class assignment, you have many responsibilities that you don't encounter with in-class writing. These include using a style book, thinking about your professor as the audience for the paper, and including the thoughts and writings of others.

Using a Particular Style.   Some of your instructors may require you to use a particular style book when you write your paper. A style book provides specific writing rules. It tells you how formal your writing has to be, exactly how to cite references, and even how to indicate the beginning of a new section or sub-section. These rules are based on the standard practice in a particular field of study. If you are writing a formal paper for an English course, you may be required to use Modern Language Association style. A journalism instructor may tell you to use the *New York Times Style Book*. Your psychology professor, and perhaps your education professor, may want you to use the style of the American Psychological Association. A biology instructor might require the Council of Biology Editors style. In chemistry you might be told to use the American Chemical Society style book. If you're assigned a major paper, your professor might indicate the appropriate style book on the assignment sheet. If not, you'd be wise to ask. Maybe you've become familiar, even comfortable, with a particular style. If so, you might want to ask if it is acceptable to follow that style.

Knowing Your Audience.   For whom are you writing? Is it for the instructor who wants to find out what you know and how well you know it? Is it for your classmates because the instructor has assigned each of you responsibilities for teaching the others? Is it for a judge or panel of judges who will assess how well your paper might inform or persuade others? Is it for the general public so that the instructor can judge your ability to inform and/or persuade others who don't know the topic? Once you know your audience, you'll have a much better idea about

1. How much you can assume your audience already knows about your topic;

2. Their preexisting attitudes, or points of view, about your topic;

3. How much detail you need to present;

exercise break 11.3

1. Think about the courses you're taking this term or courses from a previous term that required a major formal paper. Write the course titles here.

Course and Style Book

Course	Style Book

2. What style books did you use when writing these papers? Write the names of the style books next to the course titles.

3. Select one style book, and write two or three rules of style, grammar, and/or presentation that you expect to apply in your future writing assignments.

_____

_____

_____

4. The level of sophistication and complexity you need to address; and

5. The kinds of questions this audience is likely to ask.

   Even though it might sound silly, your instructor will want you to consider your audience even when you're writing a paper to be read by him or her. Think about the semester's lectures, discussions, and assignments. Are you writing on a topic covered to some extent in class or in your assigned readings? If you are, you can refer to that material and assume your audience knows that much as a starting point, unless the instructor has told you to write for a different audience.

exercise break 11.4

Think of how differently you'd discuss your desire to buy a new car depending on which of these audiences you are addressing: (1) your parents, (2) your best friend, (3) your mechanic, (4) a car salesperson, (5) your bank or credit union, and (6) your spouse or significant other. Pick two of these audiences and indicate the differences in what you'd choose to emphasize to each.

_____

_____

_____

_____

Citing Sources.   Several important incentives should compel you to use and to cite references in your presentations and papers. Among those reasons are the following:

1. Your use of numerous references lets your instructor know you took the time to research the topic. An extensive list of references indicates hard work. Hard work tends to impress instructors, which tends to result in higher grades. Be sure you have several references that support what you're saying. Be sure you're actually using all of the references you cite and that you're using them in ways that make sense.

   You may have come across one or two references that contradict the point you're trying to make. Don't necessarily toss them. You might want to mention such references to let your instructor know that you've considered other viewpoints.

2. Another reason for researching various ideas on a subject is to learn as much as you can about the topic in the time you have. You'll feel much more confident about turning in a paper if you think it's accurate and informative. Use recent sources. You'll know it's informative if it tells your professor about *recent* ideas of scholars and/or other experts. A paper that's informative is likely to earn a much higher grade.

3. If you don't cite an author whose work you're using, you're stealing that person's intellectual property, which is called **plagiarizing**.

Academic Integrity.   Beware of plagiarizing! Two serious pitfalls for novice writers are (1) not finding a way to restate someone else's ideas in their own words, that is, failing to paraphrase what the reference has written, and (2) not giving credit to authors for their ideas. You need to remember to do both. If you use another writer's words or ideas as your own, you're plagiarizing.

Plagiarism is a cardinal sin in the academic community, with dire consequences. These consequences can range from receiving no credit on an assignment, to receiving an F in the course, to being suspended or expelled from college. Whatever the disciplinary action, that professor from then on will tend to mistrust your work.

In most cases you can find a way to restate what a writer said. If you can't, maybe you don't really understand the material well enough. Maybe another rereading or two will help. An English professor recently told us about a student who thought that changing every third word would be okay. That's not how paraphrasing works. You need to put it *all* into your own words.

How to Give Credit to the Author.   You need to acknowledge where you found the ideas you're paraphrasing, using the style book's format for reporting information sources. You'll probably be required to report authors' full names, the title of the article and book or journal, the date it was published, and the exact page numbers. If you're not sure how to cite the ideas of others, refer to the style your instructor has recommended or required. If your instructor hasn't already suggested or required a style, ask.

Here are a couple of tips we've received from professors that seem to work well for most students. Keep in mind that these, like most other things you do, become easier with practice. (1) Try restating a sentence, or even a whole paragraph, as if you were trying to explain it to your parents or to a friend who isn't

Point *to* ponder

The consequences of plagiarizing can range from receiving no credit on an assignment, to receiving an F in the course, to being suspended or expelled from college.

plagiarizing: Using someone else's written work without citing that author; stealing that person's intellectual property.

© *Vivian Scott Hixson*

"Actually, I'm *not* the muse of creative writing; I'm the muse of the photocopier. But if the teaching assistant doesn't know the source we're using, I'll do just as well."

in your class. (2) Never write your paper directly from the author's text. Write from your notes. When you first jot down notes on the author's ideas, try to use your own words, and don't use complete sentences. By the time you write your third or fourth draft, the words on your pages are likely to be different than the author's original words. If you can't think of a synonym for a particularly descriptive word or phrase, use a thesaurus.

How to Use Exact Quotes.   Sometimes the words the author uses are so eloquent that you may wish to use an exact quote. If you use an exact quote, look up how to format it in your style book. And be sure to proofread the quote with special care. You don't want to misquote.

How to Give Credit.   Remember to cite authors whose ideas you're using, even when you aren't using their exact words. In addition to a formal citation, you can use such phrases as "According to *[author's name]* . . ." or "As *[author's name]* wrote . . ." or "*[Author's name]* made the following observation." This not only alerts the professor that you did your research; it also indicates that you're not trying to take credit for someone else's ideas. Again, remember to check how to format it.

■ *Other Ways to Improve Your Writing*

On-campus Writing Assistance.   Your college might offer tutoring support for writing in a tutoring center and/or through the English department. Usually staffed by students and/or professionals, the tutoring center is a place where you take a draft of your paper for help. In most colleges, this help is provided

EXERCISE BREAK 11.5

Suppose you are asked to write a report on how to avoid plagiarizing someone else's writing, and you decide to use this chapter as one of your sources. List three ways to use the information in this chapter without plagiarizing it.

_____

_____

_____

for papers that are anywhere from the first draft to the polishing-up stage. You and a writing tutor or consultant look through the draft together. The consultant asks questions about the assignment and about the points you're trying to get across. The consultant may offer suggestions on a variety of issues, from the content to the intended audience to the style you're supposed to be using to cite references.

Practice, Practice, Practice.   As do all skills, your writing will improve with practice. This is particularly true if you submit your writing to others, especially to your professors, for critical reading and suggestions. But don't neglect other ways to practice, including (1) writing to friends and family members and (2) reading a variety of written forms. Even your most casual writing in letters, a journal, or e-mail can improve your ability to organize your thoughts, to explain, and to describe. Reading widely, from newspapers and magazines to poetry to fiction to nonfiction, can also help. By reading good writing, you'll improve your own vocabulary and your understanding of how authors communicate with readers.

Make Oral Presentations

■ *Overcoming Fear*

We don't know many students who are eager public speakers when they reach college. In fact, very few are comfortable with speaking formally in front of a group even after college. We vaguely remember having read a poll of adults in which public speaking was reported as feared more than any other personal challenge or catastrophe except for one's own death. Whether that's totally accurate or not, most students don't relish the idea of giving a presentation in class. About the only students who do are debate champions. However, public speaking is different from debating; so don't be tempted to skip this portion of the chapter even if you've earned debate ribbons and medals in the past.

Why are many of us nervous about giving oral presentations? Each of us has a list of reasons, real and imagined. Some of us are afraid we'll look or sound foolish. We may expect other students to be better at it than we are, and we might expect them to be critical of what we say and how we say it. Perhaps we think our voices are too squeaky, too whiny, or too soft. We may even be convinced we look too fat, don't have attractive clothes, or can't get our hair to lie down right. And then there's the speaker's nightmare: You're so nervous that

POINT *to* PONDER

   One poll of adults revealed that public speaking is feared more than any other personal challenge or catastrophe except for one's own death.

your knees shake; your voice wavers and cracks; your palms, armpits, and fore-head sweat; you go blank; you lose your place; you speak in a monotone or stammer; you drop your notes and/or visual aids; and/or your audience gets fidgety or sneers or—perhaps worst of all—yawns.

You may be wondering why we're so aware of these symptoms. We've experienced all of them at one time or another. We're happy to report that we no longer feel this sense of dread, and we usually don't make too many mistakes during any one presentation. But this improvement in our comfort level, poise, and ability to do a good job has come from *years* of making presentations to groups of students, community members, and faculty colleagues.

case study 11.2

Consider Krishna . . .

Krishna wasn't just uncomfortable about giving speeches, he was phobic. He was excited when he received a scholarship to the university that he most wanted to attend; it was known for its outstanding computer engineering program, which was perfect for his career plans. At summer orientation, he learned that public speaking was a required core curriculum course, and he began to worry.

Krishna made an appointment with the core curriculum director early in the fall to explain why he shouldn't be expected to complete this speech requirement. He explained that he would become physically ill, would likely throw up, and would be in too much of a panic to be able to speak. He even offered to take several other courses in place of public speaking. The core director denied his request, stating that a degree from this institution meant that the student had taken all required core curriculum courses.

Krishna wanted a degree from this university, but he persisted in believing he could not possibly endure a public speaking course.

 If you were Krishna, how could you successfully solve this problem?

_____

_____

_____

_____

The core curriculum director made an appointment for herself and Krishna to meet with a communications professor. Krishna again explained his grave misgivings. The communications professor suggested several strategies and recommended that Krishna try all of them.

1. Krishna should make an appointment to see a counselor at the counseling center for this phobia. He and the counselor could work on the phobia and on relaxation techniques over the course of several months.

2. Krishna should sign up for the speech course in a five-week summer session, since the worry about the speeches was the problem. He'd have only one-third the time of the regular fifteen-week semester to worry before the term would end.

3. The communications professor also suggested that he meet with her one-on-one before the summer, so that he would become more at ease with her. If necessary, he could pretend that she was the only person in the audience during his speeches.

Krishna followed this advice and started the course in early June. He hadn't conquered his phobia, but it was under enough control for him to get through the five-week session and earn a C. He still felt ill before giving presentations, but he learned that he had enough control to throw up before going to class. For Krishna, this was success, and he now knew a life lesson: he was capable of some control over his very worst fears.

Most problems in speaking publicly come from the stresses of thinking about the presentation, not from the topic. A communications professor told us that she's observed many students whose nervousness builds up while they're waiting for their turn. They often visibly relax once they start speaking. Some have even admitted that they enjoyed the experience once they got rolling. But if you don't know the topic well enough, your insecurity about your topic compounds your stress. You need to deal with all of the reasons for stress, in the same ways you deal with the stresses of taking an exam, as discussed in Chapters 9 and 10. If you know that what you have to say is on target, you'll concentrate on what you have to say and how you want to say it, not on how it feels to be in front of your classmates.

Developing and Delivering Your Presentation

Believe it or not, no one expects you to be a polished speaker. Your instructors have never witnessed a presentation without mistakes and have seen very few in which students appeared relaxed and happy to be presenting. Think of how nervous you'd make your classmates if you were to give the perfect presentation! But you don't want to be embarrassed in front of everyone either. That's why we're listing nine helpful hints that you'll want to keep in mind when you develop and deliver an oral presentation.

1. Know your audience. Knowing your intended audience is equally as important in public speaking as in writing. In addition to the five points in the Know Your Audience section for writing papers earlier in this chapter, you also can benefit as a public speaker by asking yourself what kinds of audio visual aids might be most effective for helping you communicate with your audience.

2. Know your topic. Know what you want to say and how you plan to present it. Don't attempt to memorize or read it. Don't be tempted to write everything down exactly the way you intend to say it. If you do, you might find yourself reading your presentation instead of delivering it, and that's not effective public speaking. No one ever gives a presentation exactly as if it were a script, but having good notes will help you practice and deliver the

Apply This Now

1. Jot down the physical and emotional symptoms of stress you've experienced while waiting to give a speech.

_____

_____

_____

2. In a group of three or four students, share your lists. How have these symptoms both helped and hindered your presentations?

_____

_____

_____

BOX 11.2.   **Nine Helpful Hints for Oral Presentations**

1. Know your audience.

2. Know your topic.

3. Organize your speech into three simple parts.

4. Clue your audience about what to expect.

5. Practice, practice, practice.

6. Wear something dressier than usual.

7. Use your stress to be a better speaker.

8. Check your watch during your presentation.

9. Remember to make eye contact.

presentation. Add marginal notes to indicate when you want to use transparencies, slides, a cassette player, handouts, props, or other audio visual aids. Make sure you have a separate, legible list of your major points, in the order you want to cover them, to refer to quickly if you lose your train of thought.

3. Organize your speech into three simple parts. All you need to remember is that you must deliver (a) an introduction, (b) the body of the talk, and (c) a conclusion. Your introduction should set up the audience to anticipate what you'll talk about. The body should address all the points you mention in the introduction. Be sure to end with a conclusion that sums it all up. If you leave out any of these parts, your presentation will be much less effective; your audience may be confused about where your speech is going; and/or they may be uncertain at the end about what you've tried to say.

4. Clue your audience about what to expect. You don't want your audience to wonder what your main points are or what you want to persuade them to do or believe. As you're writing your presentation, remember to tell them very early what you intend to say; be sure your presentation says it as well as possible; and remind them at the end that you've said it.

5. Practice, practice, practice. Your most important strategy is practicing *out loud*. This may feel really awkward at first, but it's the only way you'll know how the speech sounds and approximately how long it will take. You may discover that a string of words that looks great on paper is a real tongue twister. You won't want the extra stress of worrying about whether you'll pronounce particular words correctly.

Be sure to use a clock or a timer to time every practice. Most instructors will give you a time range or set a strict time limit. By practicing out loud, you may find that your speech is too long or too short. Most inexperienced

Time to Reflect

Look back at the section of Chapter 2 on multiple intelligences.

1. Which of the eight types of intelligences would someone have to have developed well to learn effectively from an oral presentation?

_____

2. Some individuals are not well suited to learning from oral presentations. What intelligence types are *least* suited to learning this way?

_____

3. How does this knowledge help to convince you that it's necessary to carefully guide your audience by using the four helpful hints described above?

_____

_____

4. Reread the second hint. Persons with which of the intelligence types would respond well to your use of transparencies, slides, cassette players, handouts, props, or other audio visual aids?

_____

public speakers talk more quickly during the actual presentation, so if your speech is twenty to thirty seconds too long during practice, you're probably okay. If it's longer than that, you'll have to cut something out. On the other hand, if it's too short, you'll want to add remarks, such as examples or short illustrations. Practice your presentation enough times to feel comfortable about it. The first practice time should be all by yourself in front of the mirror. Then practice it again in front of a trusted friend or family member, or work with a classmate who will also practice in front of you.

Tell your listener to focus on specific points you're trying to get across to successfully complete the assignment. And let that person know whether you want her or him to just listen, to critique your speech, and/or to listen for specific problems you want to correct. This will help avoid hurt feelings and conflicts about the listener's role. It's best if you and your listener have a comfortable give-and-take relationship. With such a relationship, you'll interpret that person's observations and criticisms as helpful. The purpose of practicing in front of someone you trust is to help you avoid mistakes in front of others with whom you feel less comfortable.

After your practice presentation, try making changes as soon as possible. Then practice it at least once more. Note how long you spend on each section, or mark the place you've reached after, say, three minutes, five minutes, and so on. This will help you judge whether you're going at about the same speed when you present it in class.

6. Wear something dressier than usual. This signals that you're taking the assignment seriously. Some students also find that dressing differently makes it easier to slip into the character of a person who gives presentations, like an actor wearing a costume. Be sure what you wear doesn't distract you or your audience or cause you physical discomfort. You don't want to add another dimension of uneasiness to this exercise.

exercise Break 11.6

1. Jot down the techniques you have found to be successful for practicing a speech.

_____

_____

2. Get together with a classmate and share your lists with each other. Do your techniques differ?
   _____

   a. If they do, can you explain these differences by differences in your preferred learning styles?

   _____

   _____

   b. Can you come up with other explanations?

   _____

   _____

7. Use your stress to be a better speaker. Remember the discussion on stress in Chapter 3. Some stress is good; good stress makes you more engaged and makes your mind sharper. Harness your stress to be a better speaker. If you aren't nervous, if you're too relaxed, something is wrong; your speech will likely be flat. But you have to deal with the bad stress, the fear. Use the relaxation techniques for preparing to take tests presented in Chapter 9. They'll help combat the bad stresses you're likely to experience before it's your turn to present.

8. Check your watch during your presentation. Often, you'll see a speaker place her or his watch on the podium. Doing this makes it easier and less distracting to occasionally check the time. Think about whether you'll be speaking in a room with a wall clock. Check your watch or the clock a couple of times to see if you're taking the amount of time you thought you would. If you're talking more slowly and it's taking too long, you can either speed up your delivery or leave something out. If you're speaking too fast, take a deep breath and slow down. It's helpful to prepare something more to say, such as an example or an application of a concept, just in case you have extra time.

9. Remember to make eye contact. Don't let more than two or three sentences leave your lips without looking up and quickly locking eyes with audience members. This is the surest way to let them know you want to communicate with them. It will make you a better speaker in their eyes. And in the dominant North American culture, eye contact while you're speaking communicates credibility and trustworthiness to your audience. But practice ahead of time the way you move your eyes from your notes to the audience, to avoid having your eyes flit or your head bob. Such movements can decrease your credibility and distract your audience.

Looking at your audience also helps you gauge their reactions. But some speakers are nervous about actually locking eyes with audience members. They think they'll become flustered or distracted. If this describes you, try

exercise break 11.7

Think back to the last time you were required to make an oral presentation, whether in school or elsewhere.

1. How did you feel about it right before?

_____

2. What didn't go as planned?

_____

_____

3. What went as planned?

_____

_____

4. Overall, was it as bad an experience as you thought it might be? _____

5. What could you do in the future to improve the quality of your oral presentations?

_____

_____

glancing at noses or foreheads. It's unlikely that anyone will know the difference. And you can still pick up on useful clues. Note their body language to see if they seem to be engaged or uninterested. If you see certain heads nodding in agreement or some audience members leaning toward you or sitting up straight, they're giving you positive feedback. You and they will feel better about your presentation if you give them more of your attention. But remember to glance regularly at your instructor, no matter what feedback, if any, she or he is giving you.

© Vivian Scott Hixson

■ *Other Ways to Improve Your Public Speaking*

You may wish to choose a more formal way to improve your public speaking. Most colleges and universities offer public speaking courses. A number of colleges and universities even require students to complete such a course. Others include it among a list of options to fulfill a general education requirement. If your curriculum does require public speaking, we strongly encourage you to enroll in it as soon as your schedule allows. Work hard to successfully complete the course. Once you have, your new presentation skills and your enhanced ability to work through your fears will make you a significantly better speaker. Presentation skills will help you earn better grades in other courses and will continue to pay off even after college. You won't be as likely to develop a bad case of jitters as you anticipate your turn to speak in front of others.

exercise break 11.8

Once you've mastered public speaking skills, you'll reap many rewards. List some of the benefits for your personal and professional life that would result from enhancing your public speaking skills.

_____

_____

_____

Another excellent way to improve your public speaking is to just do it, again and again. There are many opportunities through service and social roles, such as in clubs and professional organizations. The more you do this, the more comfortable you'll be, and the more you'll hone your speaking skills.

Do your career plans include management or communications as possible goals, or do you envision yourself in public service or customer service? You'll need good writing and speaking skills to get ahead in these careers. And you'll need to know how to access and sift among various sources of information (see Appendix A). College is a wonderful place to practice.

Take it away!

Once you've had a chance to try out and to practice the ideas presented in this chapter, your college writing and presentations will

- Focus on a well-defined audience.

  Only if you know who your intended audience is can you decide what information you need to provide and how you want to say it.

- Clearly indicate whether you're using anyone else's ideas to help you make a point.

  Citing references indicates that you've done your research and that you're giving credit to those whose ideas you're using.

- Include all the points you want to make in a well-organized way.

  You want your audience to be able to follow your lead. Explaining at the very first where you're leading them and what your major points are helps the audience follow along. Then methodically cover your points in a prearranged order.

- Cause you less negative stress along the way.

  The stress of wanting to write and present well can be very helpful. Just be sure to follow one or more strategies for reducing negative stress.

This chapter and the five chapters that preceded it focused on enhancing your college success skills: taking notes, studying outside of class, preparing for and taking exams, and writing and speaking well. We hope you've been trying out the many strategies suggested in these chapters and are continuing to use the ones that work particularly well for you. Chapter 12 pulls together information from Chapters 1 through 11 and asks you to reflect on the progress you've made toward becoming a successful college student.

Questions for Critical Thought

1. Think back to the most recent major writing assignment you completed.
   a. What was the topic?
   b. What kinds of sources did you use in your research?
   c. Did a librarian help you?
   d. How many hours did you spend researching and writing notes before writing your paper?
   e. How many hours did you spend actually writing the paper?

2. Choose one of the courses you mentioned in Exercise Break 11.1 in which you are required to write a term paper. Answer the following questions.
   a. What course?
   b. When is the paper due?
   c. How long does it have to be?
   d. Is it your responsibility to select the topic?
   e. If you've already started working on it, what have you done so far?
   f. If you haven't started, when do you think you will? How do you plan to start?

3. Do you ever write for pleasure or at least find yourself enjoying the process or the feeling of accomplishment about writing letters, poems, or anything else? If so, what do you enjoy about writing?

4. What types of writing do you hate to do or at least find very uncomfortable, if any?
   a. What parts of the writing experience are hardest for you?
   b. When you have to do the type of writing you hate, do you put it off as long as possible, or do you try to get it over with as soon as you can? Why do you think you choose to approach it this way?

5. Has an instructor ever handed back your draft for a rewrite?
   a. If so, what kinds of suggestions has the instructor given that are helpful?
   b. Have you ever received comments that were unhelpful? If so, can you remember what they were?
   c. What's the major difference between the helpful and unhelpful comments?

6. Do a little research on your college's general education program. Is a course in public speaking, or a similar speech course, required? Thinking of your own pub-

lic speaking skills and your career goals, do you think that taking such a course would be beneficial? Why?

7. Think back to the last time you observed a particularly effective public speaker.
   a. What strategies did the speaker use to grab and keep your attention?
   b. Which of these strategies would you consider using in the future?
   c. Which strategies might you not use, depending on your audience?

8. Look back at the Points to Ponder that appear in this chapter.
   a. Which Point to Ponder surprised you the most?
   b. How does knowing this help you better prepare for academic success?

9. How can an understanding of concepts presented in this chapter help you outside of the college and classroom environment? Which principles and strategies are particularly relevant to success in your career and personal life?

Web Site

Visit the *Overcoming the Hurdles to Academic Success* web site for a chapter outline, review exercises, additional case studies, links to other online resources, and a practice test.

References

Beebe, S. A., and Beebe, S. J. (2000). *Public speaking: An audience-centered approach,* Fourth Edition. Boston: Allyn & Bacon.

Fontaine, Sheryl I., and Quaas, Francie. (1998). "Transforming connections and building bridges: Assigning, reading, and evaluating the college essay," in *Teaching Writing Creatively,* edited by David Starkey. Porstmouth, NH: Boynton/Cook Heinemann.

Lindemann, Erika. (1995). "Developing writing assignments," in *A Rhetoric for writing teachers,* Third Edition. New York: Oxford University Press.

12

PULL IT ALL TOGETHER

Chapter 12 Strategies

1 Develop and maintain a positive attitude about your ability to succeed.

2 Set clear life goals for yourself in all aspects of your life—education, career, civic, and personal.

3 Measure the value of your potential choices by whether they help you achieve your life goals.

4 Take responsibility for all of the choices you make throughout your life.

5 Be an active learner to achieve success in school and work, as well as in your personal and civic life.

6 Harness your stress to help you accomplish your goals.

7 Use your critical-thinking skills—analyzing, synthesizing, and bringing together various pieces of information to solve a problem—to learn more thoroughly and remember more clearly.

8 Take charge of your time, remembering to schedule your most important activities, including those important to maintaining balance between your professional responsibilities and your personal life.

9 Create or join work groups, and work on projects cooperatively with family members, so that you and the other group members can achieve more.

10 When being presented with new and important information, be sure to listen actively, try to anticipate the information being presented, and selectively take notes.

11 Practice memory-enhancing strategies: closely paying attention, repeating and organizing new information, and connecting it to what you already know, using mnemonics, and sharing strategies with friends, family, and work-group members.

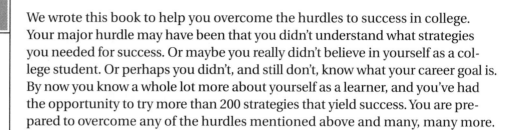

12 When you write a report or give a presentation for work or another organization, consider your audience before deciding what to include and how you want to say it.

13 Be sure to give credit whenever you're using anyone else's ideas to help you get your point across.

We wrote this book to help you overcome the hurdles to success in college. Your major hurdle may have been that you didn't understand what strategies you needed for success. Or maybe you really didn't believe in yourself as a college student. Or perhaps you didn't, and still don't, know what your career goal is. By now you know a whole lot more about yourself as a learner, and you've had the opportunity to try more than 200 strategies that yield success. You are prepared to overcome any of the hurdles mentioned above and many, many more.

To assist you with your learning process, we first wanted you to discover the ways you prefer to learn. Everyone learns in different ways. You should feel confident by now that you have the ability to learn whatever you need to learn in college. The learning strategies you choose depend on your preferred learning style, your particular strengths, and your desire to succeed. This book doesn't describe all the possible ways to analyze yourself as a learner. Nor does it describe all of the most popular learning strategies. You may already know, or you may yet discover, other strategies that are more effective for you. Our purpose has been to give you a solid foundation, and we are delighted if strategies that aren't in the book work well for you. Be sure to share them!

This chapter provides a brief overview of the book's strategies for helping you overcome the hurdles to your college success. Its purpose is to give you the opportunity to reflect on all you've learned as a result of reading the book, completing the exercises, and trying various strategies. Remember the ground rules, reproduced in Box 12.1, for successfully using strategies that really help. Because the purpose of this final chapter is for you to reflect on what works for you, it contains only Time to Reflect exercises. We hope that, as a result of completing this chapter, you'll see how far you've come as an active, engaged learner, a student who takes responsibility for shaping your own successes.

BOX 12.1.   **Ground Rules**

1. Learn a variety of academic success strategies.

2. Give each academic success strategy a try.

3. Evaluate the success of each strategy.

4. Master the strategies.

You know that to be successful in college and throughout your life, you need to do all of the following. First, you have to develop and, as much as possible, maintain a positive attitude about yourself. Second, you need to set clear goals. Third, you need to measure your potential choices by whether they help you achieve your goals. Fourth, you must take responsibility for the choices you make.

1. Maintain a positive attitude. You recognize the importance of maintaining a positive attitude about your ability to succeed. A familiar expression comes to mind: "If you can see it, you can be it!" Sometimes keeping your spirits up can be difficult. No one has a positive attitude all the time. But if you've developed a deeply held belief in yourself, you'll feel up to the hurdles of college and of life.

2. Set clear goals. You've worked on clarifying your reasons for attending college in several chapters. By now you know more about where you're headed and why. It's much easier to succeed when you've set goals for yourself, even very short-term goals. Now that you've examined your goals and what it takes to reach them, you're on your way toward identifying the hurdles you're likely to face. Once you've identified your hurdles, you're ready to prepare for them by developing skills and learning strategies to overcome them.

3. Make good choices. You understand how to use your time wisely, foregoing almost all other opportunities so as to stay on track. Most of the time you need to focus on your goals when you decide how to spend your time. Sometimes it's difficult to say no to opportunities that give immediate pleasure to you or to someone you care about. To have a balanced life, you know you need to relax and to nurture the needs of others. But it's easy to fall into bad habits and tell yourself your motives are worthy.

4. Take responsibility. You know you must accept personal responsibility for your success in college and for any choices you make that delay reaching your goals. Others can and will help you in meaningful ways, but you need to do the work. You're the one who's making the personal commitment of time and energy for your education.

© *Vivian Scott Hixson*

Time to Reflect

Look back at the goals you set for yourself in Chapter 1.

1. List the goals that are still important to you.

_____

_____

_____

2. List the goals you no longer wish to work on, and explain why you've changed your mind.

_____

_____

_____

3. If you've added any goals, list them.

_____

_____

_____

4. Are you making good progress toward reaching the goals you listed as important to you in (1) and (3)? Why?

_____

_____

_____

5. What evidence do you have of your progress?

_____

_____

_____

_____

Prepare for Academic Success

Chapters 2 through 5 focused on getting to know yourself as a learner and discovering the academic support services your college provides.

■ *Know Yourself as a Learner*

You now know a number of concepts and strategies for determining your favorite ways to learn. Now that you understand the ways you like to learn, you study in ways that work best for you. We hope you've experimented with a lot of new active-learning strategies and have decided to regularly use the ones that give you the best results. Becoming an active learner is vitally important to your success in school and beyond.

■ *Think It Through*

You've worked on strategies for increasing your ability to stay focused. In particular, you now know ways to effectively manage stress in your life. Of tremendous

Time to Reflect

As a result of reading Chapter 2:

1. Explain what you've learned about your preferred learning style(s).

_____

_____

2. Given your preferred learning style(s), describe three or four strategies you've successfully used for the first time this term.

_____

_____

_____

3. What evidence do you have that these strategies have helped?

_____

_____

_____

importance for college success, you have new ways to increase your capacity to think critically and successfully engage in problem-solving activities.

Concentration. You now know various methods to stay focused, including the prudent use of study breaks to remain alert. You've learned ways to avoid or lessen bad stress in your life and to use good stress to your advantage. Instead of trying to banish stress, you've developed strategies for harnessing it to accomplish your goals. You've learned more about your impulsive reactions to stressors in order to learn the most appropriate ways to deal with them.

Critical Thinking and Problem Solving. You know what *critical thinking* means, and you understand why it requires you to more fully understand what you learn. When you analyze and synthesize concepts, or when you bring together various pieces of information to solve a problem, you're bound to learn more thoroughly and remember more clearly.

▣ *Organize and Take Charge of Your Time*

You've studied ways to take charge of your time, experimenting with a planner to help you learn to schedule important activities. You've learned more about how, when, where, and under what conditions you study most effectively. You've learned how to make study groups work for you and other group members.

▣ *Use Campus Resources*

You've learned about several of the academic support resources available on your campus. The most important academic resources include academic advisors, classroom instructors, and the course syllabus. Your campus and your

Time to Reflect

Several chapters mentioned strategies for coping with stress.

1. List two or three new strategies you've tried in order to better manage stress.

_____

_____

2. Put a + next to any you've found to be really useful.

3. What evidence do you have that these strategies are working for you?

_____

_____

_____

Time to Reflect

As a result of reading Chapter 4 and trying the strategies discussed there:

1. In what ways have you modified your study environment since the beginning of the term?

_____

_____

2. How do you know whether this has helped?

_____

_____

_____

instructors may offer course discussion sessions, teaching assistants, tutors, and study-skills assistance. If so, you've had the opportunity to use at least some of them for additional help. If you have a documented disability, we hope you've asked for academic assistance from your special populations office or office for students with disabilities.

Master Strategies for Success

Chapters 6 through 11 focused on numerous strategies for academic success. After trying these strategies, you've probably begun to use some of them regularly. If so, you're certainly more successful in

- Taking good lecture notes;
- Increasing the amount you learn from reading your textbooks;

Time to Reflect

Look back at Chapter 5.

1. Which of the strategies from this chapter have you used for

   a. Setting up a productive meeting with an academic advisor?

   _____

   _____

   b. Finding answers to your questions about specific course material?

   _____

   _____

   c. Talking with your instructors and/or TAs outside of class?

   _____

   _____

   d. Catching up on course material when you've had to miss class?

   _____

   _____

2. What evidence do you have that these strategies have worked for you?

   _____

   _____

   _____

- Remembering more of what you've studied;
- Preparing for tests and taking tests with confidence; and
- Writing papers and making oral presentations.

▨ *Note-Taking Strategies*

 You've studied several different note-taking strategies. They include methods for organizing, listening actively, anticipating the information to be presented, being selective about what you write down, emphasizing the most important information, and abbreviating where possible. We also discussed four distinct approaches to note-taking:

1. Listing important concepts, terms, or events on the left side of the page and definitions, examples, and elaboration of those terms and events on the right side of the page;

2. Using the outline method to keep your notes organized;

3. Using a variety of writing styles, fonts, and/or colors when taking notes, such as using capital letters for major concepts and principles and regular print for details, or using different colors of ink, pencil, or highlighter

to represent different types of information or different degrees of emphasis; and

4. Using any of these approaches or perhaps another, and writing only on the right-hand side of the page, leaving ample room in an extended left-hand margin to add special notes and reminders later.

Time to Reflect

Look back at Chapter 6.

1. Which of the note-taking strategies have you tried?

_____

_____

_____

_____

_____

2. Put a + next to the ones you're still using.

3. What evidence do you have that these strategies are working for you?

_____

_____

_____

▓ *Read Your Textbooks*

We can't emphasize enough the importance of reading your textbooks. You know how to always keep your reading environment comfortable, relatively free of distractions, and supplied with the tools you need. Your reading assignments make more sense because you use a proven reading approach, such as SQ3R (survey, question, read, recite, review). You may be applying other strategies, such as taking marginal notes, answering questions as you read, quizzing yourself, and sticking to your own reading pace.

▓ *Enhance Your Memory*

You studied the way memory works. Then you studied memory-enhancing strategies. For your brain to encode and store information for the short term, you need to do some minimal work. By using memory-enhancing strategies, you can now store information long-term so that you can retrieve it well into the future.

Some memory-enhancing strategies work for everyone: closely paying attention, repeating new information, connecting new material to what you already know, organizing new information in an efficient and meaningful way, using mnemonics, and sharing strategies with friends and study-group members. Additional strategies help you remember your lecture notes and reading notes: reviewing new material soon and regularly, word processing your handwritten notes, making and using note cards, audiotaping your handwritten notes, and/or regularly studying in a study group.

Time to Reflect

Look back at Chapter 7.

1. Which of the reading strategies have you tried?

_____

_____

_____

_____

2. Put a + next to the ones you're still using.

3. What evidence do you have that these strategies are working for you?

_____

_____

_____

Time to Reflect

Look back at Chapters 3 and 8.

1. Which of the strategies are you continuing to use for

a. Being more actively involved in your learning process?

_____

_____

_____

b. Remembering classroom information?

_____

_____

c. Organizing information from classroom lectures and texts?

_____

_____

_____

2. What evidence do you have that these strategies are working for you?

_____

_____

_____

▨ *Prepare for and Successfully Take Tests*

You now have an arsenal of strategies to use before and during tests. Pretest strategies include finding out all you can about a test ahead of time, using a study guide, and using various strategies for answering multiple-choice, true/false, fill-in-the-blank, and essay questions. You also have some strategies for taking tests in nontraditional formats: group tests, open book and note tests, and take-home exams.

On Test Day.   You know to eat well, dress comfortably, bring all materials you'll need, arrive early, and settle in comfortably. For reducing anxiety and doing your best during the test, you've studied many strategies. These include reading all instructions thoroughly and looking over the entire test before starting. When possible, you write notes for yourself directly on the exam, answer items you know best first, and read every question thoroughly before answering. You ask for clarification when unsure what the question is asking. You try to answer all questions, looking at other test questions for clues to the ones you don't know. You pace yourself, take breaks if you need to, think positively, stay focused, and review your answers. *Above all, we hope you've made a personal commitment to academic honesty and integrity.*

After the Test.   You know the benefit of evaluating your test results as soon as you can, looking for why any answers were wrong. This gives you another chance to learn the material and to decide whether to change or strengthen any of your test preparation and/or test-taking strategies.

Time to Reflect

Look back at Chapters 9 and 10.

1. Which of the strategies are you continuing to use for

    a. Being better prepared for taking tests?

    _____

    _____

    _____

    b. Staying calm and remembering information during tests?

    _____

    _____

    _____

    c. Using information from returned tests to learn even more?

    _____

    _____

    _____

2. What evidence do you have that these strategies are working for you?

    _____

    _____

    _____

■ *Write Papers and Make Presentations Successfully*

You've probably had a chance to try out and practice strategies for writing college papers and making presentations. If so, you know to consider your audience before deciding what information to include and how to say it. You understand the importance of clearly stating whether you're using anyone else's ideas to help you make a point.

You want your audience to be able to follow your lead. That's why you explain at the very start where you're leading them and what your major points are. Then you methodically cover your points in order.

Citing references indicates that you've done research and that you're giving credit to those whose ideas you're using. Giving credit to sources in your papers and presentations is seriously important in college. It's as significant a commitment to academic honesty and integrity as not cheating on an exam.

Stress from wanting to write and present well is similar to the stress involved in taking tests. You've learned the positive effects of this stress. In addition, you've learned a number of strategies for reducing negative stress.

Ground Rules for Success

If you've completed any of the exercises in this chapter, you've had the opportunity to cite evidence of your success with one or more academic strategies. Congratulations! Turning back to Box 12.1, you can see that you've applied the ground rules in the use and evaluation of academic strategies. The ground rules comprise a strategy for reaching and evaluating success. Remember them. You can use them for success in all facets of your life— personal, professional, and spiritual as well as academic.

Time to Reflect

1. What written assignments and/or oral presentations were required in your courses this term?

_____

_____

2. What strategies did you use as you wrote papers and/or prepared for speeches?

_____

_____

_____

_____

3. In front of each *successful* strategy you listed in (2), write a +.

4. What evidence do you have that these strategies are working for you?

_____

_____

_____

_____

Time to Reflect

Look back at any important decision you've made while using this book.

1. How did you use the ground rules in making this decision?

_____

_____

2. What evidence do you have that the ground rules were helpful?

_____

_____

_____

Leap Over All Academic Hurdles!

You're now prepared for success in college and beyond. You know yourself as a learner. You're obviously motivated to succeed. You've learned a variety of strategies for overcoming the hurdles to college success. You're ready to leap over those hurdles to reach all of your academic goals. Good luck!

Web Site

Visit the *Overcoming the Hurdles to Academic Success* web site for a chapter outline, review exercises, additional case studies, links to other online resources, and a practice test.

A

Library Research Tips and Strategies

Appendix A Strategies

1 Hang out in the library every now and again between classes to study, read a newspaper or magazine, watch a video, or listen to music.

2 Ask multimedia lab personnel to assist you in using the computers and software to create multimedia presentations—to project text, video, sound, and graphics.

3 Ask a reference librarian for assistance. A reference librarian can direct you to research tools, specialized collections, and documents you never even knew existed.

4 Start your search early with the help of your library, making certain that you can succeed in completing the assignment with your chosen topic.

5 Find out about your library's interlibrary loan program.

6 If you don't have an exact citation or web site to search for, use one or more of the growing number of Internet search engines, using key words that indicate or describe your subject.

7 Ask for help if you need instruction to operate your library's microfiche reader, load and access a CD, or use any of the other technologies in your library.

8 If you're unsure about whether only recent articles will be acceptable for your research or writing assignment, ask your professor during office hours or right after class.

A Different Kind of Library

This appendix deals with strategies to improve your performance in library research. Under what circumstances might you need to do research in college? You may need to answer a question posed to you verbally by a professor or on an assignment sheet. You might be preparing to give an oral presentation or to hand in a major written assignment. The best place to start searching for information is your campus library. Sure, you could start on your own, perhaps by using an encyclopedia or by searching the World Wide Web. But your college library has ways to help you make a better start.

If you haven't yet set foot in your campus library or in another college library, you're in for quite a surprise. It may look like a bigger version of your high school library. It may even look a lot like your town's public library. But its purposes, its personnel, its collections, and its other resources are different from what you've experienced. And its hours of operation may really surprise you.

Multiple Libraries

You may be attending a very large university that has more than one library. If so, there's likely to be a huge library with most of the collection and one or more small libraries with collections focused on one or a few topics. Or you may be attending a community college that is part of a large metropolitan system of colleges or college campuses. Each campus or college in the system is likely to have its own library. In any case, it's possible that you'll start your search for information in one place and then determine that you need to continue your search in another.

The many differences from the libraries you're accustomed to may be overwhelming at the start. College librarians expect new students to feel this way. That's why so many college libraries offer orientation sessions. These sessions tell you where to seek information of different types, what kinds of texts and services are available, and who to ask for different kinds of help. Some courses designed for first-year college students require short library research projects that allow students to become familiar with numerous types of library resources. Some instructors even set up one or two class sessions in the library.

Reserve Book Room

College and university libraries have a room that you won't find in a public library, the reserve book room. Often instructors want their students to read portions of books, journal articles, and other sources that they make available in the library as shared texts. Instructors usually do this so that students don't have to buy these important texts. Sometimes these texts are out of print and can't be made widely available any other way. A faculty member will ask the library to put these shared materials on reserve in the reserve book room.

You use texts on reserve by going to the reserve book room and requesting them, usually by filling out a form. These texts are usually restricted to use in the library, and you are allowed to use them for a limited amount of time. The most restrictive rules might require you to return these materials after two hours. Sometimes, reserve book room materials can be checked out of the library for forty-eight hours. Other times, the instructor will restrict use to that

room; you can't even take them to another part of the library. Usually the reserve book room is in a location that's easy to find. It generally has a lot of
chairs and tables. The people who are reading texts in this room are working
under a time constraint, so they do not appreciate unnecessary talking or
other distractions.

■ Other Useful Spaces

If you don't have any assignments that require you to use the library this semester, be assured that you will, sooner or later. Meanwhile, hang out in the library every now and again between classes. Libraries can be great places to
study, read a newspaper or magazine, watch a video, or listen to music. Some
students regularly take naps in libraries; they're relatively quiet places with
comfortable furniture. Some libraries have rooms available for group study, a
very useful feature if you're assigned a group project or if you want to study together with friends. But group study rooms are so popular that in many libraries they have to be reserved in advance. More and more libraries have
snack areas, so hungry and thirsty students won't have to leave. Most libraries
have photocopy machines; some offer photocopying services. With all the texts
and services a typical college library offers, a lot of personnel are needed to
keep it running well. So your library can also be a great place to search for and
to hold a part-time job on campus.

■ Multimedia Services

Some libraries have multimedia labs. These are areas with high-end multimedia computer hardware and software, as well as audio and video tape players,
slides, videos, CDs, and cassettes. For some classes you may be required to
watch videos, view slides, or listen to music. Often the multimedia lab will
have small rooms for you to complete these assignments.

  Lab personnel can assist you in using the computers and software to create
multimedia presentations—to project text, video, sound, and graphics. These
services are useful if you have to give an oral or written presentation for which
graphics, audio or video clips, or slides can help you get your point across. The
lab assistants who help you create your presentations, as well as the machines
and materials themselves, are useful resources. At most schools students need
to provide their own diskettes, transparencies, and other supplies.

■ Reference Librarians

One or more reference librarians are usually on duty to help students find what
they need. Ask a reference librarian for assistance. Reference librarians are
among the most important resources for some of your course projects. They
are professionals who completed not only undergraduate degrees but also advanced coursework that taught them how to dig out information. A reference
librarian can direct you to research tools, specialized collections, and documents you never even knew existed. If your library doesn't have the information you need, your reference librarians can help by searching out other places
that have that information and/or by using other ways to search for it.

  Some larger colleges and universities have librarians who specialize in
helping students research the government documents collection. Many college and university libraries are government document repositories. That
means they receive every document published by one or more government

Copyright © Houghton Mifflin Company. All rights reserved.

Point *to* PONDER

The best reason to start your search early is to make certain that you can succeed in completing the assignment with your chosen topic.

agencies—federal, state and/or local. The government documents sections of most major research universities are huge, requiring a large staff of librarians to maintain the collections and to help students, faculty, and others find the information they seek.

In fact, a reference or government documents librarian can sometimes help you find too much material on a subject. You might decide that too much has been written about the subject for you to learn enough of it in the time you have. Or you might discover that the subject is much more complicated than you'd thought. Your initial foray into researching a topic can convince you that you need to drastically narrow or completely rethink your focus. However, you might have the opposite problem, even in a large library: You've chosen a subject that is so new or so narrowly focused that either you can't find enough sources or you can't understand the sources you do find. It's useful to figure out quickly if you're likely to face this scenario. Otherwise you run the risk of running out of time to switch to a different topic. This sums up the best eason to start your search early with the help of your library: to make certain that you can succeed in completing the assignment with your chosen topic.

Exhausting the Information Possibilities

Suppose your research, or even the bibliography in your textbook, indicates that you should read a text that your library doesn't have in its collection. Perhaps you've searched electronically and know of another library that has it, but it is too far away for you to access. Or maybe the topic is so new that there has been very little time for the topic to have gotten into print. There are many reasons why your college's library won't have all the information you're searching for. But there are other ways to retrieve important information, including interlibrary loan and the World Wide Web.

Interlibrary Loan

 Find out about your library's interlibrary loan program. At most colleges you can request a book or article that your library doesn't have, and your library will obtain it for you. Sometimes you have to wait a few days to a week for it. But sometimes, at some libraries and for some journal articles, you can sit down at a designated computer and request a printed copy of the article practically instantaneously. In order for you to have this quick access, your library must already have an electronic access agreement with that particular publisher.

You may be required to pay the costs to the library of obtaining what you need, either the costs of a printed copy or of shipping through interlibrary loan. Some colleges assess a general library fee or include the average cost of this service in tuition. In these situations, the service has already been paid for, shared among all students.

World Wide Web

Another source of information, but one that is tricky for you to evaluate, is the World Wide Web, usually referred to as the Web. It's tricky for students to judge the value of information they find on the Web. Anyone can put up a web page, even people who do not really know anything about the topics they cover.

Many reputable publishers, scholars, government agencies, and others share extremely useful and timely information on the Web.

 If you don't have an exact citation or web site to search for, you can still browse by using one or more of the growing number of search engines, the services on the Web that act something like library subject indexes. All you need to know are the key words that indicate or describe your subject. A search engine can connect you to numerous possibly useful sites. Even more powerful are web crawlers, powerful programs that can engage two or more search engines to complete a search. Unlike an index in your library, however, the web sites the search engine or crawler finds aren't all useful or accurate enough to merit publication. On the plus side, the references offer a greater variety of opinions and are often more up-to-date. So if you like to browse the Web to do research, be sure to include it as one of several forms of research you undertake. You'll have to be more careful and discerning about what information you choose to incorporate into your papers and presentations.

If you want to learn more about using the Internet and the Web, your library may have workshops to help you get started. Some schools offer a series of workshops, so their students can learn more and more sophisticated uses of these resources. Or you might see if your bookstore has one or more of the how-to books on this subject worth buying.

Selecting a Topic to Research

What do we mean by "selecting a topic"? We mean a whole lot more than choosing something to write about. You also need to have some idea of what kinds of things you want to say about it. Generally, this is why an instructor may require you to hand in a *thesis statement* long before the finished paper or presentation is due. A thesis statement is one sentence in which you declare a position you plan to take on a subject.

How will you know when the topic is sufficiently narrowed down but not too specific or too simple? When you narrow down your topic, you want to end up with (1) a subject that meets all the requirements of the assignment; (2) one you can understand well enough to write and/or talk about with reasonable confidence; (3) one about which you can find ten or more substantial, recent references that you can understand, but usually not as many as thirty or more; (4) a topic you think you'll like, or at least won't hate, to work on; and (5) preferably something that helps you understand both the research process and other course material better.

How do you get started in researching a topic? So much information is written on many topics that the reference librarian might suggest reading an *index* about the general field, such as psychology, business, education, international affairs, and many other general fields of study. Your library may have indexes in one or more of several forms. They may consist of numerous large and heavy bound volumes, usually with the words in tiny print, on a shelf in the reference area. Or you may find them in the reference area on microfiche, for which you'll need to use a microfiche reader. Or the index you want to look through might be accessible in CD-ROM format. In this last instance, you'll read it on a computer screen.

No matter what form it's in, the purpose of the index is to find printed references that deal with specific topics written by experts, grouped together into a

© *Vivian Scott Hixson*

general field. You need to start by knowing the topic you want to start with, or by using key words that are related to or describe your topic. When the index lists a specific reference, it provides a page summarizing that text. The summary will tell you what kinds of things the author(s) wrote about on the subject. You might be able to tell right away whether a text deals with an aspect of the subject that's helpful to you. Knowing this can save you hours of browsing through the shelves to find each text that might or might not be useful. Looking at summaries can help you pinpoint the useful texts that you want to take down from their shelves for a closer reading.

 Don't be shy about asking for instruction before attempting to operate your library's microfiche reader, if you're not sure how to load and access a CD, or if you don't know how to use any of the other technologies in your library. All reference librarians know how to use the library's technologies and have the training to show you in very little time.

Instead of starting with an index, you might want to go directly to the card catalog to find out whether your library has books on your subject. Most college libraries have electronic catalogs, which you access on a networked computer, probably in or near the reference area. A lot of community libraries also allow their patrons to access information on their collections this way. If so, looking up the subject, author, or title is already familiar to you.

It's becoming common for someone at one college to be able to search through the catalogs of other colleges and even other kinds of institutions. At some libraries you can search to find out what's available in the collections of libraries all over the world.

▇ *Writings of Experts*

Is the person whose book or article you've selected really an expert? How can you, a college student with little experience, evaluate whether texts were written by people who are generally accepted as experts? Here are some ways to tell: Was the author mentioned in a class discussion? Was the author mentioned in your textbook—either in a chapter or in the bibliography—or in several of the other articles and books you've read on the subject? If so, this is probably someone accepted as an authority in this field of study.

▪ *Timeliness of References*

How recent does a text have to be in order to be recent enough for the information to still be considered useful? This is a tough question. In some fields of study, there have been many recent discoveries, technological changes, and/or new legislation that dramatically changes what's important to know. If the area you're researching is like this, only those texts published in the last few years, or even the last few months, are still timely. Yet in other fields of study, it's appropriate to use books and articles that are twenty or more years old. It also depends on the way you approach the subject. If you are describing the history of a subject over time, then it's especially appropriate to use writings that span a number of years. If you are unsure, ask your professor during office hours or right after class.

▪ *Narrowing Your Topic*

How specific should the information be? This depends on both the audience for whom you're doing the research and how much you know about the subject when you start. Most likely, the audience is your professor. But the audience may include your classmates, especially if you'll be giving an oral presentation. You need to find references that aren't too complicated for you to comprehend. But they need to be informative enough so the professor feels confident that you have learned something by completing the assignment. If you start by knowing very little or nothing about the topic, it may be enough for you to use sources written by nonexperts, such as newspaper and magazine reporters. But before you decide that's okay, you should check with your professor. Sometimes an important article includes a lot of mathematical equations you can't understand. If the course doesn't require you to know this level of math, you can often get by with skipping that part of the author's argument.

The major purpose of libraries used to be to serve as repositories for written words and other types of documents. College libraries have been transformed in the past ten years or so. Now they serve more as portals for accessing information from other libraries and from numerous other sources around the world. Books and journals aren't your most important library resources. Instead, the librarians who help you access information and create your own documents on site and elsewhere are your most valuable library resources.

Point *to* ponder

▪ **The librarians who help you access information and create your own documents on site and elsewhere are your most valuable library resources.**

Take it Away!

This appendix explained the numerous facets of a typical college library. Knowing what your library has to offer can help you complete assignments, do research, and even enjoy pleasure reading.

- College libraries include numerous resources and functions that make them very different from high school and community public libraries.

  You may have one or more libraries on your college campus that include a reserve book room, lounges, multimedia services, and specialized collections, most notably government documents. Reference librarians are available to help you search for information.

- If your library doesn't have paper copies of documents you need, you can still retrieve the information.

    Libraries store some important information on microfiche and CD-ROMs. If your library doesn't have the information in any format, you can use interlibrary loan to have it delivered from another institution. Or you might possibly retrieve it from the Web.

- Before you decide on your topic for a research assignment, you need to see what research resources are available to you.

    The topic will need to be narrow enough that you won't have too much researching to do, but broad enough to find an adequate number of references.

- You'll have to make decisions about which authors are respected as experts.

    It can be difficult to decide whose research is respected, especially if you conduct your research on the Web. You can ask your professor, pay special attention to people mentioned in class or in your textbook, and ask librarians for advice.

- Consider reference librarians to be your best library resources.

    Reference librarians are experts in finding useful information. Their purpose is to help all library patrons find useful research materials.

 ## Questions for Critical Thought

1. What different kinds of libraries had you been to before college? What were your purposes for using them? Did you enjoy going to the library?

2. Think back to the most major writing assignment you were assigned in high school.
    a. What was the topic?
    b. What kinds of sources did you use in your research?
    c. Did a librarian help you?
    d. How many hours did you spend on researching and writing notes before writing your paper?
    e. How many hours did you spend actually writing of the paper?

3. Have you stepped inside your college library yet? Why? What are your impressions so far?

4. Look back at the Points to Ponder that appear in this appendix.
    a. Which Point to Ponder surprised you the most?
    b. How does knowing this help you better prepare for academic success?

5. How does the information presented in this appendix help you in your life outside of the classroom and college environment? Which strategies are particularly relevant to success in your career and personal life?

Web Site

Visit the *Overcoming the Hurdles to Academic Success* web site for a chapter outline, review exercises, additional case studies, links to other online resources, and a practice test.

Reference

List, Carla. (1993). *Introduction to library research,* Second Edition. New York: McGraw-Hill.

B

using computers

 Appendix B Strategies

1 To be prepared for employment after college, develop not only comfort with using computers but also competency in some specific computer uses.

2 Attend at least one of the computer orientation sessions offered on your campus.

3 If your campus doesn't offer computer orientation sessions, ask your instructors if they know of ways for you to learn more about using campus computers.

4 If your campus computer labs are in high demand, experiment and trade stories with your classmates to find computer lab times that work best for your schedule.

All college campuses provide some access to computers and some instruction for their use. More and more colleges and universities require all their students to achieve some level of computer literacy before graduation, sometimes in a course designed specifically for that purpose. One university in south Texas teaches all English composition courses in computer labs, and all of its core curriculum math courses include a two-hour computer lab component each week.

Your campus may provide other examples that are very different from these. Even if your school doesn't have a computer literacy policy, find opportunities to use computers to help you prepare for professional work. Almost all jobs that require a college education require employees to use computers as part of everyday work. To be prepared for employment after college, you'll need to develop not only comfort with using computers but also competency in some specific computer uses.

Point *to* PONDER

More and more colleges and universities require that all of their students achieve some defined level of computer literacy before graduation.

Your User Account

Most colleges require students to open computer/network user accounts before they can access computer programs. Some issue computer accounts as soon as a student has been accepted for enrollment. This allows new students to access information that's helpful for advising, registration, and other programs for getting started. Making students have individual computer access accounts benefits both the students and the institution. Your account will have a password, which will protect your privacy and restrict access to it. This also allows the campus to monitor computer usage and provide better security for the system.

Computer Courses

Most colleges and universities offer academic majors and minors in computer science, computer applications, and/or other programs that involve significant computer use. Examples of other programs include management information systems, geographic information sciences, computer-aided design, mathematics, computer-generated art, cinema, industrial engineering, library science, technical writing, journalism, and even music composition and performance.

Getting Started

Luckily, computers are becoming easier to use, more user-friendly. Many colleges and universities provide free computer orientation sessions and ongoing training for faculty and students. Computer orientation sessions are useful even if you're already an experienced computer user. Your campus may offer computer applications that are new to you, and your instructors may require you to use these applications. Attend at least one of the computer orientation sessions offered on your campus. Such sessions are often advertised in the student newspaper and announced in classes. You can ask a librarian or someone at the computer lab or the tutoring or learning center. These workshops can save you hours of frustration while dramatically improving your efficiency.

Point *to* PONDER

Computer orientation sessions are useful even if you're already an experienced computer user. Your campus may offer computer applications that are new to you, and your instructors may require you to use these applications.

Copyright © Houghton Mifflin Company. All rights reserved.

If your college doesn't offer such orientations, ask around for help: Most computer labs are staffed by lab assistants, usually students, who can answer at least some of your questions. You might ask a classmate who's been at the college for a while if she or he is willing to help you. If your instructors require you to complete assignments on a computer, they may arrange special sessions to help you learn how to utilize campus computers. If not, ask if they know of ways for you to learn more about using campus computers. Don't be embarrassed to ask questions or to admit you don't know how to get started. Each college has its own procedures, and both the hardware and the software can differ considerably from what you're used to. It's not at all unusual for students new to a college to ask for help.

Computer Labs

On many campuses, the demand for computer labs has dramatically increased over the past few years. Each year, more courses include assignments that can or must be completed on a computer. Some computer labs are available only for students taking certain classes that require special, very powerful computers. Sometimes you have to show up at a computer lab very early in the morning or very late at night to get a computer without waiting. If you face these situations, experiment and trade stories with your classmates to find computer lab times that work best for your schedule.

Different schools are coping with this congestion in different ways. Some have extended lab hours until very late at night or early in the morning, and/or have placed additional labs in residence hall common areas, student rooms in residence halls, the library, and/or the student union. Some schools make it easy for students to use campus computers from off-campus locations with their own personal computers and modem access. Some schools monitor the type of use, automatically logging off those who spend more than some maximum time. Others yet have provided their students with their own computers. Find out and record where and when your campus has labs open.

Networks

Some campuses are investing in the development of wireless local area networks (LAN) and/or Internet access. With the right hardware installed, wireless access allows people in specific, usually limited locations on campus to use laptop computers to access programs available on the network, as if they're wired into the network.

The Internet is a worldwide network, an electronic information superhighway. It's a pathway that can link your computer to anyone in the world—but only if you and the person you're trying to link to are both Internet subscribers. The Internet has been around for a number of years, and it's radically transformed the way we obtain information, communicate with one another, publish our ideas, and transact business. It's also making us examine what we think about such important concepts as privacy and decency and how we define what a publication is. It's even changed the way a growing number of individuals meet and date each other. If you access campus resources from home, you do so on the Internet. You need the right hardware and software; your campus computer services department can tell you what you need.

A local area network (LAN) is a campus-wide network, the electronic information local highway. It's the pathway that can link your computer to other people and programs on campus.

The World Wide Web

The World Wide Web (WWW, or Web) is the name given to all the publicly available sites you can visit via your computer on the Internet. If you don't know the address, you have to first access a web browser. (For more details on web searches, see Appendix A.)

Some sites have more than one web page, one or more screens that give you information. If a site has multiple web pages, you can view more detail on a subject by clicking on the designated spot on the computer screen. Various web pages at a single site are interconnected, so you can go back and forth from one to another, and sometimes move to related web sites. In order to access some sites, you must be a subscriber. Examples are publications, such as magazines, newspapers, and newsletters.

Many colleges and universities have created web sites on which potential students and others can learn more about them. Some allow prospective students to fill out applications right on the Web and transmit them electronically. During your first, or next, journey into the Web, check to see whether your school has a web site.

Electronic Mail

Email, short for electronic mail, is correspondence to and from individuals and groups over a computer network. If you have a computer account on the Internet, you can send email all over the world. All you need to know is the email address of the person or group to whom you want to send mail. Email is great, especially if your close friends and/or family members are far away. The person you're contacting doesn't have to be available at the time you're writing. Another really big plus is the cost as compared to the cost of a long-distance phone call. An emailed message costs you nothing.

Internet2

Not all campuses are ready to provide general access to the Internet. Those that aren't are trying to catch up as fast as they can. But if your campus can't provide this for you, take heart. Educators and scientists around the country are busily developing and extending Internet2, which will be incredibly faster and more efficient. They predict it will be available for general use within a year, and it may already be available at your institution. For more information on Internet2, visit the web site www.internet2.edu/index.html.

take it away!

This appendix explained the numerous ways in which your campus can help you use computers as part of your learning experience. Knowing what your college has to offer can help you complete assignments, do research, increase your computer literacy, and maybe choose a major in a computing field.

- Many colleges provide numerous computing resources.

  You may have one or more open computer labs on your college campus. Your college may offer instruction on using computer hardware and/or software. Most likely, you'll need to open a computer account in order to access these resources.

- Many colleges provide access to both local area networks and the Internet.

  With local area network and Internet access, you can communicate with others using email. You can also reach the World Wide Web for research.

Questions for Critical Thought

1. What different kinds of computer applications had you used before entering college? What were your purposes for using them? Did you enjoy using a computer?

2. Have you stepped inside one of your college's computer labs yet? Why? What are your impressions so far?

3. Look back at the Points to Ponder that appear in this appendix.
   a. Which Point to Ponder surprised you the most?
   b. How does knowing this help you better prepare for academic success?

4. How does the information presented in this appendix help you in your life outside of the classroom and college environment? Which strategies are particularly relevant to success in your career and personal life?

Web Site

Visit the *Overcoming the Hurdles to Academic Success* web site for a chapter outline, review exercises, additional case studies, links to other online resources, and a practice test.

index